European Union and its Neighbours in a Globalized World

Volume 36

The series publishes monographs and edited volumes in the field of European and international law and policy. A special focus is put on the European neighbourhood policy, current problems in European and international law and policy as well as the role of the European Union as a global actor. The series supports the publishing and distribution of research results of cross-border research consortia. Besides renowned scientists the series is also open for publication projects of young academics. The series emphasizes the interplay of the European Union and its neighbouring countries as well as the important role of the European Union as a key player in the international context of law, economics and politics.

Nikolaos Gaitenidis

The Rights of Cultural Identity in the Case Law of the European Court of Human Rights

In Search of a Fair Balance between Multiple Diversities, European Values and State Interests

Springer

Nikolaos Gaitenidis
International and European Studies
University of Macedonia
Thessaloniki, Greece

ISSN 2524-8928 ISSN 2524-8936 (electronic)
European Union and its Neighbours in a Globalized World
ISBN 978-3-032-23044-7 ISBN 978-3-032-23045-4 (eBook)
https://doi.org/10.1007/978-3-032-23045-4

This Springer imprint is published by the registered company Springer Nature Switzerland AG
The registered company address is: Gewerbestrasse 11, 6330 Cham, Switzerland

Prologue

Cultural diversity has become an integral part of daily life in European societies, but effectively recognizing, managing, and safeguarding this diversity poses complex challenges at both national and international levels. Respecting cultural diversity not only presents practical and theoretical difficulties but also involves legal and political claims, as well as conflicts and tensions.

Exploring the relationship between fundamental rights and cultural identity is a challenging endeavor. Various international legal instruments, such as the International Covenant on Civil and Political Rights, the International Covenant on Economic, Social and Cultural Rights, and the European Convention on Human Rights, include rights that can be invoked to support the claims of cultural minorities. This relationship between human rights and cultural identity can be seen as two-fold: on one hand, international human rights standards provide a framework for the expression and evolution of multiple cultural identities, and on the other hand, human rights act as safeguards against the exploitation of cultural identity to justify abusive practices that contradict human values.

Despite being a vast body of international law, it is often difficult to strike a fair balance between respecting distinct cultural identities, state interests, and solid constitutional values within international human rights law. This challenge is particularly pronounced in Europe, where diverse identities intersect with different legal systems, constitutional traditions, and shared values. Accommodating cultural diversity and reconciling differences seem like an ongoing and complex task, especially considering that culture and identity are not static but evolve over time and in interaction with other cultures.

Nikolaos Gaitenidis undertakes the task of providing insights into the complexities of the "multiple diversities" present in Europe today. Through an examination of case law from the European Court of Human Rights, he develops a coherent framework for managing diversity based on human rights and fundamental freedoms. His research analyzes various cases where human rights were invoked to protect cultural claims, highlighting efforts to strike a fair balance between diversity and homogeneity. While his research does not delve into specific details exhaustively, it serves as a valuable resource for human rights scholars and policymakers.

Additionally, his work is supported by an extensive international bibliography, contributing to and enriching academic knowledge in this field.

This research comes at a critical juncture of political and social transformations in Europe. The rise of xenophobia, racism, and nationalism in many European countries has fostered a perception that multiculturalism and tolerance have failed. Concurrently, there is an increase in fundamentalist and separatist sentiments within Europe and its neighboring regions. A deeper understanding of how traditional cultures protect the well-being of their societies can shed light on the shared foundation of human dignity, which underpins the promotion and protection of human rights.

Department of International and European Studies
University of Macedonia,

GreeceThessaloniki P. Naskou Perraki
2023

Preface

This book was written as part of the Erasmus+ Jean Monnet Project "Intercultural dialogue, EU Values and Diversity" implemented by the Department of International and European Studies at the University of Macedonia in Greece. I am thankful to this project for funding my study visits to various academic institutions where I had the opportunity to engage with distinguished professors and gather valuable material. I would also like to express my gratitude to the academic coordinator of the project, Associate Professor Despoina Anagnostopoulou, for always believing in me, supporting me in all my endeavors, and providing years of guidance and patience. Special thanks goes to Professor Paroula Naskou Perraki for offering valuable insights, correcting my mistakes, and graciously writing the prologue for this book. Lastly, I am sincerely grateful to my editor, project coordinators, and publishers for their excellent work in bringing this book to fruition.

I dedicate this book to my family and friends with deep gratitude for the lessons of tolerance and mutual understanding they have taught me. Thank you all for the light you bring to my life.

Thessaloniki
2025

Nikolaos Gaitenidis

Acknowledgments

Co-funded by
the European Union

Funded by the European Union. Views and opinions expressed are, however, those of the author(s) only and do not necessarily reflect those of the European Union or the European Education and Culture Executive Agency (EACEA). Neither the European Union nor EACEA can be held responsible for them.

About the Jean Monnet Project EUVadis at the University of Macedonia, Greece

This monograph presents the research outcomes of the Jean Monnet Project *"Policy Discourses on Intercultural Dialogue, EU Values, and Diversity"* (known with the acronym *EUVadis*), conducted at the Department of International and European Studies of the University of Macedonia, Greece and co-funded by the European Commission (EACEA), ERASMUS+ Jean Monnet Action Programme.

The Jean Monnet Project EUVadis was awarded to the University of Macedonia in July 2018, following its selection for co-funding by the ERASMUS+ Jean Monnet Action Program. The Project EUVadis started in September 2018, halted its progress during the COVID-19 pandemic period and was concluded at the end of 2022.

Its purpose was to stimulate research, reflection, and dialogue in the field of European integration studies, as well as promote debate, the flow of knowledge and the provision of new research insights, with a particular emphasis on EU values, diversity, and intercultural dialogue from a multidisciplinary perspective.

Research under the Jean Monnet Project was conducted across four key thematic axes, which included the organization of roundtable discussions, conferences and research:

- Axis One: Fundamental Rights, Values, and Diversity
- Axis Two: European Identities, Inclusion, and Equality
- Axis Three: Citizenship, Security, and External Relations
- Axis Four: EU Security Watchspot, EU Security Database, and relevant Guest Lectures, designed to report, discuss and analyze current EU security affairs, collect commentaries on security, EU legislation, as well as case law on terrorism by the EU Court of Justice and the European Court of Human Rights. The whole axis was coordinated by Associate Professor Fotini Bellou, University of Macedonia, Head of the EU Security Watchspot.

Additionally, two seminars were held, titled *"The Challenges for European Societies"* and *"Intercultural Dialogue as a European Project"*. The research was further enriched by study visits of the Project's researchers to universities and research institutes in the United States (New York) and Canada (Quebec).

This ambitious initiative would not have been possible without the co-funding provided by the ERASMUS+/Jean Monnet Action, which significantly enhanced the research capabilities and outreach of the researchers at the University of Macedonia.

Additional information, along with manuals and working papers, are uploaded on the official website of the Jean Monnet Project EUVadis at jmpeuvadis.uom.gr, a webpage designed and managed by Ms. Angeliki-Aliki Hapsanidou-Vidaki, graduate of the Department of International and European Studies, University of Macedonia.

Competing Interests The author has no competing interests to declare that are relevant to the content of this manuscript.

Contents

Chapter 1
Introduction

Contents

Cultural, religious, racial and ethnic diversity has been a permanent characteristic of European societies and the recent increase in migration and refugee flows have attributed different variables on this issue. It is, however, the enhancement of democratic principles, the growing concern for human rights as well as the empowerment of minority groups that have led in increased claims for cultural recognition by minority groups and individuals.

The issue of recognizing and managing diversity constitutes a multifaceted and controversial field of interest, at national and international level. Campaigns and political actions arose under the umbrella of "identity politics" and "politics of recognition" which are parallel and complementary to anti-racist and anti-discrimination policies. Thus, challenges to the institutions and processes by which Western states manage religious, cultural and ethnic differences have emerged.[1] These policies vary significantly, not only between European states but also at the regional and local level, while in recent years the interest seems to be shifting to international dialogue and international decision-making fora. However, despite the fact that "identity politics" are now quite widespread, policy and decision-makers seem quite hesitant in recognizing cultural identity claims of immigrants and minority groups. This hesitation stems not only from restrictive political ideologies but also from the

[1] Vertovec and Wessendorf (2006), pp. 171–187.

N. Gaitenidis, *The Rights of Cultural Identity in the Case Law of the European Court of Human Rights*, European Union and its Neighbours in a Globalized World 36, https://doi.org/10.1007/978-3-032-23045-4_1

fear of legitimizing cultural practices that are incompatible with democratic principles and the core constitutional values of the European public order.[2]

Indeed, the policies of multiculturalism had been on the forefront during the late 1980s and 1990s in order to accommodate difference and diversity and avoid assimilation. However, as Casals observes "*a retreat in this accommodationist trend, affecting a variety of programmes and regulations aimed at institutionalising diversity and promoting a difference-based model of integration. As a political trend, the backlash against multiculturalism is especially noticeable in Europe, where the model has come under intense pressure in countries that had (officially or semi-officially) recognized and granted specific entitlements to minority cultures. The case of the Netherlands, where publicly supported multiculturalist programmes had been central since the 1980s, has come to epitomize the main patterns of a broader shift. The model started to be under pressure in the late 1990s, when the growing presence of non-Western immigrant communities, especially Muslim minorities, came to be represented as a threat. Initially, the critique of both immigration and multiculturalism by a number of influential public intellectuals helped to validate the growing popular dissatisfaction, ultimately paving the road for the institutional setback. At the outset, discontent focused on multiculturalism as a model characterized by an excess of toleration that runs the risk of producing an ethnically segregated society*".[3]

As a result, a shift is observed regarding the recognition of different cultural identities from the political arena to claiming rights to courts, domestic and international, with the European Court of Human Rights taking a prominent role in the interpretation of fundamental rights, such as freedom of conscience, freedom of association and freedom of religion, in cultural and religious disputes.[4]

1.1 The Dimensions of Cultural Identity

The term "culture" has many references, such as cultural products, i.e. arts and literature, the cultural process, or culture as a way of life. In addition, culturecan develop and mutate over time as it is not a static, but a dynamic concept. It is not a product, but a process, with an objective and a subjective dimension. The objective dimension of culture is reflected in visible characteristics, such as language, religion or customs, while the subjective dimension in common attitudes and ways of thinking, feelings and activities. Finally, culture has an individual and a collective meaning: cultures are developed and shaped by communities, with which individuals identify, in the construction of their personal cultural identity.[5]

---

[2] Eisenberg (2009), pp. 2–5.

[3] Torbisco-Casals (2016), p. 377.

[4] Torbisco-Casals (2016), p. 403.

[5] Donders (2010), p. 15.

Cultural identity or identities is a complex construct and difficult to define as it is shaped by many interconnected dimensions that are constantly evolving. According to Chen "*Cultural identity refers to identification with, or sense of belonging to, a particular group based on various cultural categories, including nationality, ethnicity, race, gender, and religion. Cultural identity is constructed and maintained through the process of sharing collective knowledge such as traditions, heritage, language, aesthetics, norms and customs. As individuals typically affiliate with more than one cultural group, cultural identity is complex and multifaceted. While formerly scholars assumed identification with cultural groups to be obvious and stable, today most view it as contextual and dependent upon temporal and spatial changes. In the globalized world with increasing intercultural encounters, cultural identity is constantly enacted, negotiated, maintained, and challenged through communicative practices*".[6]

The delimitation of the concept of cultural identity is based on a number of defining criteria that are considered "objective", such as common origin, genealogy, language, culture, religion and ties to a specific geographical place. The individuals, through their biological heritage, grow and assimilate the cultural elements, the "mentality" and the "genius" of the people to whom they belong.[7] The claim that a practice, a place or an activity is important for the identity of the individual is interpreted as a mirror of the person's self-perception. Therefore, access to them is fundamental for someone's personal development. At the same time, the claim that an inherent trait, such as race or ethnicity, is at the core of one's identity, means that someone's existence is perceived in part or in whole in reference to that trait.[8]

At the same time, the development of the cultural identity of the individual is directly influenced by the process of socialization. In this way, each person forms a different cultural identity depending on the group or groups of interaction at any given time. Therefore, the concept of cultural identity is fluid and multifaceted prone to "intersectionality", i.e. the fact that an individual can be identified as "different" due to many features of their identity. Each characteristic can be the cause of different forms of discrimination and subjugation.[9] In addition the concept of cultural identity is twofold: it concerns both its collective existence and its individual.[10]

Cultural identity as a concept presents several characteristics and properties: (a) cultural identity is not static but flexible, (b) cultural identities frequently overlap with other cultures and identities, (c) cultures include subcultures that shape an individual's identity, (d) cultural identity is communicated to others and is perceived by others in many ways that may include stereotypes, (e) the modes of expression that a cultural community share (symbols, customs etc.), demonstrate a shared

---

[6] Chen (2014), p.1.

[7] Cuche (2001), pp. 148–149.

[8] Eisenberg (2009), p. 18–24. See also, Shelton (2016), pp. 1–18.

[9] Cuche (2001), p. 161.

[10] Eisenberg (2009), p. 25.

identity, (f) there are three components to cultural identity, i.e. individual (how an individual interprets his cultural identity based on experiences), relational (how individuals interact with one and another) and communal identity (communication in the creation, affirmation and negotiation of shared identity), g) cultural identity changes due to several factors which are social, political, economic and contextual.[11]

1.2 Human Rights and Cultural Identity

The importance of respect for cultural identity lies in the fact that it concerns the individual and collective sense of "belonging", i.e. the self-determination of the individual and the way in which he experiences, expresses and fulfills his identity in the private and public area. In this light, respect for cultural identity is an integral part of human dignity.[12]

The theoretical link between human rights and cultural identity has been identified in many international law texts, for example in the UNESCO Universal Declaration for Cultural Diversity. According to Article 4 of the Declaration "*The defence of cultural diversity is an ethical imperative, inseparable from respect for human dignity. It implies a commitment to human rights and fundamental freedoms, in particular the rights of persons belonging to minorities and those of indigenous peoples. No one may invoke cultural diversity to infringe upon human rights guaranteed by international law, nor to limit their scope*". The Article entails a two--sided relationship regarding the relationship of human rights and cultural diversity. On the one hand, respect for different cultural identities is guaranteed through the international human rights framework. On the other hand cultural practices that are clearly in conflict with international human rights norms cannot be justified in the name of the maintaining diversity of cultures. As Donders notes "*It is broadly agreed that human rights and cultural diversity have a mutually interdependent and beneficial relationship. Many human rights, such as the rights to freedom of expression, freedom of religion, freedom of assembly, as well as the rights to take part in cultural life and to education, play a direct role in the promotion and protection of cultural diversity. At the same time, the enjoyment of human rights is promoted by a pluralistic society*".[13]

Respect for diverse cultural identities poses practical and theoretical challenges mainly because it is an ambiguous field of legal and political claims. First of all, it concerns the protection of rights both at the individual and the collective level. The first case concerns the protection of individuals from discriminatory practices and the guarantee of the principle of equality, and relates to the protection of certain

[11] Yea-Wen and Hengjun (2016), pp. 1–3.

[12] Stamatopoulou (2006), p. 1391. See also, Donders (2010), p. 15. See also, Shelton (2016), p. 3.

[13] Donders (2013), p. 123.

fundamental rights, such as the right to self-determination, the right to expression, religious freedom, participation in cultural and social life, the right to equality, the right to education and the emerging right to the protection of cultural identity.[14] The second case concerns mainly the taking of measures and the granting of special rights for the protection of individuals or groups and minorities from forced assimilation and the freedom to preserve their cultural identity.[15] In other words, if cultural identity consists of a set of values, beliefs, customs as well as linguistic or religious peculiarities that distinguish an individual or group of individuals (often defined as a system of rules), then the protection of cultural identity implies the establishment of a socioeconomic environment that respects and encourages individuals and groups to access, produce and disseminate their distinct cultural expressions.[16]

Despite the fact that several international institutions, tasked with overseeing the implementation of international human rights treaties, have affirmed the value of cultural diversity for human dignity in a pluralistic society, the exact relationship between cultural identity and human rights law remains unclear and represents a field for further exploration under different perspectives and disciplines.[17] In addition, despite the fact that the integration of cultural identity in human rights acts is not an innovation, an autonomous right to cultural identity has not been recognized to date. Supporters of the adoption of an independent right insist that the current system of human rights protection does not meet the demands of individuals and communities for the recognition and protection of their cultural identity. On the other hand, critics of this adoption argue that the concept of cultural identity is too vague to be "translated" into a right, which could lead to the approval of controversial cultural practices. As Donders concludes "*although it is true that cultural rights have generally been neglected and that the protection of cultural identity as an important value and element of human dignity would fit into the human rights sphere, translating cultural identity into a separate right is neither desirable nor necessary. It is not desirable because translating the vague and general concept of cultural identity into a right would risk abuse or suppression of individual rights and freedoms within a cultural context. It is not necessary because existing cultural rights in the broad sense already offer possibilities for the protection of cultural identity*".[18]

However, Donders observes that over the last years international law and international case law have been developed and evolved and "*it seems that cultural identity is increasingly seen also as a more self standing or substantive right to be enjoyed by individuals and by communities. Indeed, the collective subject of the right to cultural identity is increasingly recognized*". In addition Donders remarks

[14] Henrard (2007), pp. 13–15.

[15] An academic disagreement should be noted: a large portion of the scientific community disagrees with the special treatment of specific groups of individuals, believing that this violates the principle of formal equality. See for example Barry (2001), pp. 55–60.

[16] Eisenberg (2009), p. 8.

[17] Donders (2013), p. 2.

[18] Donders (2002), p. 337.

that "*the risks of a right to cultural identity have been addressed in international human rights law. The possible tension between the collective right to cultural identity and individual freedoms, as well as the problem of harmful cultural practices, have been dealt with in standard-setting as well as in monitoring processes. Several international legal instruments have specified that cultural diversity or cultural rights cannot be used to infringe upon other human rights. Moreover, limitation clauses to human rights, including cultural rights, have been included and used to protect the rights of others or broader societal interests. The balancing of these different interests, individual, collective and societal, is an important task of States in the implementation of cultural rights and it is an important aspect of the monitoring work of international and regional bodies*".[19]

References

Barry B (2001) Culture and equality: an egalitarian critique of multiculturalism. Polity Press, Cambridge

Chen VHH (2014) Cultural identity Key Concepts in Intercultural Dialogue, 22. https://centerforinterculturaldialogue.files.wordpress.com/2014/07/key-concept-cultural-identity.pdf

Cuche D (2001) The concept of culture in the social sciences. Typothito - G. Dardanos, Athens (in Greek)

Donders Y (2002) Towards a right to cultural identity? Antwerp, Intersentia, Bruxelles

Donders Y (2010) Do cultural diversity and human rights make a good match? Int Soc Sci J 61(199):15–35

Donders Y (2013) International human rights and cultural diversity: balancing act. Romanian J Comp Law 4(2):123–138

Donders Y (2018) Towards a right to cultural identity? Yes, indeed! Diritti Umani e Diritto Internazionale 12(3):523–548

Eisenberg A (2009) Reasons of identity, a normative guide to the political and legal assessment of identity claims. Oxford University Press, Oxford

Henrard K (2007) Equal rights versus special rights? Minority protection and the prohibition of discrimination. European Commission Directorate-general for employment and social affairs. Office for Official Publications of the European Communities, Luxembourg

Shelton D (2016) On identity. George Washington Int Law Rev 49(1):1–18

Stamatopoulou E (2006) Cultural rights and contemporary realities: the right to participate in cultural life. Armenopoulos 9:1391–1041. (in Greek)

Torbisco-Casals N (2016) Multiculturalism, identity claims, and human rights: from politics to courts. Law Ethics Human Rights 10(2):367–404

Vertovec S, Wessendorf S (2006) Cultural, religious and linguistic diversity in Europe: an overview of issues and trends. In: Penninx R, Berger M, Kraal K (eds) The dynamics of international migration and settlement in Europe. University of Amsterdam Press, Amsterdam

Yea-Wen C, Hengjun L (2016) Cultural Identities. Oxf Res Encyclopedias:1–25. https://doi.org/10.1093/acrefore/9780190228613.013.20

[19] Donders (2018), pp. 523–548.

Chapter 2
Culture, Cultural Rights and the Cultural Dimension of Human Rights

Contents

For the purposes of the research, it is necessary to conceptually separate cultural rights, in the narrow sense of the term, and fundamental rights, which include a dimension related to the protection of cultural identity. Cultural rights have received less attention from the political and academic community and, consequently, are conceptually and legally less developed than political, economic and social rights. One reason for their slow conceptual and normative development is the ambiguity of the term "culture". The academic literature identifies several other reasons for the neglect of cultural rights in addition to the fluid and changing meaning of the term "culture", such as the fear of direct or indirect recognition of the issue of cultural relativity of fundamental rights that may degrade their universal character, their consideration as a "luxury" by part of the international political community and political difficulties at the international political and diplomatic level. Finally, one of the most important difficulties is the threat the recognition of collective cultural identities entails for the nation-state, but also for the cultural majority.[1]

UNESCO defines culture as " *the set of distinctive spiritual, material, intellectual and emotional features of society or a social group, and that it encompasses, in addition to art and literature, lifestyles, ways of living together, value systems, traditions and beliefs*".[2] The importance of cultural rights lies in the fact that they

[1] Stamatopoulou (2006), pp. 1338–1339.

[2] UNESCO Universal Declaration on Cultural Diversity (2001), preample.

N. Gaitenidis, *The Rights of Cultural Identity in the Case Law of the European Court of Human Rights*, European Union and its Neighbours in a Globalized World 36, https://doi.org/10.1007/978-3-032-23045-4_2

concern the individual and collective sense of a person's identity and "belonging", i.e. the self-definition of the individual and the way in which they experience it, express it and fulfill themselves in the private and public area. In this light, they are an integral part of human dignity.[3]

The way in which cultural rights are defined in international law largely depends on the different approaches to the concept of culture. Under a "narrow" view of culture, as the cultural products of arts, literature, tangible and intangible cultural heritage, cultural rights could include the protection of cultural heritage, as well as the right to participate in cultural life and access to products of culture. By including in the concept of culture the process of artistic and scientific creation, cultural rights should include the rights of freedom of expression, artistic and intellectual freedom, as well as the rights associated with the protection of the moral and economic interest of artists and producers, including copyright. Finally, if culture also includes a way of life, the term includes the sum of the material and intellectual activities and products of a community, thus cultural rights include the right to self-determination, including cultural development, the right to freedom of thought and religion, the right to association, the right to education, as well as the rights to preserve and develop culture.[4]

There are also three approaches regarding the protection and promotion of cultural rights. The first emphasizes the individual dimension of these rights. In this respect, it recognizes individuals as bearers of cultural rights, who must be protected from abuses of state power, group or sub-group. The second puts forward the collective dimension of cultural rights, considering groups, such as indigenous peoples or minorities, as bearers of cultural rights seeking their protection from the states in which they live. Finally, the third interest group recognizes cultural rights in states, trying to protect small or less powerful states from larger or more powerful ones. Cultural rights are primarily defined as individual rights in the provisions of international human rights law. However, although, according to international law, only individuals can claim these rights, it is clear that their enjoyment is closely linked to other individuals and to communities. For example, the individual right to participate in cultural life can be exercised by individuals only as members of a, broad or smaller, cultural community.[5] Finally, other approaches divide cultural rights into three categories that reflect their evolution from the passive enjoyment of culture to active participation in cultural production and the protection of cultural identity: (a) the right to cultural participation, which includes the right to free participation; the freedom of religious conscience, the right to benefit from culture etc. (b) the right to education at all levels, including vocational education, (c) the right

[3] Stamatopoulou (2006), p. 1391. See also, Donders (2010), p. 15.

[4] Marks (2003), pp. 293–324. See also Donders (2010), p. 18–19. It should be noted that despite the fact that there is an extended corpus of international legislation regarding the right to intellectual property, this right is considered primarily to be part of international commercial law. Stamatopoulou (2006), p. 1394.

[5] Donders (2010), p. 20.

to cultural identification i.e. the right to choose a culture or civilization, language, cultural heritage etc.[6]

Within the general human rights framework, cultural rights are of particular importance in promoting and preserving cultural diversity. The broad concept of culture, which includes not only cultural products, but also identity aspects such as association, language, religion and education, means that cultural rights include many different human rights that refer to the cultural identity of individuals and of communities as part of their human dignity such as the right to privacy, family life, housing and health. Cultural rights reflect the individual as well as the collective dimension of human rights and have a multidimensional character. As such, they embody the indivisibility, interdependence and interconnectedness of all human rights.[7]

2.1 Universality and Cultural Relativism of Rights

The idea of universality of human rights can be traced in antiquity, and the idea of natural law. The perception of universality, is based on the hypothesis that human rights are inherent to human nature and their dynamic is unchanged, therefore, they belong to every person and apply to all human societies in identical degree, irrespective of their cultural differences. The assumption that a particular value or moral judgment is universal implies that its significance is recognized by all of humanity, without significant exceptions. Indeed, the *raison d'etre* of human rights is to allow people to fulfill the needs they perceive as necessary for their lives and for these needs to be degenerated into societal values. On the other hand, the perception of these values may be very different and even diametrically opposite in a multicultural society or between different societies.[8] As John-Stewart Gordon summarizes "*According to most scholars in the field, human rights are primarily moral rights of high priority that are universally valid, independent of any legal recognition by particular nation-states or of particular times and places. All human beings are endowed with these rights simply by virtue of their humanity. In this respect, human rights are commonly seen as inborn, unalterable and inalienable. In addition, they are considered the minimal standards necessary to protect the most vital and precious interests and values of human beings—for example, their freedom, safety, equality, political participation and social security, to name just a few*".[9]

[6] Meyer-Bisch (1993), pp. 35–36.

[7] Donders (2010), pp. 20–32.

[8] Lenzerini (2014), pp. 1–4.

[9] Gordon (2015), pp. 21–35.

The theory of cultural relativism argues that human values are not universal but they vary largely depending on the different cultural backgrounds.[10] According to the cultural relativism theory, each culture or nation should be judged on its own values and standards of conduct and not on the values or standards of another culture or nation.[11] Proponents of the theory of cultural relativism argue that there is no moral judgment with universal force. In the context of human rights, this support means that local cultural traditions, determine the existence and the application of human rights in a given society.[12] The application of the theory of cultural relativism in the context of the protection, promotion, interpretation and application of fundamental rights implies that they could be interpreted in different ways depending on the different cultural, ethnic and religious traditions.[13] In this light human rights are defined sometimes as either an exclusive product of western culture, or as general and broad values which can employ various interpretations.[14]

It has been argued that cultural relativism could be a dangerous threat to effectiveness of international law and the international framework of human rights protection. If the state's compliance with international standards is governed solely by cultural tradition, then the indifference, abuse and violation of human rights should be considered legitimate and the respect of human rights will be subject solely in the state discretion, and not in international standards.[15] In addition, the mass migration in Western Europe brought to the forefront of academic interest new discussions on universality of human rights: questions arise as to whether immigrants should be forced to adopt western norms and values or whether the requirements of multiculturalism could make some exceptions, resulting in courts taking different cultures into account in their assessments.[16]

Like most sectors of the international law, international human rights law constitutes a modern accomplishment of humanity that is new to all cultures. Human rights reflect the dynamic, coordinated international community efforts to promote one common system of protection of human life and dignity. Flexibility in the interpretation of human rights is already facilitated with the establishment of minimum standards and incorporation of cultural rights. In this context, states have the maximum cultural margin of appreciation without compromising the risk of human rights violation. This view is also reflected in the Vienna Declaration and the

---

[10] See more details for the development of theory of cultural relativism in sociological and anthropological thought at Zechenter (1997), pp. 323–329.

[11] *Pararas* (2011*), pp. 45–75.*

[12] *Téson (*1985*)*, pp. 869–898. See also, Lenzerini (2014), pp. 4–5.

[13] Ayton-Shenker (1995), pp. 1–6. See also, Kekes (1996), pp. 12–20. See also Lenzerini (2014), pp. 4–5.

[14] Roy and Annicchino (2013), p. 16. The divergence regarding the protection and restriction of freedom of expression between the constitutional framework of the United States and the states of Europe is an illustrative example of the relative application of universal fundamental rights See more, Nieuwenhuis (2000), pp. 195–214.

[15] Ayton-Shenker (1995), pp. 1–6.

[16] Roy and Annicchino (2013), pp. 18–19.

Programme of Action, which confirms the Universal Declaration of Human Rights as a "common standard" for all. The Vienna Declaration was adopted in June 1993 by the World Conference on Human Rights in Vienna, and it strengthens the universality of human rights stating that "*all human rights are universal, indivisible and interconnected*". This means that political, cultural, economic and social rights must be considered indispensable, of equal value that apply to all persons. The Vienna Declaration reports to first paragraph, that "The universal character" of all human rights and fundamental freedoms is "beyond any doubt". The Vienna Declaration predicts explicitly that promotion and protection human rights must take into account culture, stating that "*While the significance of national and regional particularities and various historical, cultural and religious backgrounds must be borne in mind, it is the duty of States, regardless of their political, economic and cultural systems, to promote and protect all human rights and fundamental freedoms*".[17] While the Declaration takes a clear position in favor of universality, it recognizes a possible significance of national and regional specificities and various historical, cultural and religious contexts. That is, the Vienna Declaration seems to support a "culturally sensitive universality".[18]

The flexibility of the interpretation and application of human rights and the different perceptions of how to protect them also seem to be accepted in the context of the European Convention on Human Rights. In particular, Article 56 par. 3 on the territorial application of the Convention, which states that the provisions of the Convention iukrain certain territories will be applied taking into account local requirements. In addition, recognizing the different legal and cultural traditions of each state, the European Court of Human Rights has incorporated in its case law the "margin of appreciation doctrine", admitting that it is difficult to detect single European standards for human rights protection.[19] The margin of appreciation provides the necessary flexibility required to avoid controversies between the Court and the States and provides a fair balance between the sovereignty of member states and the obligations arising from the Convention.[20] Similarly, the Court of the European Union recognizes the relevance of the protection of human rights between Member States, holding that "*It is not indispensable in that respect for the restrictive measure issued by the authorities of a Member State to correspond to a conception*

[17] Vienna Declaration and Program of Action (1993), part I par. 5. The exact same wording is repeated in the Resolution of the UN General Assembly GA res 60/167, Human rights and cultural diversity, 7 March 2006.

[18] Lenzerini (2014), p. 12. At the same time, academic literature highlights the role of states' reservations in international human rights treaties as a tool for preserving cultural pluralism. Donders (2013a, b), pp. 205–239.

[19] See Ostrovsky (2005), pp. 47–64.

[20] Fenwick (2005), pp. 34–37. See cases ECHR, *Pretty v. the United Kingdom,* Application *No.* 2346/02, 29 July 2002 and ECHR, Handyside v. The United Kingdom, Application *No.* 5493/72, 7 December 1976.

shared by all Member States as regards the precise way in which the fundamental right or legitimate interest in question is to be protected".[21]

It could be argued that the European public order adopts a "moderate" approach to cultural relativism (moderate cultural relativism) based on the assumption that regional and local variants for human rights are acceptable, but, at the same time, they can not affect a common core of fundamental rights, which are universal[22] and represent a hard won consent of the international community, not the cultural imperialism of a specific area or a set of traditions.[23]

2.2 Identity Protection in International and European Law

The legal recognition of cultural diversity and the protection of cultural identity lie mainly in the right of everyone to declare the identity they desire and to behave accordingly, thus it concerns their personal autonomy and development. In this light, it refers to international or regional human rights conventions, for example the 1948 Universal Declaration of Human Rights, the United Nations International Covenant on Civil and Political Rights, the United Nations International Covenant on Civil and Political Rights, the International Convention on the Elimination of Racial Discrimination of 1966, etc.

Fundamental rights explicitly mentioned in culture are enshrined in principle in international law and in Article 27 of the Universal Declaration of Human Rights, which provides that "Everyone has the right freely to participate in the cultural life of the community, to enjoy the arts and to share in scientific advancement and its benefits" and "*E* Everyone has the right to the protection of the moral and material interests resulting from any scientific, literary or artistic production of which he is the author". Article 13 of the International Covenant on Economic, Social and Cultural Rights provides that "*The States Parties to the present Covenant recognize the right of everyone to education. They agree that education shall be directed to the full development of the human personality and the sense of its dignity, and shall strengthen the respect for human rights and fundamental freedoms. They further agree that education shall enable all persons to participate effectively in a free society, promote understanding, tolerance and friendship among all nations and all racial, ethnic or religious groups, and further the activities of the United Nations for the maintenance of peace*". Paragraph 3 of the same Article states that "*The States Parties to the present Covenant undertake to have respect for the liberty of parents and, when applicable, legal guardians to choose for their children schools, other than those established by the public authorities, which conform to such*

[21] Judgment of the Court (First Chamber) of 14 October 2004, Omega Spielhallen- und Automatenaufstellungs-GmbH v Oberbürgermeisterin der Bundesstadt Bonn, C-36/02, ECLI:EU:C:2004:614.

[22] Lenzerini (2014), p. 8.

[23] Ayton-Shenker (1995), pp. 1–6.

minimum educational standards as may be laid down or approved by the State and to ensure the religious and moral education of their children in conformity with their own convictions". In addition, Article 15 of the International Covenant on Economic, Social and Cultural Rights stipulates that States Parties recognize the right to take part in cultural life, to enjoy the benefits of scientific progress and its applications, to benefit from the protection of the moral and material interests resulting from any scientific, literary or artistic production of which he is the author. Article 27 of the International Covenant on Civil and Political Rights provides that "*In those States in which ethnic, religious or linguistic minorities exist, persons belonging to such minorities shall not be denied the right, in community with the other members of their group, to enjoy their own culture, to profess and practice their own religion, or to use their own language*".[24]

According to the above, the "narrow" group of cultural rights includes the right to education, the right to participate in cultural life, the right to benefit from scientific progress and its applications, the right to benefit from the protection of moral and material interests, which arise from every scientific, literary or artistic work and finally the freedom for scientific research and creative activity. The "broad" group of cultural rights includes the aforementioned rights, but also other economic, political and social rights related to culture, such as the rights to freedom of religion, freedom of expression and freedom of association, while several international Organizations such as the Council of Europe and the Inter-American Commission on Human Rights have included the right to life, the right to health and the right to family life and residence.[25]

Undoubtedly, the role that UNESCO is also very important. UNESCO has adopted a number of acts affecting the management of cultural diversity, such as the Convention against Discrimination in Education, the 2001 UNESCO Declaration on Cultural Diversity, the 1995 Declaration of Principles for Tolerance, and the 1978 UNESCO Declaration on race and racial prejudice, the 2005 UNESCO Convention for the Protection and Promotion of the Diversity of Cultural Expressions of 2005.[26] At regional level, the 1990 Copenhagen Document on the Human Dimension which was adopted in the framework of the Organization for Security and Cooperation in Europe (OSCE) is worth mentioning. The document calls on member states to take positive action to ensure equality.[27]

The self-identification of the European Union as a "defender" of diversity, combined with the principle of solidarity between member states, respect for minorities and the protection of human rights, lead to the implementation of policies that

---

[24] See more at Stamatopoulou (2007), p. 121.

[25] It should be noted that despite the rich international law on intellectual property rights, this right is considered to be more in the realm of international commercial law. Stamatopoulou (2006), p. 1394.

[26] See Xanthaki (2010), pp. 21–48.

[27] Organization for Security and Co-operation in Europe, Document of the Copenhagen Meeting of the Conference on the Human Dimension of the CSCE, Copenhagen 1990. See, Tavernier (1994), p. 27.

promote diversity and protect the distinct cultural identities. During the last decade, however, skepticism has emerged regarding the "failure" of the pluralist/multicultural model. Human rights, based on the European Convention of Human Rights and the constitutional traditions of the member states, are recognized by the Court of the European Union as general principles of the European Union Law.[28] In addition, the Court of the European Union has declared in the *Nold* case that fundamental rights set out in other international treaties,[29] such as the International Covenant on Civil and Political Rights and the International Covenant on Economic, Social and Political Rights are also part of the general principles of the Union law, consequently article 27 of the International Covenant on Civil and Political Rights and article 15 of the International Covenant on Economic, Social and Political Rights serve in the interpretation of the Treaties.[30] This model was mainly accused of establishing "parallel worlds" within societies without any mutual contact, which undermined social peace, as well as promoting essentialization of culture. Thus, the concept of "integration" is re-defined, as the necessary answer to multiculturalist policies in immigrant-receiving countries.[31]

The Treaty of Lisbon highlights new dimensions on the Union's commitments to the protection of human rights are significantly increased in a way that has implications for the protection of cultural identity. Article 2 of the Treaty of the European Union provides that "*The Union is founded on the values of respect for human dignity, freedom, democracy, equality, the rule of law and respect for human rights, including the rights of persons belonging to minorities. These values are common to the Member States in a society in which pluralism, non-discrimination, tolerance, justice, solidarity and equality between women and men prevail*". In addition, respect for cultural diversity acquires a fundamental value in the European Union because it is explicitly recognized in Article 22 of the now binding Charter of Fundamental Rights of the European Union: "*The Union shall respect cultural, religious and linguistic diversity*".[32]

The Council of Europe has taken several initiatives to protect the cultural identity of the individual, for example the 1995 Council of Europe Framework Convention for the Protection of National Minorities, which entered into force in 1998, the European Convention on Legal Status of Migrant Workers of 1977 and the European Charter for Local and Minority Languages of 1992.[33] However, the European

[28] Judgment of the Court of 17 December 1970, Internationale Handelsgesellschaft mbH v Einfuhr- und Vorratsstelle für Getreide und Futtermittel, Case 11–70, ECLI:EU:C:1970:114 and Judgment of the Court of 28 October 1975, Roland Rutili v Ministre de l'intérieur, Case 36–75, ECLI:EU:C:1975:137. See also, Tridimas (2022), p. 82.

[29] Judgment of the Court of 14 May 1974, J. Nold, Kohlen- und Baustoffgroßhandlung v Commission of the European Communities, Case 4–73, ECLI:EU:C:1974:51.

[30] Donders (2003), p. 117–148. See also, Weiler (2009), pp. 73–101.

[31] Kostakopoulou (2010), pp. 5–18. See also, von Bogdandy (2008), pp. 244–246.

[32] Swiebel (2009), pp. 22–23. See also, Di Federico (2011), pp. 15–54.

[33] Advisory Committee on the Framework Convention for the Protection of National Minorities (2006),. See also, General UN Office of the High Commissioner for Human Rights (199), Fact

Convention on Human Rights is the most important document for the protection of fundamental rights on the European continent. In the sphere of the European public order, human rights law has been generated, assessed and interpreted through the case-law of the European Court of Human Rights, one of the most influential and well developed mechanisms of human rights protection in the world. The link between cultural diversity and human rights is also established by the European Court of Human Rights, where individuals and communities invoke human rights to protect interests in relation to their cultural identity. As a result, the European Court of Human Rights has produced a large corpus of case-law in which the recognition of cultural interests was claimed.[34]

Based on the above, the investigation of the nature, extent and content of the rights that directly or indirectly contribute in the protection of cultural identity is necessary in order to provide more clarity and comprehensibility on how human rights provide the fair framework of addressing identity claims effectively; More specifically, human rights, as developed by international and regional organizations, have the potential to provide a fair theoretical and practical framework for ensuring the respect of cultural identities while at the same time they provide the necessary and reasonable restrictions to cultural practices that are not compatible with a democratic society.

2.3 Cultural Identity, Human Rights, and the Challenge of Multiculturalism in Europe

The protection of cultural identity through human rights frameworks engages a broad spectrum of fundamental rights, which are firmly established in both international and European law. For instance, Article 18 of the Universal Declaration of Human Rights (1948) and Article 9 of the European Convention on Human Rights explicitly guarantee the right to freedom of thought, conscience, and religion, encompassing the individual's ability to practice and express their cultural and religious identity. These legal provisions form a cornerstone for safeguarding cultural identity, ensuring that individuals and communities can maintain their distinct traditions, beliefs, and practices without discrimination. Other relevant rights, such as freedom of expression (Article 19 UDHR, Article 10 ECHR), the right to participate in cultural life (Article 27 UDHR, Article 15 ICESCR), and the right to non-discrimination (Article 14 ECHR), further reinforce the protection of cultural identity as an integral aspect of human dignity.

However, the rise of multiculturalism (both as a social reality and as a policy) in Europe has significantly redefined the meaning and boundaries of human rights protection, presenting both opportunities and challenges. Cultural diversity,

Sheet No. 18 (Rev.1), Minority Rights, February 1998, No. 18 (Rev.1).

[34] Letsas (2013), pp. 106–141. See also, Topidi (2021), pp. 1–18.

characterized by the coexistence of diverse cultural, ethnic, and religious groups within European societies, has prompted a reevaluation of how human rights frameworks accommodate cultural diversity while upholding universal principles. On one hand, multiculturalism enriches societies by fostering pluralism and encouraging the recognition of diverse identities. On the other hand, it raises complex questions about balancing individual and collective rights, particularly when cultural practices conflict with universal human rights norms or with the values of secular, liberal democracies. For example, debates surrounding religious symbols in public spaces, such as the wearing of headscarves or burqas, highlight tensions between the right to religious freedom and societal interests like gender equality or public security. Such cases, often adjudicated by the European Court of Human Rights,[35] illustrate the dynamic and contested nature of human rights in multicultural contexts.

This challenge in Europe lies in navigating these tensions while ensuring that human rights protections remain inclusive and equitable. Cultural identity, as a fluid and intersectional construct, complicates the application of human rights law, as states must address overlapping identities and potential conflicts between cultural practices and fundamental rights. For instance, minority groups may demand collective rights to preserve their cultural heritage, such as language or traditional practices, while individuals within those groups may assert their right to opt out of certain practices that they perceive as restrictive.[36] This creates a delicate balancing act for policymakers and courts, who must reconcile the collective right to cultural identity with individual autonomy and broader societal interests.

Moreover, multiculturalism challenges the traditional universality of human rights by highlighting their contextual application. In Europe, where migration and globalization have intensified cultural diversity, human rights frameworks are increasingly tested by competing claims of cultural relativism versus universalism. The integration of cultural identity into human rights law thus requires a nuanced approach that respects diversity while preventing the justification of practices that violate fundamental rights, such as those related to gender equality or freedom from harm.

Drawing on the preceding discussion, this book seeks to address the following central research question: *How can European human rights frameworks effectively reconcile the protection of cultural identity with the challenges of multiculturalism, ensuring both the preservation of diverse identities and adherence to universal human rights principles?*

This question seeks to explore the evolving role of human rights in addressing cultural identity within multicultural European societies, focusing on the practical and theoretical implications of balancing diversity with universal norms.

This analysis focuses on the European Convention of Human Rights and the related case law of the European Court of Human Rights as it represents the most comprehensive international system of human rights protection with a considerable

---

[35] For example, ECHR, *S.A.S. v. France*, Application no. 43835/11, 1 July 2014.

[36] Kymlicka (1995).

influence in the European public order. The book presents the most prominent cases in which the European Court of Human Rights assesses identity claims. The first section focuses on cases in which members of minority cultures have attempted to invoke protection guaranteed by the European Convention on Human Rights in order for their cultural specificities be protected. The second part explores the ways in which human rights are used as restrictions on the expression of cultural identity for example in order to address the issue of intra-group diversity and the conflicts that have arisen between an individual and the cultural group of his affiliation.

The terms "cultural Identity" and "cultural diversity" are inherently broad, encompassing dimensions such as ethnicity, religion, language, and cultural practices, which are often fluid and intersectional thus posing significant challenges for legal and policy frameworks. For this reason, scholars have highlighted the need to contextualize diversity within specific legal and cultural frameworks to avoid vague generalizations.[37] Recognizing these critiques, this book deliberately adopts a broad approach to cultural identity, as a multifaceted construct that intersects with human rights law. Rather than narrowing the scope to a single aspect of identity, such as religious freedom or minority language rights, this study argues that a comprehensive perspective is essential to capture the interconnected nature of cultural identity and its implications for human rights in Europe's pluralistic societies. This approach is necessary to address the holistic nature of cultural identity, which encompasses individual, relational, and communal dimensions. By examining how the European Court of Human Rights navigates the tensions between cultural diversity and universal human rights principles, this study avoids the fragmentation inherent in focusing on a single dimension of diversity. Instead, it seeks to provide a comparative analysis of the Court's approach to cultural identity across various rights, such as freedom of religion (Article 9 ECHR), freedom of expression (Article 10 ECHR), and non-discrimination (Article 14 ECHR), to identify patterns and gaps in judicial reasoning.

References

Ayton-Shenker D (1995) The Challenge of Human Rights and Cultural Diversity, United Nations Background Note http://www.un.org/rights/dpi1627e.htm

Di Federico G (2011) Fundamental rights in the EU: legal pluralism and multi-level protection after the Lisbon treaty. In: Di Federico G (ed) The EU charter of fundamental rights, from declaration to binding instrument. Springer, London, pp 15–54

Donders Y (2003) Protection of cultural rights in Europe: none of the EU'S business. Maastricht J Eur Comp Law 10(2):117–148

Donders Y (2010) Do cultural diversity and human rights make a good match? Int Soc Sci J 61(199):15–35

Donders Y (2013a) Cultural pluralism in international human rights law: the role of reservations. ACIL 2:1–34

[37] Romainville (2014).

Donders Y (2013b) Cultural pluralism in international human rights law: the role of reservations. In: Vrdoljak AF (ed) The cultural dimension of human rights. Oxford University Press, Oxford, pp 205–239
Fenwick H (2005) Civil liberties and human rights. Cavendish Publishing Limited, London
Gordon JS (2015) Human rights and cultural identity. Baltic J Law Politics 8(2):112–135
Kekes J (1996) The morality of pluralism. Princeton University Press, New Jersey
Kostakopoulou D (2010) Introduction. In: van Oers R, Ersbøll E, Kostakopoulou D (eds) A re-definition of belonging?, language and integration tests in Europe. Martinus Nijhoff Publishers, Leiden, pp 1–23
Kymlicka W (1995) Multicultural citizenship: a Liberal theory of minority rights. Oxford University Press, Oxford
Lenzerini F (2014) The Culturalization of human rights law. Oxford University Press, Oxford
Letsas G (2013) The ECHR as a living instrument: its meaning and its legitimacy. In: Føllesdal A, Wilhelms W, Ulfstein G (eds) *Constituting Europe* the *European court of human rights in a national*, European and global context. Cambridge University Press, Cambridge, pp 106–141
Marks SP (2003) Defining cultural rights. In: Iin Bergsmo M (ed) Human rights and criminal justice for the downtrodden—essays in honour of Asbjorn Eide. Martinus Nijhoff Publishers, The Hague, pp 293–324
Meyer-Bisch P (1993) Les droits culturels forment-ils une catégorie spécifique de droits de l'homme? In: Meyer-Bisch P (ed) Les droits culturels, une catégorie sous développée de droits de l'homme. Editions universitaires, Fribourg, pp 17–43
Nieuwenhuis A (2000) Freedom of speech: USA vs Germany and Europe. Netherlands Q Human Rights 18(2):195–214
Ostrovsky AA (2005) How the margin of appreciation doctrine preserves Core human rights within cultural diversity and legitimises international human rights tribunals. Hanse Law Rev 1(1):47–64
Pararas PI (2011) *Constitutional culture* and human *rights*. Ant. Sakkoulas, Athens - Komotini (in Greek)
Romainville C (2014) Cultural diversity as a multilevel and multifaceted legal notion operating in the law on cultural policies. Int J Cultural Policy 22(2):273–290
Roy O, Annicchino P (2013) Human rights between religions, cultures, and universality. In: Vrdoljak AF (ed) The cultural dimension of human rights. Oxford University Press, Oxford, pp 7–25
Stamatopoulou E (2006) Cultural rights and contemporary realities: the right to participate in cultural life, Armenopoulos 9: 1391–1041 (in Greek)
Stamatopoulou E (2007) Cultural rights in international law, article 27 of the universal declaration of human rights and beyond. Martinus Nijhoff Publishers, Leiden
Swiebel J (2009) The European Union's policies to safeguard and promote diversity. In: Prügl E, Thiel M (eds) Diversity in the European Union. Palgrave Macmillan, London, pp 21–36
Tavernier P (1994) Minorités et facteur de tensions en Europe. In: Grigoriou P (ed) Questions de minorités en Europe. Presses Interuniversitaires Européennes, Bruxelles, pp 17–33
Téson F (1985) International human rights and cultural relativism. Va J Int Law 25:869–898
Topidi K (2021) Religious minority identity in the work of the advisory Committee of the Framework Convention for the protection of National Minorities: a multifaceted challenge in evolution. Religion 12:1–18
Tridimas T (2022) The general principles of EU law, 3rd edn. Oxford University Press, Oxford
von Bogdandy A (2008) The European Union as situation, executive, and promoter of the international law of cultural diversity—elements of a beautiful friendship. Eur J Int Law 19(2):241–275
Weiler JHH (2009) Fundamental rights and fundamental boundaries: common standards and conflicting values in the protection of human rights in the European legal space. In: Kastoryano R (ed) An identity for Europe, the sciences Po series in international relations and political economy. Palgrave Macmillan, New York, pp 73–101

Xanthaki A (2010) Multiculturalism and international law: discussing universal standards. Human Rights Q 32(1):21–48
Zechenter EM (1997) In the name of culture: cultural relativism and the abuse of the individual. J Anthropol Res 53(3):319–347

Part I
Human Rights as Defenders of Cultural Identity

Chapter 3
The Right to Enter or Exit a Culture

Contents

It could be argued that individuals' cultural identity and cultural affiliations are not a matter of choice, as many of the characteristics that shape a person's identity are innate or inherited, such as race and ethnic origin. However, the importance of "cultural participation" has been emphasized by highly acclaimed theorists as a condition of individual autonomy as it provides the individual with guidelines for the personal pursuit of well-being.[1]

Cultural identity is increasingly understood as a dynamic and fluid construct, shaped by evolving social, political and personal contexts. Traditional perspectives that view culture as a static entity tied to fixed geographic or ethnic boundaries have been overtaken by modern theories emphasizing its adaptability. Hall posits that cultural identity is not a fixed essence rooted in immutable traditions but a "positioning" continually negotiated through interactions with others and societal structures.[2] This fluidity enables individuals to navigate multiple affiliations, reshaping their sense of self in response to changing experiences and contexts. Kymlicka highlights the role of cultural participation as a cornerstone of personal fulfillment, emphasizing the freedom to embrace, modify, or reject cultural norms. This perspective challenges essentialist notions that confine individuals to rigid cultural categories, instead acknowledging the intersectionality and multiplicity of modern identities.[3] As Bradley notes, individuals may simultaneously engage with multiple cultural spheres or shift between them over time.[4]

---

[1] See more, Kymlicka (1989), *pp. 38;* Kymlicka (1995), pp. 59–80; Kymlicka (2001), pp. 28–35. It should be noted that Kymlicka's view has been criticized by members of the academic community to be overly optimistic. Cultural participation provides options to the individual, but at the same time it takes away part of the individual's choices by imposing moral limitations. See more, Pierce (2012), p. 17.

[2] Hall (1997), pp. 51–59.

[3] Kymlicka (1995), pp. 59–80.

[4] Bradley (2018), pp. 1–21.

N. Gaitenidis, *The Rights of Cultural Identity in the Case Law of the European Court of Human Rights*, European Union and its Neighbours in a Globalized World 36, https://doi.org/10.1007/978-3-032-23045-4_3

The individual's freedom to choose his own system of cultural references is a key element of human rights and of fundamental freedoms. In one given time or in different stages of their lives, people may develop different cultural relations. Nobody should be a "prisoner" of a cultural group, community, system of thought or worldview, but should be free to resign from past choices and to make new ones, under the condition that they are consistent with universal values.[5]

The Friborg Declaration on Cultural Rights (Articles 3 and 4) affirms that individuals, alone or with others, have the right to freely choose and change their cultural identity, which must be respected regardless of its expression. This right is closely linked to freedoms of thought, conscience, religion, opinion, and expression, and no one may be forced to adopt or assimilate into a cultural community

[5]European Manifesto for Multiple Cultural Affiliations, para 5. The Fribourg Declaration on Cultural Rights states that every person, alone or together with others, has the right to choose a cultural identity and that it is respected regardless of the forms in which it is expressed. The exercise of this right is mainly intertwined with the freedom of thought, conscience, religion, opinion and expression. In addition, everyone is free to choose whether or not to identify with one or more cultural communities, without being hindered by limits or obstacles, as well as being free to change their choice. No one can be forced into a cultural identity or assimilated into a cultural community against their will. The launch of the Fribourg Declaration on Cultural Rights was declared on May 7, 2007 at the University of Fribourg and May 8, 2007 at the Palais des Nations in Geneva. The text was presented by the Observatory of Diversity and Cultural Rights (which headquarters are at the Interdisciplinary Institute of Ethnics and Human Rights at the Fribourg University) together with the Organisation Internationale de la Francophonie and UNESCO. The Fribourg Declaration is supported by more than fifty human rights high profiles, as well as a platform of NGOs. See more at: https://culturalrights.net/en/documentos.php?c=14&p=161. This right is also recognized in the Council of Europe Framework Convention for the Protection of National Minorities, Article 3, par. 1 which provides that "*Every person belonging to a national minority shall have the right freely to choose to be treated or not to be treated as such and no disadvantage shall result from this choice or from the exercise of the rights which are connected to that choice*". The importance of this right is emphasized by the "landmark" case *Sandra Lovelace v. Canada* of the UN Human Rights Commission. The applicant lost her status as an indigenous (Maliseet Indian) after marrying a non-Indian, under Canadian law. As a result, after her marriage ended and she returned to the camp to live with her parents, she was not allowed to purchase a home in the Tobique Reservation and was denied access to special federal programs in education, housing and social welfare. She also lost the ability to practice traditional hunting and fishing, and all the cultural benefits related to her living with her family and friends in the reserve. The Commission decided that people, who were born and brought up in a camp, have maintained ties and want to maintain further ties to that community, are considered part of that group within the meaning of Article 27 of the International Covenant on Civil and Political Rights. Therefore, Lovelace was a member of the Maliseet because she was raised in the reserve and had only been married outside of it for a few years. In addition, the Commission found that the interference with the applicant's right to enjoy her culture also lies in the fact that there are no communities outside the camp that share the same language and culture. Finally, the Commission decided that refusing Lovelace to live in the camp was neither reasonable nor necessary to preserve the group's identity; therefore, denying her indigenous status was a violation of Article 27 of the International Covenant on Civil and Political Rights. Sandra Lovelace v. Canada, Communication No. 24/1977: Canada 30/07/81, UN Doc. CCPR/C/13/D/24/1977. The relevant law was modified in 1985 for the elimination of gender discrimination in determining the indigenous status. Barth (2008), pp. 134–154. See also, similar case Ivan Kitok v. Sweden, Communication No. 197/1985, CCPR/C/33/D/197/1985 (1988).

against their will. This right to choose a cultural identity is integral to the free development of one's personality and it embodies self-determination, allowing individuals to shape their lives based on their inclinations and beliefs, free from state-imposed standardization.[6] While no specific provision exists in the European Convention on Human Rights (ECHR) or the EU Charter of Fundamental Rights, this right is protected under Article 8 ECHR as part of "private life".[7]

Article 8 of the European Convention on Human Rights is applied with regard to the right of the individual to freely choose his own cultural or ethnic identity, and for this choice to be respected. For example, in the *Ciubotaru v. Moldova* case, the Court considered the refusal of the Moldovan authorities to register the national (Romanian) origin requested by the applicant in the process of replacing his Soviet identity card with a Moldovan identity card, on the grounds that his parents were not registered as "Romanians" on their birth and marriage certificates. The European Court of Human Rights held that a person's national identity is an essential aspect of his private life under Article 8 of the Convention and concluded that Moldovan law and practice created insurmountable obstacles for someone wishing to declare a national identity other the one registered for his parents by the Soviet authorities. Although the Court accepted that the authorities could refuse a request when it is based on a purely subjective and unfounded justification, the legal practice in Moldova makes it impossible for the applicant to provide all objective evidence to support his request, such as verifiable ties to the Romanian ethnic group.[8] Objective reasons that characterize nationality or ethnic identity are, according to the Court, the common language, religious belief or cultural and traditional practices and background, name and affiliation with other members of the group.[9]

The religious dimension of this right is of particular importance and is well developed by the international case law is, as freedom of religious conscience includes the freedom to choose, maintain, change or abandon a specific religion, as well as to choose or abandon religion in general, non-religion or atheism, without the occurrence of any adverse consequences. Religious freedom in this form is inadmissible of restrictions regarding admission, abandonment, accepting another religion or ascribing to no religion at all. This does not preclude that certain conditions must be met, determined by the internal/national law.[10] This point of view, of the non-intervention of the state in the procedures of admission or expulsion of members

---

[6] Pikramenos (2019).

[7] ECHR, *Pretty v. the United Kingdom,* Application *No.* 2346/02, 29 July 2002.

[8] ECHR, Ciubotaru v. Moldova, Application no. 27138/04, 27 April 2010.

[9] ECHR, Sejdić and Finci v.Bosnia and Herzegovina, Application nos. 27,996/06 and 34,836/06, 22 December 2009. See more, Lenzerini (2014), pp. 148–149. See also Donders (2018), pp. 176–177. The relevant law was modified in 1985 for the elimination of gender discrimination in determining the indigenous status. Barth (2008), pp. 134–154.

[10] Dagtoglou (1991), pp. 360–378. The view is also supported that, in reference to cultural, non-religious groups, the conditions in question for the admission or abandonment of a minority culture should not discriminate on the basis of gender, religion, or family ties. See, Sandra Lovelace v. Canada, Communication No. 24/1977: Canada 30/07/81, UN Doc. CCPR / C /13/ D /24/1977.

from a religious community, is also adopted by the European Court of Human Rights.[11]

The same applies to the prohibition of prosyletism. Primarily, it should be pointed out that since the choice of religion or belief is part of the *forum internum,* which does not allow for restrictions, a general prohibition of prosyletism or change of faith by the state is in conflict with the norms of international human rights law. A state also has a positive obligation to ensure that freedom of religion or belief of individuals within its territory and under its jurisdiction.[12] These observations seem to bring the *forum internum* into conflict with the *forum externum* of the right to religious freedom, that is, the manifestation of religious beliefs. In particular, the question arises whether the prohibition of prosyletism, violates the freedom to manifest the religious beliefs. The case law of the European Court of Human Rights is particularly enlightening regarding this issue. Specifically, the landmark *Kokkinakis v. Greece*[13] *case* is considered one of the most fundamental in the entire jurisprudence of the Court. The applicant was a Jehovah's Witness from Sitia (Crete). He and his wife visited in March 1986 the home of a Christian woman and engaged in a discussion with her regarding religious beliefs. Her husband, called the police who arrested them. Kokkinakis was convicted of proselytizing according to the Greek law. The applicant appealed to the European Court, alleging a violation of Article 9. The Court agreed with the applicant that his conviction for the offense of proselytizing undoubtedly infringed his right to freedom of manifestation of his religion. The Court pointed out that a "*distinction has to be made between bearing Christian witness and improper proselytism. The former corresponds to true evangelism, which a report drawn up in 1956 under the auspices of the World Council of Churches describes as an essential mission and a responsibility of every Christian and every Church. The latter represents a corruption or deformation of it. It may, according to the same report, take the form of activities offering material or social advantages with a view to gaining new members for a Church or exerting improper pressure on people in distress or in need; it may even entail the use of violence or brainwashing; more generally, it is not compatible with respect for the freedom of thought,*

[11] ECHR, Svyato - Mykhaylivska Parafiya v. Ukraine, Application No. 77703/01, 14 June 2007.

[12] In cases where non-state actors interfere with an individual's right to "have or adopt" a religion or belief of his choice, the requirements of Article 18 of the International Covenant on Civil and Political Rights and other relevant international instruments also imply a positive obligation on the state to protect persons from such interference. States must ensure that persons within their territory and persons under their jurisdiction, including members of religious minorities, practice the religion or belief of their choice without coercion or fear. If non-state actors interfere with this freedom, and in particular with the individual's freedom to change or maintain an individual's religion, the state is obliged to take appropriate measures to investigate, bring the perpetrators to justice and compensate the victims. General Assembly, A/60/399, Report of the Special Rapporteur of the Commission on Human Rights on freedom of religion or belief, Asma Jahangir, 30 September 2005, par. 52–53.

[13] ECHR, *Kokkinakis v. Greece,* Application no. 14307/88, 25 May 1993. Naskou Perraki (2006), pp. 321–325.

conscience and religion of others".[14] Thus, the Court observed that the Greek courts did not sufficiently identify the unfair means used to influence the cantor's wife, in violation of Article 9.[15]

Based on this case, the European Court of Human Rights distinguished between the right to disseminate and teach religious beliefs and the unlawful act of improper prosyletism. The first case is part of the freedom of manifestation of religion that can be exercised publicly, and within the circle of those who share their faith but also individually in a private space and includes the right to try to convince others. The second case can take the form activities that offer materials or social advantages for the purpose of acquisition of new members, the exercise of inappropriate pressure to people who are at risk or in need, the use of violence or brainwash. Therefore, it is not a compatible practice with the respect for freedom of thought, consciousness and religion but on the contrary it constitutes a distortion and a perversion of this right.[16] Thus, in 1998 in the *Larrisis and Others v. Greece case*[17] the European Court heard an interesting proselytizing case involving three Greek air force officers who belonged to the Church of Pentecost and who had been found guilty of proselytizing by a Greek court. The Court vindicated Greece on the part of the plaintiffs' conviction for proselytizing, due to the hierarchical dependence inherent to the military structure, taking into consideration the particular characteristics of military life and its effects on the situation of individual members of the armed forces, but condemned Greece on the part of proselytizing civilians.[18] At this point, a reservation is necessary: According to Naskou-Perraki the Court traced the distinction between abusive prosyletism and proper witness to the findings of an outdated report by the Christian World Council of Churches. Thus, the Court chose, in a religiously one--sided way, the elements for the proportionality check of the limitations to the religious freedom, namely the way of jeopardizing freedoms of others (offering advantages, abusive pressure, use of force, brainwashing) and the seriousness of the risk (corruption and distortion of the Christian testimony). The reservation lies in the fact that issue of the dissemination of religious beliefs is regulated on an *ad hoc* basis by the second paragraph of Article 18 of the International Covenant on Civil and Political Rights, according to which "*No one shall be subject to coercion which would impair his freedom to have or to adopt a religion or belief of his choice*". Consequently, the fair balance between measures restricting religious freedom and the need to protect the rights of proselytes is disturbed, not only when a general ban

---

[14] ECHR, *Kokkinakis v. Greece,* Application no. 14307/88, 25 May 1993, par. 48.

[15] Papapolychroniou (2008), p. 97. Also, Kastanas (2013), pp. 363–393. See also, Evans (2017), pp. 83–98.

[16] Report of the Special Rapporteur on freedom of religion or belief, Asma Jahangir - Missionto Sri Lanka, E/CN.4/2006/5/Add.3, par. 70–78.

[17] ECHR, Larrisis and Others v. Greece, Application No s. 23372/94; 26,377/94; 26,378/94, 24 February 1998.

[18] Pollis (1999), pp. 184–185.

on the propagation of beliefs is imposed, but also when less restricting measures are applied, instead of those chosen to prevent cases of coercion.[19]

It can be concluded that the right to choose a culture or a religion includes the freedom to change or "exit" a culture without adverse consequences for the individual's choice.[20] The European Court of Human Rights considers that the right to exit constitutes the absolute guarantee of freedom of thought, conscience and religion. Therefore, Article 9 of the European Convention on Human Rights does not guarantee an opposition right within a religious body. In case of disagreement on the subjects of doctrine between one religious community and one of its members, the religious freedom of the individual is secured through the freedom to withdraw from the community.[21]

The concept of the exit rights is based on the perception of the individual as a member of a group, who nevertheless maintains the autonomy to determine their life. The right of exit focuses on the practical possibility of a rupture between individual preferences, beliefs or rights and the preferences and beliefs of one's group. Thus, the right to exit can provide an opportunity for the individual to leave oppressive conditions and join a lifestyle with more personal freedom. However, the declaration of this right, without social and legal institutions and mechanisms for its implementation, is problematic and inadequate.[22] In addition, the realization of the right of exit is related to an abstract right, that of "entry" into the mainstream culture. In this respect, the right of entry should provide the opportunity for involvement in the civic and political life of the dominant culture, without this transition

---

[19] Naskou Perraki (2006), pp. 346–347. According to the UN Human Rights Committee "*Article 18.2 bars coercion that would impair the right to have or adopt a religion or belief, including the use of threat of physical force or penal sanctions to compel believers or non-believers to adhere to their religious beliefs and congregations, to recant their religion or belief or to convert. Policies or practices having the same intention or effect, such as, for example, those restricting access to education, medical care, employment or the rights guaranteed by article 25 and other provisions of the Covenant, are similarly inconsistent with article 18.2. The same protection is enjoyed by holders of all beliefs of a non-religious nature*". UN Human Rights Committee (HRC), CCPR General Comment No. 22: Article 18 (Freedom of Thought, Conscience or Religion), 30 July 1993, CCPR/C/21/Rev.1/Add.4, par. 5.

[20] For several theorists of multiculturalism, and especially of the liberal approach, the right to leave a culture or religion is the most basic condition for the consolidation of tolerance to different cultural practices. See, Kukathas (2003), p. 112.

[21] See ECHR, Karlsson v. Sweden, Application no. 12356/86, decision of the Commission of 8 September 1988, ECHR, Spetz and Others v. Sweden, Application no. 20402/92, decision of the Commission of 12 October 1994, ECHR, Williamson v. the United Kingdom, Application no. 27008/95, decision of the Commission of 17 May 1995, ECHR, Holy Synod of the Bulgarian Orthodox Church (Metropolitan Inokentiy) and Others v. *Bulgaria*, Application nos. 412/03 and 35,677/04, 22 January 2009. However, in many cases the exit from a minority culture is practically impossible or can bring about damaging consequences for the life and development of the individual. As Levy concludes, everything about a culture is an exit barrier. A culture, the exit from which is completely inexpensive, is not a culture. Levy (2000), p. 112.

[22] Ben-Porath (2010), p. 1023.

necessarily entailing a complete renunciation of ties to the minority culture of the individual's origin.

The main condition for the actual possibility of exercising an individual's right to exit is the existence of a wider open society.[23] Moreover, the systematic involvement, both legal and social, of the state institutions is a necessary condition for the fulfillment of the right to entry. For example, providing protection to victims of religious violence, providing all levels of education that provide opportunities for skill development, the implementation of integration programs similar to immigrant integration programs, the provision of health services that take into account cultural specificities, support in the search for housing and access to financial services etc.[24]

The right to exit a cultural community implies a corresponding right to "enter" either the mainstream culture or another minority group. Under the principle of autonomy, a state cannot force a religious community to accept or expel members.[25] This right of entry requires measures to support participation in civic and political life within the dominant culture, without requiring individuals to abandon their minority cultural identity. An open, inclusive society that respects individual choices is essential for enabling such transitions.[26]

Based on the above, the European Court of Human Rights strikes a fair and necessary balance in protecting both the individual's right to autonomy and the community's collective interests. By recognizing the right to enter or exit a culture as part of the broader framework of private life and religious freedom, the Court ensures that personal identity is safeguarded without undermining the cohesion of society. The case law illustrates that while freedom of cultural and religious self-determination is absolute in the *forum internum*, its external manifestation must still respect the rights and freedoms of others. This nuanced approach avoids both extremes: neither imprisoning individuals in identities they no longer embrace nor allowing unrestricted practices that could harm others. Ultimately, the ECHR's jurisprudence provides a workable model for balancing autonomy, diversity, and social harmony, ensuring that the right to cultural choice is meaningful in practice.

References

Barth WK (2008) On cultural rights, the equality of nations and the minority legal tradition. Martinus Nijhoff Publishers, Leiden

Ben-Porath S (2010) Exit rights and entrance paths: accommodating cultural diversity in a Liberal democracy. Perspect Polit 8(4):1021–1103

Bradley N (2018) Essentialism in the concept of culture: gauging belief. J Intercult Commun 21:1–21

[23] Kukathas (1992), p. 134.

[24] Ben-Porath (2010) p. 1025–1029.

[25] ECHR, Svyato-Mykhaylivska Parafiya v. Ukraine, Application no. 77703/01, 14 June 2007.

[26] Kukathas (1992), p. 134.

Dagtoglou P (1991) Constitutional law, individual rights, vol. a. Antonis N. Sakkoulas, Athens--Komotini (in Greek)
Donders Y (2018) Towards a right to cultural identity? Yes, indeed! Diritti Umani e Diritto Internazionale 12(3):523–548
Evans M (2017) The freedom of religion or belief in the ECHR since Kokkinakis: or quoting Kokkinakis. Religion Human Rights 12:83–98
Hall S (1997) Cultural identity and diaspora. In: Woodward K (ed) Identity and difference. SAGE Publications, pp 51–59
Kastanas H (2013) Article 9. In: Sisilianos LA (ed) European convention on human rights, interpretation by article. Nomiki Vivliothiki, Athens, pp 363–393. (in Greek)
Kukathas C (1992) Are there any cultural rights? Political Theory 20(1):105–139
Kukathas C (2003) The Liberal archipelago: a theory of diversity and freedom. Oxford University Press, New York
Kymlicka W (1989) Liberalism, community, and culture. Oxford University Press, Oxford
Kymlicka W (1995) Multicultural citizenship: a Liberal theory of minority rights. Oxford University Press, Oxford
Kymlicka W (2001) Politics in the vernacular: nationalism, multiculturalism, and citizenship. Oxford University Press, Oxford
Lenzerini F (2014) The Culturalization of human rights law. Oxford University Press, Oxford
Levy TJ (2000) The multiculturalism of fear. Oxford University Press, Oxford
Naskou Perraki P (2006) Religious Freedom. In: Naskou-Perraki P, Kistakis G (eds) Greek cases in Strasbourg, volume I, 1991–2001. Ant. N. Sakkoulas, Thessaloniki-Athens, pp 321–353. (in Greek)
Papapolychroniou S (2008) Interpretative pluralism as a condition for inclusion of minority values in law: the example of religious minorities in Greece and the "dominant" religion. In: Christopoulos D (ed) The unrecognized issue of minorities in the Greek legal order. Minority Groups Research Center, Kritiki Publications, Athens, pp 89–126. (in Greek)
Pierce AJ (2012) Collective identity, oppression, and the right to self-ascription. Lexington Books, London
Pikramenos MN (2019) What does it mean that I can freely develop my personality? (in Greek). https://www.syntagmawatch.gr/my-constitution/ti-simainei-oti-boro-na- anaptyxo-elefthera-tin-prosopikotita-mou/
Pollis A (1999) Greece: a problematic secular state. In: Tsitselikis K, Christopoulos D (ed), Legal Issues of Religious Otherness in Greece, Center for Research on Minority Groups, Ed. Kritiki & KEMO, Athens, pp. 165–197. (in Greek)

Chapter 4
The Right to Equality

Contents

The principles of equality and non-discrimination concern differences in behavior arising from human activity.[1] As key principles of international human rights law they also embed the right to be different. Until recently, the principles of equality and non-discrimination were perceived as secondary and difficult to apply. For example, Article 14 of the European Convention on Human Rights, which refers to non -discrimination is only applied in conjunction with some other substantive provision of the Convention. Article 1 of Protocol No. 12 extended the scope of the principle of non discrimination.[2]

It is argued that equality and non-discrimination in human rights law express the positive and negative content of the same principle and that is why the two concepts are used interchangeably.[3] In the context of the European Convention of Human Rights the two terms are used as identical without a conscious choice as to their true meaning. This view is also expressed in the explanatory memorandum to Additional Protocol 12 to the European Convention on Human Rights.[4]

[1] Kanellopoulos (2010), p. 330.

[2] Allen (2007), p. 10. See also McCrudden (2003), p. 10.

[3] McKean (1983), p. 288.

[4] Council of Europe, Protocol No. 12 to the Convention for the Protection of Human Rights and Fundamental Freedoms, Explanatory Report, (ETS No. 177) Rome, 4.XI.2000. It should be noted that the European Union adopts the same view. See for example Judgment of the Court (First Chamber) of 27 January 2005, Europe Chemi-Con (Deutschland) GmbH v Council of the European Union, C-422/02 P, ECLI:EU:C:2005:56. Tridimas (2006), p. 64.

N. Gaitenidis, *The Rights of Cultural Identity in the Case Law of the European Court of Human Rights*, European Union and its Neighbours in a Globalized World 36, https://doi.org/10.1007/978-3-032-23045-4_4

4.1 Prohibition of Discrimination

Having equal rights is not the same as being treated equally. Indeed, equality and non-discrimination not only imply that equal situations should be treated equally (direct discrimination), but also that unequal situations should be treated unequally (indirect discrimination).[5] Prohibiting indirect discrimination makes greater progress in protecting cultural identity. This progress lies mainly in the fact that it "illuminates" practices and criteria, which while seemingly neutral, tend to favor the dominant/majority culture. In this respect, this approach does not ignore *de facto* cultural, religious or social differences, but instead urges them to be taken into account, thus reducing the "cost" of the individual's participation in a cultural, religious or ethnic minority group.[6]

Any discussion on the principle of equality in pluralistic societies could not avoid examining possible conflicts between equality and other values or the general interest. For example, in the *Mann case Singh v. France,* the European Court of

[5] Donders (2010), pp. 15–35.

[6] Fredman (2001), p. 24. It should be noted that in the framework of the European Union a comprehensive anti-discrimination legislation have been developed. In the secondary law of the European Union there are mainly two Directives for combating discrimination, the Directive 2000/43/EC, on the implementation of the principle of equal treatment of persons regardless of their racial or ethnic origin and the Directive 2000/ 78/EC establishing a general framework for equal treatment in employment and work. The two Directives apply to all persons, in the public and private sector. However, they differ in their scope. Thus, the Racial Discrimination Directive applies in cases concerning the conditions of access to employment and self-employment, vocational training, social protection, education, housing etc. However, it only applies in cases of discrimination due to ethnic or racial origin. The Employment Equality Directive, despite the fact that it includes a wider set of protected characteristics, applies only to cases relating to the field of work, i.e. conditions of access to employment, self-employment and work, including selection criteria and conditions recruitment, regardless of the sector of activity and at all levels of the professional hierarchy, including promotions, access to all types and all levels of vocational guidance, vocational training, retraining and vocational reorientation, including the acquisition of practical work experience, work conditions and terms of employment, including dismissal and remuneration, membership and participation in an organization of workers or employers or in any organization whose members practice a particular occupation, including benefits sponsored by such organizations. The two Directives do not apply in cases of different treatment due to nationality, which is mainly regulated by Directive 2004/38/EC on the right of citizens of the Union and their family members to move and reside freely in the territory of the Member States. Also the Court of the European Union has developed an extensive body of case law regarding the prohibition of discrimination for example, Judgment of the Court (Grand Chamber) of 15 July 2021, IX v WABE eV and MH Müller Handels GmbH v MJ, Joined Cases C-804/18 and C-341/19, ECLI:EU:C:2021:594, Judgment of the Court (Second Chamber) of 10 July 2008, Centrum voor gelijkheid van kansen en voor racismebestrijding v Firma Feryn NV, C-54/07, ECLI:EU:C:2008:397, Judgment of the Court (Grand Chamber) of 14 March 2017, Samira Achbita and Centrum voor gelijkheid van kansen en voor racismebestrijding v G4S Secure Solutions NV, C-157/15, ECLI:EU:C:2017:203, Judgment of the Court (Grand Chamber) of 16 July 2015, "CHEZ Razpredelenie Bulgaria" AD v Komisia za zashtita ot diskriminatsia, C-83/14, ECLI:EU:C:2015:480, Judgment of the Court (Second Chamber) of 13 October 2022, S.C.R.L. (Vêtement à connotation religieuse), C-344/20, ECLI:EU:C:2022:774. See more at FRA (2018a, b), pp. 34–38.

Human Rights was confronted with the question whether the French obligation to appear bareheaded on photographs on identity documents was compatible with the rights protected by the European Convention on Human Rights. The Court has ruled that it is a necessary measure for public safety and protection of public policy, in particular in the context of checks carried out during the driver's movement. Thus, the Court decided that the ban on the wearing of the religious turban of the Sikhs in the photo of the driving license and therefore the restriction of Articles 8 and 9 in conjunction with Article 14 of the European Convention on Human Rights was justifiable for reasons of public safety and public order.[7]

As far as the religious or ethnic identity of individuals is concerned, the case law of the European Court of Human Rights is quite rich in examples of the application of virtually neutral rules, which, however, tend to embrace the practices of the dominant culture, especially in cases where the general "public interest" is concerned.[8] A typical example is the case of the UK's urban planning laws, which were at odds with the nomadic way of life of Roma or gypsies. The *Buckley v. the United Kingdom case highlights the* European Court of Human Rights' reluctance *to deepen the principle of equality, effectively equating the notion of the public interest with the perception of the dominant social group. In particular, the Court, although acknowledging the special way of life and vulnerable social position of the gypsy minority, ruled that the authorities' refusal to grant a caravan permit to a privately owned area which was not an official gypsy settlement, for reasons of proper planning, pursued a legitimate aim necessary in a democratic society, within the limits of the discretion (margin of appreciation) of the national authorities.*[9]

In the landmark *Thlimmenos v. Greece* case, a Jehovah's Witness was convicted of a felony for having refused to enlist in the army at a time when Greece did not provide alternative service to conscientious objectors (*legem secundum*) to military service. A few years later he was refused appointment as a chartered accountant on the grounds of his conviction despite his having scored very well in a public competition for the position in question. The Court found a violation of Article 14 in conjunction with Article 9, since the authorities had failed to differentiate from other persons convicted of serious crimes. Thlimmenos's crime was different as it resulted from the very exercise of his freedom of religion, and could not, unlike

[7] ECHR, Mann Singh v. France, Application No. 24479/07, 21 November 2008. It should be noted that the same applicant made a claim concerning the prohibition to wear a turban on the photograph on his passport (instead of his driver's license) in front of the UN Human Rights Committee. In (Mann) Singh v. France (HRC, 26/09/2013, CCPR/C/108/D/1928/2010), the Human Rights Committee decided that prohibiting a Sikh to wear a turban on the identity photograph, without convincingly explaining how such a measure is necessary for guaranteeing the public safety, violates the individual's right to manifest his religion (Article 18 of the ICCPR). See more, Strasbourg Observers academic blog (2013), para 3.

[8] Fredman (2001), p. 33.

[9] ECHR, Buckley v. the United Kingdom, Application No. 20348/92, 7 February 1992.

other convictions for serious criminal offences, imply any dishonesty or moral turpitude likely to undermine his ability to exercise this profession.[10]

The *Ahmad v. The United Kingdom* case is an example that demonstrates the burden of some religious minorities when their religious practices are not compatible with the structured working conditions based on Christian values. The case concerned the forced resignation of a Muslim teacher from his job when his request for leave on Fridays so that he could pray in the mosque, according to his "strict" religious traditions was not accepted. The British court ruled that the applicant's right to express his religious beliefs should be restricted in favor of the rights of third parties, i.e. the educational authorities under the contract he had signed, as well as the rights of the students he was obliged to teach. The case went to the European Commission of Human Rights, which rejected the appeal on the basis of a narrow interpretation of equality, as it considered that only other religious minorities could be the comparative criterion. That is to say, the Commission considered that since all religious minorities were obliged to conform to the standards of the majority religion, the applicant was not subject to 'less favorable treatment', noting that in most countries only the religious holidays of the majority of the population were considered public holidays.[11]

In *Kosteski v. Former Yugoslav Republic of Macedonia*, the applicant was fined for taking a one-day holiday without permission to celebrate the Muslim religious holiday Bayram. The national court noted that Kosteski did not give any evidence concerning his beliefs and, thus, was not discriminated. The European Court of Human Rights restated this decision by stressing that a manifestation of belief in the particular case was not proven. According to the Court, the employer's request to prove the employee's religious affiliation in order to legitimately enjoy certain privileges in the workplace does not breach Article 9 in conjunction with Article 14 of the Convention. More specifically, the Court stated that it does not find it unreasonable that an employer may regard absence without permission or apparent justification as a disciplinary matter. Where the employee then seeks to rely on a particular exemption, it is not oppressive or in fundamental conflict with freedom of conscience to require some level of substantiation especially when that claim concerns a privilege or entitlement not commonly available. The ritual precepts of some religions can, sometimes, conflict with the professional obligations of their followers and require that their employer (public or private) take specific measures to reconcile them. However, Article 9 of the Convention does not guarantee, as such, the right of the worker to take time off from work on religious holidays. When the national law establishes a special privilege or exemption for members of a religious community, especially in matters of employment, it is not contrary to Article 9 to place the burden on the interested party on providing at least a minimum

[10] ECHR, Thlimmenos v. Greece, Application No. 34369/97, 6 April 2000.

[11] ECHR, Ahmad v. The United Kingdom (1982) 4 EHRR 126. See also, ECHR, X. v the United Kingdom, Application no. 8160/78, 12 March 1981. See Fredman (2001), p. 34.

justification of the reality of his belonging to this community in order to benefit from this special treatment.[12]

The European Court of Human Rights in the *Stec and Others v. the United Kingdom*[13] argued that in certain cases, the failure to try to correct inequalities through different treatment could be considered a violation of Article 14. Similarly, in the *Chapman v. The United Kingdom* the Court stated that the vulnerable position of the gypsies as a minority means that some special attention should be paid to their needs and their different way of life. In this respect, there is a positive obligation on the part of the states under Article 8 to facilitate the gypsy way of life.[14] The Court also observed the emerging international consensus between state parties of Council of Europe, which recognizes the special needs of minorities and the obligation of states to protect their security, identity and lifestyle, not only for the purpose of safeguarding the interests of minorities, but also for the purpose of conservation of cultural diversity as a societal value.[15]

The cases of *Lavida and others v. Greece*[16] and *Sampanis and others v. Greece*[17] should be mentioned, in which the Court concluded that the compulsory attendance of Roma children in a primary school in which the only students were other Roma children consists a violation of Article 14 of the European Convention on Human Rights in conjunction with Article 2 of the 1st Protocol to the Convention (right to education).

In *Wa Baile v. Switzerland* (2024),[18] the ECtHR unanimously ruled that a Black Swiss man's identity check at Zürich railway station constituted racial profiling, violating Article 14 (prohibition of discrimination) and Article 8 (right to private life) of the ECHR, both procedurally and substantively, as well as Article 13 (right to an effective remedy). Unlike *Basu v. Germany*[19] and *Muhammad v. Spain* (2022),[20] which focused on individual intent, the Court recognized the systemic nature of racial profiling in Swiss policing, citing inadequate training and legal frameworks. It shifted the burden of proof to Switzerland, which failed to justify the check. However, the Court's single-categorical approach overlooked intersectional factors (e.g., perceived immigrant status), limiting its transformative potential.[21] Similarly, in the case of *Seydi and Others v. France* (2025) the Court rejected five of the six applications for failing to meet the evidentiary threshold of "strong, clear, and

---

[12] ECHR, Kosteski v. Former Yugoslav Republic of Macedonia, Application No. 55170/00, 13 July 2006. See also, Wolff (2021), pp. 259–286.

[13] ECHR, *Stec* and Others *v. the United Kingdom, Applications nos. 65,731/01 and 65,900/01, 12 April 2006.*

[14] ECHR, Chapman v. the United Kingdom, Application No, 27238/95, 18 January 2001.

[15] ECHR, DH and Others v. the Czech Republic, Application No. 57325/00, 13 November 2007.

[16] ECHR, Lavida and Others v. Greece, Application no. 7973/10, 30 May 2013.

[17] ECHR, Sampanis and others v. Greece, Application no. 59608/09, 11 December 2012.

[18] ECHR, *Wa Baile c. Suisse,* Requêtes nos 43,868/18 et 25,883/21, 20 février 2024.

[19] ECHR, Basu v. Germany, Application no. 215/19, 18 October 2022.

[20] ECHR, *Muhammad v. Spain,* Application no. 34085/17, 18 October 2022.

[21] Dube (2024).

concordant inferences," but it found a violation in the case of Karim Touil, who had been stopped three times in ten days, including one instance involving verbal abuse and violence. For the Court, these circumstances created a strong presumption of discrimination, which the French state failed to rebut with objective justification.[22]

Although the Court did not address the wider issue of systemic racial profiling, the judgment is significant in two respects. First, it clarifies that identity checks fall within the scope of private life and may therefore trigger scrutiny under non-discrimination provisions. Second, it signals to states that repeated, unexplained stops of ethnic minorities cannot be justified as routine policing. The ruling strengthens individual protections against discriminatory practices and places pressure on states to ensure that police powers are exercised with transparency, accountability, and respect for human dignity.[23]

Based on the above, it can be concluded that the prohibition of discrimination under the ECHR requires more than formal equality; it demands recognition of the structural disadvantages faced by minorities and a willingness to treat unequal situations unequally where necessary. The Court's case law shows that rules which appear neutral often privilege the majority culture, and therefore indirect discrimination must be addressed if equality is to be meaningful. Over time, the Court has expanded the concept of equality to encompass modern phenomena such as racial profiling, as demonstrated in *Wa Baile v. Switzerland* and *Seydi and Others v. France*, where identity checks targeting ethnic minorities were found to fall within the scope of private life and discrimination analysis. This development reflects a broader understanding of how systemic practices, rather than overt laws, perpetuate inequality.

At the same time, the jurisprudence highlights a persistent tension between protecting individual rights and respecting public order or majority values. While the Court applies especially strict scrutiny to racial discrimination,[24] its approach to religious discrimination remains more reserved,[25] partly because religion is considered a matter of individual choice.[26] Still, the Court increasingly acknowledges that both racial and religious identities are integral to human dignity, and that states have positive obligations to remove hidden barriers, ensure effective participation of minorities, and promote cultural diversity.[27] In this way, Article 14 evolves into a powerful instrument not only against overt exclusion but also against subtler practices like profiling, thereby strengthening genuine equality in pluralistic societies.

---

[22] ECHR, Seydi and Others v. France, Requête no 35844/17, 26 juin 2025.

[23] Farrior (2024), pp. 94–141.

[24] ECHR, Timishev v. Russia, Applications nos. 55,762/00 and 55,974/00, 13 December 2005.

[25] ECHR, Hoffman v. Austria, Application No. 12875/87, 23 June 1993.

[26] Pitt (2007), p. 225.

[27] Benedi Lahuera (2009), pp. 748–749.

4.2 Protection of Vulnerable Groups

The vulnerability criterion, developed by the European Court of Human Rights (ECtHR) within its Article 14 jurisprudence, was initially introduced to strengthen anti-discrimination protections by narrowing the state's margin of appreciation when dealing with disadvantaged groups. This framework, which has roots in cases such as *Chapman v. United Kingdom* (2001)[28] and crystallized with *D.H. and Others v. Czech Republic* (2007),[29] identifies groups such as Roma communities, asylum seekers, persons with disabilities, and victims of domestic violence as requiring "special protection."[30] Arnardóttir shows that while this seems like a novel doctrine, it often mirrors earlier "suspect grounds" reasoning, where discrimination on the basis of race, gender, or religion already triggered strict scrutiny.[31]

What the vulnerability criterion contributes is an explicit recognition of structural disadvantage and social exclusion, connecting law to lived experiences of marginalization. Cultural identity often becomes central: in *Chapman*, the Court highlighted the Roma's traditional lifestyle as part of their vulnerability, while in *Oršuš and Others v. Croatia* (2010),[32] it stressed the Roma's turbulent history and cultural distinctiveness in finding indirect discrimination in segregated schooling. These cases illustrate how the vulnerability framework has served as a conduit for acknowledging and, to some extent, protecting minority cultural identity.[33]

Yet, as both So Yeon Kim and Arnardóttir argue, the vulnerability criterion is applied inconsistently and risks entrenching paternalism when cultural identity is at stake. For example, in *Muñoz Díaz v. Spain* (2009),[34] the Court acknowledged the Roma applicant's marriage, celebrated under Roma cultural traditions, as relevant to her vulnerability in being denied a widow's pension. This recognition affirmed her cultural identity, but the Court did not always extend similar reasoning in cases involving other minority practices. Likewise, in *B.S. v. Spain* (2012),[35] where an African woman working as a prostitute alleged police abuse, the Court noted her "particular vulnerability" at the intersection of race, gender, and social status, but this emphasis still framed her identity primarily through weakness rather than agency. Arnardóttir emphasizes that the Court's vulnerability reasoning is socially contextual, rooted in histories of prejudice and exclusion, but warns that it can slip into essentializing groups as inherently fragile.[36]

---

[28] ECHR, Chapman v. the United Kingdom, Application No. 27238/95, 18 January 2001.

[29] ECHR, *D.H. and Others v. Czech Republic,* Application No. 57325/00, 13 November 2007.

[30] Kim (2021), p. 617.

[31] Arnardóttir (2017), p. 150.

[32] ECHR, Oršuš and Others v. Croatia, Application no. 15766/03, 16 March 2010.

[33] Arnardóttir (2017), pp. 150–171.

[34] ECHR, Muñoz Díaz v. Spain, Application no. 49151/07, 8 December 2009.

[35] ECHR, B.S. v. Spain, Application no. 47159/08, 24 July 2012.

[36] Arnardóttir (2017), pp. 150–171.

When cultural identity is subsumed under vulnerability, minority groups risk being perpetually cast as passive victims instead of active rights-holders. A stronger framework would shift from group-based vulnerability to one grounded in **individual autonomy and dignity**, protecting cultural identity as an inherent right rather than a marker of fragility. This would not only mitigate stereotypes but also ensure a more principled and consistent Article 14 jurisprudence, aligning minority cultural protection with a robust vision of substantive equality.[37]

A more robust approach would pivot from group-based vulnerability to a framework centered on individual autonomy and dignity. This shift would prioritize protecting cultural identity as an inherent right, grounded in the principle that individuals should freely live according to their traditions and identities without discrimination. Such a reorientation could mitigate the risk of stereotyping while fostering a more inclusive and consistent jurisprudence, ensuring that cultural identity is safeguarded not because of perceived weakness but as a fundamental aspect of human dignity. This analytical reframing demands further scrutiny of the ECtHR's case law to assess whether a dignity-based approach could better balance the protection of minority rights with the empowerment of individuals within those communities.[38]

4.3 Protection from Racist Violence

During the last few years, Europe has been tested by the consequences of serious economic and political developments taking place both inside and outside its territory. Within this edgy environment, racism is nurtured, shaped and reinforced as a phenomenon on such alarming dimensions that it is commonly accepted that its treatment, in order to be effective, needs to be multifaceted and the intervention of the criminal legislator is now imperative, or at least justified.[39]

Racism and xenophobia are in direct conflict with the principles of freedom, democracy, respect of human rights and fundamental freedoms, and the rule of law. Furthermore, according to the European Court of Human Rights, tolerance and respect of the equal dignity of all human beings are the foundation of a democratic, pluralistic society.[40] The European Court of Human Rights has affirmed that "*the authorities must use all available means to combat racism and racist violence, thereby reinforcing democracy's vision of a society in which diversity is not perceived as a threat but as a source of its enrichment*".[41] Thus, the prohibition of certain forms of racism and related intolerance is part of the wider framework of

[37] Kim (2021), pp. 617–632.

[38] Arnardóttir (2017), pp. 150–171; Kim (2021), pp. 617–632.

[39] Giannakoula (2018), pp. 89–110.

[40] ECHR, Erbakan v. Turkey, Application no. 59405/00, 6 July 2006.

[41] ECHR, Nachova and others v, Bulgaria, Application nos. 43,577/98 and 43,579/98, 6 July 2005.

combating discrimination as racism prevents equal participation in the social environment.[42]

The activation of criminal law in the specific field, at International, European and national level, aims in particular to respond to the need to combat the manifestations of racism, in order to protect the persons who suffer from them and the groups to which they belong and additionally to control the upheavals and consequent risks created for social cohesion and the democratic order. In this respect, two main forms of racist and intolerant manifestations are prosecuted, namely the criminalization of hate speech and the combating of hate crimes.[43]

4.3.1 Protection from Hate Speech and Historical Denialism

Many criminal codes in Europe have prohibited hate speech and treat it as a criminal offense. However, the application of a universal, common definition of hate speech remains a difficult and controversial issue,[44] with many arguments in favor of the repression of this form of intolerance through criminal law and an equal amount of arguments against the criminalization of hate speech.[45] According to the Committee of Ministers of the Council of Europe, hate speech covers all forms of expressions that spread, incite, promote or justify racial hatred, xenophobia, anti-Semitism or other forms of hatred based on intolerance.[46] Also, according to the Additional Protocol to the Convention on Cybercrime concerning the criminalization of acts of a racist and xenophobic nature committed through computer systems of the Council of Europe "racist and xenophobic material" means any written material, any image or any other representation of ideas or theories, which advocates, promotes or incites hatred, discrimination or violence, against any individual or group of individuals, based on race, color, descent or national or ethnic origin, as well as religion if used as a pretext for any of these factors. Each Party shall adopt such legislative and other measures as may be necessary to establish as criminal offences under its domestic law, when committed intentionally and without right, the following conduct: distributing, or otherwise making available, racist and xenophobic material to the public through a computer system. According to the European Commission against Racism and Intolerance (ECRI), hate speech is "*the use of one or more particular forms of expression – namely, the advocacy, promotion or incitement of the denigration, hatred or vilification of a person or group of persons, as well any harassment, insult, negative stereotyping, stigmatization or threat of such person or*

[42] Anagnostopoulou (2019), pp. 169–171.

[43] Giannakoula (2018), p. 90.

[44] Rokša Zubčevič et al. (2017), p. 8.

[45] Bromell (2022), pp. 167–187.

[46] Recommendation No. R (97) 20 of the Committee of Ministers on "hate speech", adopted on 30 October 1997.

persons and any justification of all these forms of expression – that is based on a non- exhaustive list of personal characteristics or status that includes "race", color, language, religion or belief, nationality or national or ethnic origin, as well as descent, age, disability, sex, gender, gender identity and sexual orientation".[47] The European Court of Human Rights understands hate speech as speech that "*incite, promote or justify racial hatred, xenophobia, anti-Semitism or other forms of hatred based on intolerance*" as a starting point in its related judgments.[48]

The most comprehensive definition of hate speech is provided by the European Union Council Framework Decision 2008/913/JHA on combating certain forms and expressions of racism and xenophobia by means of criminal law.[49] The Framework Decision, on Article 1, recognizes as "hate speech" the following forms of speech: a) Publicly inciting to violence or hatred directed against a group of persons or a member of such a group defined by reference to race, color, religion, descent or national or ethnic origin. b) Public dissemination or distribution of tracts, pictures or other material that incites to violence or hatred directed against a group of persons or a member of such a group defined by reference to race, color, religion, descent or national or ethnic origin. c) Publicly condoning, denying or grossly trivializing crimes of genocide, crimes against humanity and war crimes as defined in

---

[47] European Commission against Racism and Intolerance (ECRI), General Policy Recommendation No 15 on "hate speech" 8.12.2016.

[48] ECHR, Gündüz v. Turkey, Application no. 35071/97, fourth December 2003.

[49] Council Framework Decision 2008/913/JHA of 28 November 2008 on combating certain forms and expressions of racism and xenophobia by means of criminal law, OJ L 328, 6.12.2008, p. 55–58. The Framework Decision is aimed at defining a common, EU wide criminal law approach to certain racist and xenophobic conducts, in order to ensure that the same behavior constitutes an offence in all Member States and that effective, proportionate and dissuasive penalties are provided for natural and legal persons having committed or being liable for such offences. Report from the Commission to the European Parliament and the Council on the implementation of Council Framework Decision 2008/913/JHA on combating certain forms and expressions of racism and xenophobia by means of criminal law, COM(2014)27 final. In addition, according to Article 20, par. 2, of the International Covenant on Civil and Political Rights (ICPPR) of 1966 "any advocacy of national, racial or religious hatred that constitutes incitement to discrimination, hostility or violence shall be prohibited by law". Furthermore, Article 4 of the Convention for the Elimination of Racial Discrimination (CERD) reads as follows: "*States Parties condemn all propaganda and all organizations which are based on ideas or theories of superiority of one race or group of persons of one color or ethnic origin, or which attempt to justify or promote racial hatred and discrimination in any form, and undertake to adopt immediate and positive measures designed to eradicate all incitement to, or acts of, such discrimination and, to this end, with due regard to the principles embodied in the Universal Declaration of Human Rights and the rights expressly set forth in Article 5 of this Convention, inter alia: a) Shall declare an offence punishable by law all dissemination of ideas based on racial superiority or hatred, incitement to racial discrimination, as well as all acts of violence or incitement to such acts against any race or group of persons of another color or ethnic origin, and also the provision of any assistance to racist activities, including the financing thereof; b) Shall declare illegal and prohibit organizations, and also organized and all other propaganda activities, which promote and incite racial discrimination, and shall recognize participation in such organizations or activities as an offence punishable by law; c) Shall not permit public authorities or public institutions, national or local, to promote or incite racial discrimination*".

Articles 6, 7 and 8 of the Statute of the International Criminal Court, directed against a group of persons or a member of such a group defined by reference to race, color, religion, descent or national or ethnic origin when the conduct is carried out in a manner likely to incite to violence or hatred against such a group or a member of such a group. d) Publicly condoning, denying or grossly trivializing the crimes defined in Article 6 of the Charter of the International Military Tribunal appended to the London Agreement of 8 August 1945, directed against a group of persons or a member of such a group defined by reference to race, color, religion, descent or national or ethnic origin when the conduct is carried out in a manner likely to incite to violence or hatred against such a group or a member of such a group.[50]

The criminalization of hate speech has sparked a considerable amount of controversy as a number of scholars consider that a democratic society has the obligation to tolerate even the opinions that are racist, hateful and intolerant.[51] After all, the European Court of Human Rights has declared that "*Freedom of expression constitutes one of the essential foundations of [a democratic] society, one of the basic conditions for its progress and for the development of every man. Subject to paragraph 2 of Article 10 [of the European Convention on Human Rights], it is applicable not only to 'information' or 'ideas' that are favourably received or regarded as inoffensive or as a matter of indifference, but also to those that offend, shock or disturb the State or any sector of the population. Such are the demands of that pluralism, tolerance and broadmindedness without which there is no 'democratic society'. This means, amongst other things that every 'formality', 'condition', 'restriction' or 'penalty' imposed in this sphere must be proportionate to the legitimate aim pursued*".[52]

When dealing with cases concerning incitement to hatred and freedom of expression, the European Court of Human Rights uses two approaches which are provided for by the European Convention on Human Rights: (a) the approach of exclusion from the protection of the Convention, provided by Article 17 (prohibition of abuse of rights), where the comments in question amount to hate speech and negate the fundamental values of the Convention, and (b) the approach of setting restrictions on freedom of expression, as provided by the Article 10, para 2, of the Convention; this approach is applied in cases where the expression that is examined, although falls under the definition of hate speech, is not apt to destroy the fundamental values of the Convention. Internet news portals which, for commercial and professional purposes, provide a platform for user-generated comments assume the "*duties and responsibilities*" associated with freedom of expression in accordance with Article 10 para 2 of the Convention where users disseminate hate speech or comments amounting to direct incitement to violence.[53] In such cases the European Court of Human Rights takes into consideration a) the content of the speech and b) the

---

[50] See more at Peršak (2022), pp. 85–119. See also, Belavusau (2012), pp. 20–25.

[51] Yves Kuhn (2019), pp. 119–147. See also, Pegorier (2018), pp. 97–126.

[52] ECHR, Handyside v. The United Kingdom, Application *No.* 5493/72, 7 December 1976.

[53] European Court of Human Rights (2022), p. 1.

potential impact on the religious faith of the persons concerned. For example in the Giniewski case the ECtHR ruled that the critical analysis of the papal encyclical "The Shining of Truth" did not constitute an "unreasonably offensive" article and did not incite intolerance or disrespect.[54]

In the *Norwood v. the United Kingdom*, the applicant had displayed in his window a poster supplied by the British National Party, of which he was a member, representing the Twin Towers in flame. The picture was accompanied by the words "Islam out of Britain – Protect the British People". As a result, he was convicted of aggravated hostility towards a religious group. The applicant argued, among other things, that his right to freedom of expression had been breached. The Court declared the application inadmissible (incompatible *ratione materiae*). It found in particular that such a general, vehement attack against a religious group, linking the group as a whole with a grave act of terrorism, was incompatible with the values proclaimed and guaranteed by the Convention, notably tolerance, social peace and non-discrimination. The Court therefore held that the applicant's display of the poster in his window had constituted an act within the meaning of Article 17 (prohibition of abuse of rights) of the Convention, and that the applicant could thus not claim the protection of Article 10 (freedom of expression) of the Convention.[55]

In the case of *Jersild v Denmark*, the Court held broadcasting a documentary of a racist organization does not constitute hate speech; it rather intends to present a social phenomenon of general interest to the public.[56] More recently, in the case *Šimunić v. Croatia*, the applicant, a football player, was convicted of a minor offence of addressing messages to spectators of a football match, the content of which expressed or enticed hatred on the basis of race, nationality and faith. He submitted in particular that his right to freedom of expression had been violated. The Court declared the applicant's complaint under Article 10 (freedom of expression) of the Convention inadmissible as being manifestly ill-founded, finding that the interference with his right to freedom of expression had been supported by relevant and sufficient reasons and that the Croatian authorities, having had regard to the relatively modest nature of the fine imposed on the applicant and the context in which he had shouted the impugned phrase, had struck a fair balance between his interest in free speech, on the one hand, and society's interests in promoting tolerance and mutual respect at sports events as well as combating discrimination through sport on the other hand, thus acting within their margin of appreciation. The Court noted in particular that the applicant, being a famous football player and a role-model for many football fans, should have been aware of the possible negative impact of provocative chanting on spectators' behavior, and should have abstained from such conduct.[57]

---

[54] ECHR, Giniewski v. France, Application no. 64016/00, 31 January 2006. See also, Stavrinaki (2017), pp. 475–518.

[55] ECHR, Norwood v. the United Kingdom, Application no. 23131/03, 16 November 2004.

[56] ECHR, Jersild v.Denmark, Application No. 15890/89, 23 September 1994.

[57] ECHR, Šimunić v. Croatia, Application No. 20373/17, 22 January 2019. See more European Court of Human Rights (2022), pp. 5–27.

The *Soulas and Others v. France* case concerned the criminal proceedings brought against the applicants, following the publication of a book entitled "The colonisation of Europe", with the subtitle "Truthful remarks about immigration and Islam" for inciting hatred and violence against Muslim communities from northern and central Africa. The Court held that the domestic courts had underlined that the terms used in the book were intended to give rise in readers to a feeling of rejection and antagonism, exacerbated by the use of military language, with regard to the communities in question, which were designated as the main enemy, and to lead the book's readers to share the solution recommended by the author, namely a war of ethnic re-conquest. It considered that the interference in the latter's right to freedom of expression had been "necessary in a democratic society".[58]

In the case *Pavel Ivanov v. Russia*, the applicant, owner and editor of a newspaper, was convicted of public incitement to ethnic, racial and religious hatred through the use of mass-media. He authored and published a series of Articles portraying the Jews as the source of evil in Russia, calling for their exclusion from social life. He accused an entire ethnic group of plotting a conspiracy against the Russian people and ascribed Fascist ideology to the Jewish leadership. Both in his publications, and in his oral submissions at the trial, he consistently denied the Jews the right to national dignity, claiming that they did not form a nation. The applicant complained, in particular, that his conviction for incitement to racial hatred had not been justified. The Court declared the application inadmissible (incompatible *ratione materiae*). It had no doubt as to the markedly anti-Semitic tenor of the applicant's views and agreed with the assessment made by the domestic courts that through his publications he had sought to incite hatred towards the Jewish people. Such a general, vehement attack on one ethnic group is directed against the Convention's underlying values, notably tolerance, social peace and non-discrimination. Consequently, by reason of Article 17 (prohibition of abuse of rights) of the Convention, the applicant could not benefit from the protection afforded by Article 10 (freedom of expression) of the Convention.[59]

More recently, the case *E.S. v. Austria* triggered a new round of debates, at an international level, about the limits of freedom of expression when they meet with the right to respect the religious sentiment of others.[60] The case concerned the criminal conviction of the applicant for disparaging religious doctrines. The applicant held several seminars entitled "Basic Information on Islam" at the right-wing Freedom Party Education Institute. Several statements she had made during these (public) seminars had been directed against the doctrines of Islam, which essentially conveyed the message that Muhammad had had paedophilic tendencies. The Court noted that the subject matter is of a particularly sensitive nature, and that the (potential) effects of the impugned statements depend, to a certain degree, on the situation

[58] ECHR, Soulas and Others v. France, Application no. 15948/03, 10 July 2008.

[59] ECHR, Pavel Ivanov v. Russia, Application no. 35222/04, 20 February 2007. European Court of Human Rights (2022), p. 5. See also, Chainoglou (2017), pp. 136–150.

[60] Bougiakiotis (2018), para. 1.

in the country where the statements were made at the time and the context in which they were made. The Court therefore considers that the domestic authorities had a wide margin of appreciation in the instant case, as they were in a better position to evaluate which statements were likely to disturb the religious peace in their country. More importantly the Court observed that the applicant's purpose was not to contribute to a public debate, but to attack a religion. Thus, the association of Muhammad with pedophilia, without taking into account the historical background, on the one hand did not allow a serious discussion on this subject, on the other hand contained elements of religious intolerance.[61]

Similarly, in *Garaudy v. France* case, the Court considered that the content of the applicant's remarks had amounted to Holocaust denial, and pointed out that denying crimes against humanity was one of the most serious forms of racial defamation of Jews and of incitement to hatred of them. Disputing the existence of clearly established historical events did not constitute scientific or historical research; the real purpose was to rehabilitate the National Socialist regime and accuse the victims themselves of falsifying history. As such acts were manifestly incompatible with the fundamental values of the Convention; the Court applied Article 17 and held that the applicant was not entitled to rely on Article 10.[62]

It has been accepted that national rules regarding Holocaust denial serve purposes such as maintaining public order, preventing crime, protecting the dignity of victims who have perished under the Nazi regime, and the preservation of the reputation of the Jews. For example, in the case of *H.W.P. and K.v. Austria*, the Commission relied on the necessity of "national security" and "crime prevention" as a basis to justify a criminal conviction for the promotion of leaflets which claimed that the murder of six million Jews by the Nazis was a lie.[63] A later case, *Nationaldemokratische Partei Deutschlands v. Germany*, concerned a city ordinance that imposed an obligation on an organization to ensure that, in the context of a conference, the Nazi persecution of the Jews would not be questioned. The Commission held that the need to "prevent crime" and "protect the honor and rights of Jews" justified the restrictions imposed on expression.[64] The Commission and the Court have repeatedly emphasized that the restrictions provided by the States should be justified and proportionate, granting a wide "margin of appreciation" to the States, which is based on the specific historical past of each country. However, in a case concerning the conviction of "public defense of war crimes or crimes of collaboration", following the publication of a newspaper Article presenting in a positive light certain acts of Philippe Pétain, the Court held that the conviction was "prescribed by law" and pursued a legitimate aim. The Court, however, ruled that the case does not belong to the category of "clearly defined historical facts", such as

---

[61] ECHR, *ES v. Austria*, Application No. 38450/12, 25 October 2018. See also, Stratilatis (2014), pp. 725–749.

[62] ECHR, Garaudy v. France, Application no. 64496/17, 7 July 2003.

[63] ECHR, H.W.P. and K. v. Austria, Application no. 12774/87, 12 October 1989.

[64] ECHR, Nationaldemokratische Partei Deutschlands v. Germany, Application No. 25992/94, 29 November 1989. See also, Pech (2009), p. 28.

the Holocaust, the denial or revision of which does not fall under the protection of Article 10 of the European Convention on Human Rights due to Article 17, which concerns the prohibition of the abuse of rights. In addition, the Court found that the facts mentioned in publication had taken place 40 years ago. Despite the fact that it was likely to reopen the controversy and resurface of hurtful memories, the passage of time does not allow the publication to be treated in the same way as in the case of more recent events. The Court therefore ruled on the criminal conviction of the applicants disproportionate and unnecessary in a democratic society.[65]

The European Court of Human Rights did not provide an explanation of the term "clearly defined historical facts". Thus, in the *Doğu Perinçek v. Switzerland* case, the European Court of Human rights considered that, the context in which the applicant's comments were made (denial of the Armenian genocide) had not been marked by heightened tensions or special historical overtones in Switzerland. Taking into account the specific circumstances of the case and the proportionality between the means used and the aim sought to be achieved, the Court concluded that that it had not been necessary, in a democratic society, to subject the applicant to a criminal penalty in order to protect the rights of the Armenian community at stake in the case. The Court in this case made a distinction between "clearly established historical facts", such as the Holocaust, and subject that are still open to public and academic debate. According to the Court, the limit beyond which it is possible to invoke Article 17 is determined by the question whether the purpose of the speech was to incite hatred or violence, with the aim of destroying the rights of others. Historical research is by definition open to debate, without necessarily drawing final conclusions or absolute truths.[66]

4.3.2 Protection from Hate Crime

Article 4 of the EU Council Framework Decision 2008/913/JHA on combating certain forms and expressions of racism and xenophobia by means of criminal law refers to any other criminal offence committed with a racist and xenophobic and biased motivation. With regard to such offences, Article 4 of the Framework Decision obliges Member States to ensure that such racist and xenophobic motivation is considered as an aggravating circumstance, or alternatively that such motivation may be taken into account in the determination of the penalties. Thus, hate crimes consist of two elements: a) The act must be a crime under the Criminal Code; b) The crime must have been committed with a bias motivation. Hate crime is the most severe expression of discrimination and a core fundamental rights abuse.[67]

[65] ECHR, Lehideux and Isorni v. France, Application No. 24662/94, 23 September 1998.

[66] ECHR, Doğu Perinçek v. Switzerland, Application no. 27510/08, 15 October 2015. See, Pegorier (2018), p. 99. See also, Pietrobon (2020), pp. 164–174.

[67] FRA (2016), p. 7.

Based on the above, a hate crime, or crime with racist characteristics, is a crime committed because of the singular characteristics of the race, color, national or ethnic origin, descent, religion, disability, sexual orientation, identity or gender characteristics of the victim. It is any act that constitutes an offense under criminal law and is motivated by the characteristics of the victim. These crimes usually include violence, such as threats, vandalism and damage to property, bodily harm or even murder. However, a crime with racist characteristics can be any other criminal offense committed against an individual or a group of persons because of their supposed characteristics. Racist crimes can also affect individuals or legal entities associated with a group of persons, such as human rights defenders and /or journalists. In this sense, a hate crime may also involve the destruction of a monument and the desecration of a place of worship.[68]

The issue of racist violence has been also addressed by the European Court of Human Rights. In the case *Vona v. Hungary*, the Court found that the dissolution of the association "Hungarian Guard" (Magyar Gárda) by domestic courts was a lawful restriction of the applicant's rights under Article 11 of the Convention. The Court made the ruling on the basis that the activities of the association, which included a series of paramilitary rallies in several villages with large Romani populations across Hungary as well as the advocacy for racially-motivated policies, which intimidated the Romani population and violated their fundamental rights. The Court found that the Hungarian authorities were therefore entitled to take preventive measures to protect democracy and ban the association.[69] Thus, according to the Court, the state has the right to take measures that limit the freedom of association, insofar as the measures are necessary to prevent the danger represented to the functioning of democracy by a large-scale intimidation tactic. Moreover, the Court expressly stated that a state cannot be required to wait until a political movement has taken action to undermine democracy, or resort to violence, before intervening. In particular, it held that states have the right to take preventive measures to protect democracy if they identify a sufficiently imminent threat that affects the rights of others, such as members of the Roma minority and undermines the fundamental values of a democratic society. One of these values is the coexistence of members of society without racial discrimination.[70]

In the case of *Angelova and Iliev v. Bulgaria,* the applicants, a mother and son, complained about the racially motivated killing of their respective son and brother by seven teenagers and the subsequent failure of the Bulgarian authorities to investigate and prosecute those responsible. The Court held that there had been a procedural violation of Article 2 (right to life) of the Convention, finding that the Bulgarian authorities had failed to fulfill their obligation under Article 2 to effectively investigate the death of the applicants, taking into account the racial motivations of the attack and the need to maintain the confidence of minority groups in the ability of

---

[68] OSCE (2022), pp. 15–18.

[69] ECHR, Vona v. Hungary, Application no. 35943/10, 9 July 2013.

[70] Geller and Gergely (2013), para 1–8.

the authorities to protect them from the threat of racist violence. Furthermore, noting the widespread prejudice and violence against the Roma during the relevant period and the need to continually reaffirm society's condemnation of racism and maintain the confidence of minorities in the authorities, the Court found that the authorities failed to make the required distinction from other non-racially motivated offenses which constituted an unjustified treatment incompatible with Article 14 of the Convention. The Court therefore held that there had been a violation of Article 14 in conjunction with Article 2 of the European Convention of Human Rights.[71]

Similarly, the case *Stoica v. Romania* concerned the beating of Roma teenager by a police officer, during a clash between police officers and a group of persons of Roma origin, despite the fact that the police officer was warned that the victim had recently undergone head surgery. In addition, the applicant claimed that he had been ill-treated by the police and that the subsequent investigation into the incident was inadequate. He also alleged that the mistreatment and the decision not to prosecute the police officer were motivated by racial bias. The Court held that there had been a violation of Article 3 (prohibition of inhuman or degrading treatment) of the Convention, both in its procedural and substantive aspects, as the Romanian authorities had not carried out an adequate investigation. The Court further held that there had been a violation of Article 14 (prohibition of discrimination) of the Convention in conjunction with Article 3 of the European Convention; neither the prosecutor who was responsible for the criminal investigation, nor the Romanian government could present any argument that the incident was racially neutral. Instead, the evidence showed that the police officers' conduct was clearly racially motivated. There, the Court reiterated that "*when investigating violent incidents, State authorities have the additional duty to take all reasonable steps to unmask any racist motive and to establish whether or not ethnic hatred or prejudice may have played a role in the events. Failing to do so and treating racially induced violence and brutality on an equal footing with cases that have no racist overtones would be to turn a blind eye to the specific nature of acts that are particularly destructive of fundamental rights*".[72]

The cases of *Sakir v. Greece*[73] and *Gjikondi and others v. Greece*[74] concerned the failure of Greek authorities to effectively investigate the racist motive of hate crimes. The *Sakir case* concerns the violation by the authorities of their obligation under the European Convention on Human Rights, to conduct an effective investigation into a violent attack against an immigrant which resulted in his injury. In particular, the Court found that the authorities had failed to investigate the possible racist motive for this attack (breach of the procedural part of Article 3 of the European Convention of Human Rights). The case of *Gjikondi and others* concerned the murder of a

---

[71] ECHR, *Angelova and Iliev v. Bulgaria,* Application No. 44862/04, 26 July 2007.

[72] ECHR, *Stoica v. Romania*, Application No. 42722/02, 4 March 2008.

[73] ECHR, Sakir v. Greece, Application no. 48475/09, 24 May 2016. See also, Prevedourou (2021), pp. 749–750.

[74] ECHR, Gjikondi and others v. Greece, Application no. 17249/10, 21 March 2018.

foreigner and, inter alia, the failure to investigate the possible racist motives of the perpetrators which amounted to a violation of the procedural part of Article 2 of the Convention.

Based on the aforementioned cases, *it can be concluded that as far as hate crimes is concerned, a state may be held accountable on the following grounds: a) failure to effectively investigate or take into account the racist motive of a crime and b) mistreatment of persons by authorities based on racist motivations.*[75] *However,* based on the Courts reasoning in the *Nachova and others v. Bulgaria* case,[76] Henrard identifies a certain level of reluctance in addressing cases of discriminatory violence and observes that "*the Court has been reticent to adopt the special allocation of the burden of proof. This reluctance was clearly visible in the Grand Chamber judgment in the Nachova case, concerning the killing of two fugitive Roma men by Bulgarian policemen. In contrast to the Chamber, the Grand Chamber rejected the special allocation of the burden of proof, because it would impose a too demanding burden of (negative) proof on the government (that no racial animus informed the killings). The Grand Chamber did not accept that flawed police investigations as such were sufficient to constitute a prima facie case of racial discrimination. It proceeded to make a firm distinction between the procedural obligation to properly investigate such incidents, and investigate a potential discriminatory motive on the one hand and the substantive obligation to refrain from discriminatory killings on the other. The Grand Chamber in Nachova did identify three relevant criteria for the use of the special allocation of the burden of proof: 'the specificity of the facts, the nature of the allegations made, and the Convention right at stake*".[77] However, by analyzing and comparing the cases *Antayev and others v Russia,*[78] *Begheluri and others v Georgia*[79] and *Abdu v Bulgaria,*[80] which concerned discriminatory violence by public authorities or lack of protection by the public authorities against racist violence by private parties, Henrard concludes that "*the Court's jurisprudence in relation to cases on alleged invidious discrimination arguably no longer reveals general reluctance to finding a prohibited instance of discrimination. Indeed, the Court appears to be stepping up its levels of protection in several respects. First of all, the Court has clearly developed a steady line of jurisprudence revealing a high level of scrutiny for disadvantageous treatment on the basis of race/ethnicity and religion. It may be more explicit about the suspect nature of race in comparison to religion, but de facto similar levels of scrutiny are evident. Second, the Court seems to be – slowly but surely – more willing to share the burden of proof in discrimination cases. In particular, more recent case law reveals that the Court is in some*

[75] See also, ECHR, Milanović v. Serbia, Application no. 44614/07, 14 December 2010. See also, OSCE/ODIHR (2009), p.16. See also, FRA (2018a, b), p. 2.

[76] ECHR, Nachova and others v. Bulgaria, Application no. 43577/98 and 43,579/98, 6 July 2005.

[77] Henrard (2016), p. 163.

[78] ECHR, Antayev and others v Russia, Application no. 37966/07, 3 July 2014. See also, Prevedourou (2021), pp. 749–752.

[79] ECHR, Begheluri and others v Georgia, Application no. 28490/02, 7 October 2014.

[80] ECHR, Abdu v Bulgaria, Application no. 26827/08, 11 March 2014.

cases ready to identify a prima facie case of direct discrimination on grounds of ethnicity and/or religion. Admittedly, the Court still needs to develop further criteria in this respect, since the Court only accepts a prima facie case when there is very strong proof'.[81]

References

Allen QCR (2007) Article13 EC, evolution and current contexts. In: Meenan H (ed) Equality law in an enlarged European Union. Cambridge University Press, Cambridge, pp 38–72

Anagnostopoulou D (2019) The prohibition of hate speech in the international framework of the United Nations. In: Kouroupis K, Karagouni V (eds) Consolidating the European area of justice, the protection of fundamental rights—justice training program for a European area of justice. Nomiki Vivliothiki, pp 169–181. (in Greek)

Arnardóttir OM (2017) Vulnerability under article 14 of the European convention on human rights: innovation or business as usual? Oslo Law Rev 4(3):150–171

Belavusau U (2012) Fighting hate speech through EU law. Amsterdam Law Forum 4(1):20–25

Benedi Lahuera S (2009) Race equality and TCNs, or how to fight discrimination with a discriminatory law. Eur Law J 15(6):738–756

Bougiakiotis E (2018) *E.S. v Austria*: Blasphemy Laws and the Double Standards of the European Court of Human Rights, U.K. Const. L. Blog, https://ukconstitutionallaw.org/

Bromell D (2022) Regulating free speech in a digital age - hate, harm and the limits of censorship. Springer, London

Chainoglou K (2017) The right to historical truth and historical memory versus historical revisionism and Denialism: a human rights analysis. In: Chainoglou K, Strawson J, Collins B, Phillips M (eds) Injustice, memory and faith in human rights. Routledge, Abingdon, New York, pp 136–150

Donders Y (2010) Do cultural diversity and human rights make a good match? Int Soc Sci J 61(199):15–35

Dube N (2024) Wa Baile v. Switzerland: An implicit acknowledgment of racial profiling as structural discrimination. Strasbourg Observers, https://strasbourgobservers.com/2024/03/26/wa-baile-v-switzerland-an-implicit-acknowledgment-of-racial-profiling-as-structural-discrimination/

European Court of Human Rights (2022) Fact sheet: Hate speech, June 2022: https://www.echr.coe.int/documents/fs_hate_speech_eng.pdf

Farrior S (2024) Basu v. Ger. And Muhammad v. Spain (Eur. Ct. H.R.). Int Leg Mater 63(1):94–141

FRA (2016) Ensuring justice for hate crime victims: professional perspectives. Publications Office of the European Union, Luxembourg. https://fra.europa.eu/sites/default/files/fra_uploads/fra-2016-justice-hate_crime-victims_en.pdf

FRA (2018a) Handbook on European non-discrimination law—2018 edition. Publications Office of the European Union, Luxembourg. https://fra.europa.eu/sites/default/files/fra_uploads/fra-2018-handbook-non-discrimination-law-2018_en.pdf

FRA (2018b) Unmasking bias motives in crimes: selected cases of the European Court of Human Rights. https://fra.europa.eu/sites/default/files/fra_uploads/fra-2018-unmasking-bias-motives-paper_en.pdf

[81] Henrard K., opt. cit., p. 165.

Fredman S (2001) Combating racism with human rights: the right to equality. In: Fredman S (ed) Discrimination and human rights, the case of racism. Oxford University Press, Oxford, pp 9–44
Geller J, Gergely D (2013) Vona v.Hungary: Freedom of association and assembly can be restricted to protect Minority Rights. Strasbourg Observers academic blog https://strasbourgobservers.com/2013/08/07/vona-v-hungary-freedom-of-association-and-assembly-can-be-restricted-to-protect-minority-rights/
Giannakoula A (2018) The criminal law dealing with racism: current challenges and targets. In: Deligianni C, Gaitenidis N, Koniaris V (eds) Protection of fundamental rights: contemporary issues in the European space. Papazisis Publications, Athens, pp 89–110. (in Greek)
Henrard K (2016) The European court of human rights, ethnic and religious minorities and the two dimensions of the right to equal treatment: jurisprudence at different speeds? Nord J Hum Rights 34(3):157–177
Kanellopoulos PI (2010) The law of the European Union, treaty of Lisbon, 5th edn. Sakkoula, Athens - Thessaloniki (in Greek)
Kim SY (2021) Les vulnérables: evaluating the vulnerability criterion in article 14 cases by the European court of human rights. Leg Stud 41(4):617–632
McCrudden C (2003) The new concept of equality. Academy of European Law, Trier, pp 2–24. http://www.era-comm.eu/oldoku/Adiskri/02_Key_concepts/2003_McCrudden_EN.pdf
McKean W (1983) Equality and discrimination under international law. Clarenden Press, Oxford
OSCE (2022) Hate crime Laws: a practical guide, 2nd edn. OSCE. Office for Democratic Institutions and Human Rights (ODIHR), Warsaw. https://www.osce.org/files/f/documents/1/4/523940.pdf
OSCE/ODIHR (2009) Hate crime Laws - a practical guide. Published by the OSCE Office for Democratic Institutions and Human Rights (ODIHR), Warsaw. https://www.osce.org/files/f/documents/3/e/36426.pdf
Pech L (2009) The Law of Holocaust Denial in Europe: Towards a (qualified) EU-wide Criminal Prohibition, Jean Monnet Working Paper 10/09, NYU School of Law, pp. 1–53. http://www.jeanmonnetprogram.org/papers/09/091001.pdf
Pegorier C (2018) Speech and harm: genocide denial, hate speech and freedom of expression. Int Criminal Law Rev 18(1):97–126
Peršak N (2022) Criminalising hate crime and hate speech at EU level: extending the list of Eurocrimes under article 83(1) TFEU. Crim Law Forum 33(2):85–119
Pietrobon A (2020) State Negationism and the rule of law. In: Gattini A, Garciandia R, Webb P (eds) Human dignity and international law. Brill, Leiden, pp 164–174
Pitt G (2007) Religion or belief: aiming at the right target. In: Meenan H (ed) Equality law in an enlarged European Union. Cambridge University Press, Cambridge New York, pp 202–230
Prevedourou E (2021) Article 14. In: Sarmas I, Kontiadis X, Anthopoulos C (eds) ECHR, interpretation by article. Sakkoulas, Athes—Thessaloniki, pp 720–764. (in Greek)
Rokša Zubčevič A, Bender S, Vojvodid J (2017) Media regulatory authorities and hate speech. Council of Europe https://edoc.coe.int/en/media/7431-media-rgulatory-authorities-and-hate-speech.html
Stavrinaki T (2017) Article 10. In: Sisilianos LA (ed) European convention on human rights, interpretation by article. Nomiki Vivliothiki, pp 475–518. (in Greek)
Strasbourg Observers academic blog (2013) Mann Singh wins turban case in Geneva after losing in Strasbourg https://strasbourgobservers.com/2013/11/19/mann-singh-wins-in-geneva-after-losing-in-strasbourg/
Stratilatis C (2014) On the distinction between statements of fact and value judgments: a comment on Petrenco v. Moldova. Annuaire International des Droits de l'Homme VIII:725–749
Tridimas T (2006) The general principles of EU law, 2nd edn. Oxford University Press, Oxford
Wolff T (2021) True believers?—sincerity and article 9 of the European convention on human rights. Eur Const Law Rev 17(2):259–286
Yves Kuhn P (2019) Reforming the approach to racial and religious hate speech under article 10 of the European convention on human rights. Hum Rights Law Rev 19:119–147

Chapter 5
Respect of Religious Convictions, Blasphemy, Defamation of Religion and Anti-blasphemy Extremism

Contents

Defamation of religion and "blasphemy" remain highly contentious subjects especially in our modern era when religions are becoming a political issue and can incite terror and violence. The debate focuses mainly on the equilibrium between freedom of expression or respect for religious beliefs. From a constitutional perspective it is a conflict between two constitutionally protected goods.[1]

Within the framework of the Council of Europe, the Parliamentary Assembly dealt with the question of whether and to what extent respect for religious beliefs should restrict freedom of expression in its Resolution 1510 (2006) on freedom of expression and respect of religious beliefs. The Assembly expressed the view that freedom of expression should not be subject to further restrictions in order to satisfy the increased sensitivity of particular religious groups but stressed that the hate speech against any religious group is incompatible with the European Convention

[1] *Venice Commission (*2010*), pp. 18–20.* In addition, the issue of "defamation of religion" has repeatedly addressed the United Nations since 1999, with several non-binding resolutions condemning the "defamation of religion". Resolutions on the fight against "defamation of religions" have passed by the UN on an annual basis from 1999 to 2010, for example Commission of Human Rights Resolutions 2000/84 E/CN.4/RES/2000/84, 26 April 2000, 2001/4 E/CN.4/RES/2001/4, 18 April 2001, 2002/9, E/CN.4/RES/2002/9, 15 April 2002, 2003/4, E/CN.4/RES/2003/4, 14 April 2003, 2004/6, E/CN.4/RES/2004/6, 13 April 2004 και 2005/3, E/CN.4/RES/2005/3, 12 April 2005. The most recent resolution of the UN Council of Human Rights, the fight against Defamation of Religions, inter alia condemned the ban construction of minarets in Switzerland. UN Human Rights Council, Combating defamation of religions: resolution / adopted by the Human Rights Council, 15 April 2010, A/HRC/RES/13/16.

N. Gaitenidis, *The Rights of Cultural Identity in the Case Law of the European Court of Human Rights*, European Union and its Neighbours in a Globalized World 36, https://doi.org/10.1007/978-3-032-23045-4_5

on Human Rights. In its Recommendation 1805 (2007) on blasphemy, religious insults and hate speech against persons because of their religion, the Parliamentary Assembly considered that national law should only punish expressions of religious matters which deliberately and seriously disrupt public order and call for public violence.[2]

According to case law of the European Court of Human Rights the right to freedom of expression "*is not only about information or ideas which are accepted or regarded as non-offensive or uniform but also as offensive or shocking or disturbing State or a part of the population. These are imposed by pluralism, tolerance and broadness of the spirit, without which there is no "democratic society". Those who create, present, distribute or exhibit works of art contribute to the exchange of ideas and opinions, which is fundamental to a democratic society. Thus, the state is obliged not to interfere improperly with their freedom of expression. Artists and promoters do not, of course, enjoy some immunity from the limitations referred to in paragraph 2 of Article 10. Anyone exercising his or her freedom of expression is subject, in the words of this paragraph, to "duties and responsibilities". Their extent will depend on their condition and the means they use*".[3]

In *Otto-Preminger-Institut v. Austria*, the European Court of Human Rights was called upon to decide on the issue of freedom of arts and its conflict with religious sentiments. In 1985, the Austrian non-profit company Otto Preminger Institut programmed the screening of the film "Erotic Session" by director Werner Schroeter. Before the film was screened, at the request of the Catholic bishop of the region, the Austrian authorities seized the film. These actions were considered by the Austrian courts to be lawful, and the Institute has appealed to the European Court of Human Rights for violating freedom of the art as an expression of its freedom of expression, arguing that, on the one hand, it is a satirical work and cannot therefore be regarded as a contempt or insulting religion, on the other hand, that project monitoring was carried out with the same will of the viewer. The Court held that the Austrian authorities' interference with freedom of expression through the confiscation of the film constitutes a legitimate outcome of the weighing of the right to freedom of religion and the right to freedom of the arts and therefore does not violate Article 10 of the Convention. In interpreting Article 9 of the Convention, the Court accepted that "*Those who choose to exercise the freedom to manifest their religion, irrespective of whether they are members of a religious majority or minority, should reasonably expect not to be excluded from any criticism. They should tolerate and accept the denial by others of their religious beliefs and even the dissemination of other beliefs hostile to their faith*". However, the way in which opposition or refusal is expressed in religious beliefs and doctrines is a matter that may involve the responsibility of the state, in particular the responsibility to ensure the peaceful enjoyment of the

[2] Council of Europe, Parliamentary Assembly Resolution Resolution 1510 (2006), Freedom of expression and respect for religious beliefs and Council of Europe, Parliamentary Assembly Recommendation 1805 (2007), Blasphemy, religious insults and hate speech against persons on grounds of their religion.

[3] ECHR, Vereinigung Bildender Künstler v. Austria, Application no. 68354/01, 25 January 2007.

rights enshrined in Article 9. Indeed, in extreme cases, the influence of specific methods of opposition or denial on religious beliefs may be such as to prevent those who hold such beliefs from exercising their freedom to maintain and express them. The Court added that "*Article 9, which enshrines religious freedom can legitimately be perceived as being infringed by the provocative depictions of objects of religious significance, which can be considered as a malicious violation of the spirit of tolerance which is a hallmark of a democratic society*". That is, the European Court of Human Rights, while accepting that religious beliefs can clearly be the subject of criticism and opposition, considers at the same time that the way in which opposition or denial to certain religious beliefs or doctrines is expressed may justify intervention by the state. The Court did not comment on what restrictions are necessary and appropriate in the case but rather referred to the theory of the "margin of appreciation", according to which "it is not possible to export to Europe a unified concept of the importance of religion in society, nor is it possible to reach a comprehensive definition".[4]

A similar approach persisted in the *Wingrove v. the United Kingdom* case. The applicant argued that the refusal by the competent authorities to grant a marketing authorization to the film "Ecstasy Visions" violated his right to freedom of expression. The 18-minute video was inspired by the life of Saint Therese and among other things contained a love story of the heroine with Christ. The Court held that the intervention of the authorities in the freedom of the artist fulfilled the criteria of proportionality, that is, provided for by law, pursuing a legitimate aim, namely the protection of the rights of third parties against contemptuous, abusive, vulgar and ridiculous ways of the presence of religious symbol, and was necessary in a democratic society.[5] As Bratza comments "*If the Otto-Preminger case can itself be explained on its own facts as being a decision influenced by the risk of public outrage and the preserving of religious peace in a particularly sensitive region, the same cannot be said of the Wingrove case. This concerned a refusal to award a certificate permitting the distribution of a short video depicting Saint Teresa's erotic visions of Christ on the Cross. The certificate had been refused not on grounds of obscenity but on grounds of blasphemy. Here there was no risk of public outrage being caused to Christians by a video that was likely, in any event, to have a very limited market, whatever its artistic merits. The Court nevertheless upheld the decision to refuse a certificate on the grounds that it served the legitimate aim of protecting the rights of others not to be gratuitously offended in their religious beliefs. The questions may be asked whether the Court struck a fair balance between the conflicting ECHR rights and, in particular, whether the distinction drawn between expressions critical of or hostile to a religion or its members for which no exemption can reasonably be expected and those that are 'gratuitously offensive' to the*

---

[4] ECHR, Otto-Preminger-Institut v. Austria, Application no. 13470/87, 20 September 1994. See also Kuhn (2019), p. 123.

[5] ECHR, Wingrove v. the United Kingdom, Application no. 17419/90, 25 November 1996.

religion concerned constitutes a sound basis for the Court's resolution of the conflict".[6]

The European Court of Human Rights, by judgment of 13 September 2005, concluded that the Turkish authorities did not violate freedom of expression by condemning a book publisher for the publication of insults against "God, religion, the Prophet, and the Sacred Book". The CEO of Berfin Publishing House in France was sentenced to two years' imprisonment, which was later turned into a fine. The Strasbourg Court accepted that this interference with the applicant's right to freedom of expression was provided by law and pursued the legitimate objectives of preventing disorder and protecting the morals and the rights of others. Whether the measure of conviction of the applicant was necessary in a democratic society, the Court referred to the need to balance the applicant's right to convey his ideas and religious theories to the public on the one hand and the right of others to respect freedom of thought, conscience and religion, on the other. The Court reiterated that religious people must show tolerance in the denial of their religious beliefs by others, even the spread of beliefs hostile to their faith. However, provocative opinions and abusive attacks on one's religion should be distinguished. The Court has therefore accepted that believers could legitimately feel that certain extracts of the book constituted an unjustified and offensive attack on them. Consequently, the conviction of the publisher was a measure aimed at providing protection against offensive attacks on issues considered sacred by Muslims. As the book was not seized and the publisher was required to pay a small fine, the Court concluded that the Turkish authorities did not violate the right to freedom of expression.[7]

It is worth noting, however, that in the most recent case of *Sekmadienis v. Lithuania*, it was decided that the ban on posting a clothing advertising poster that depicted the Virgin Mary and Jesus Christ in modern everyday clothing was a disproportionate restriction of freedom of expression. With this decision, the European Court of Human Rights "shifts" its reasoning in the weighing process and emphasizes an objective criterion, i.e. that the content of the poster did not incite to acts of violence or hatred and did not disturb public order; The Court did not take into account the subjective criterion of the religious feeling of believers.[8]

In all the above-mentioned cases, the Court referred to the "margin of appreciation" doctrine on the nature and scope of restrictive measures, whereas in the last two cases it is noteworthy that there is no reference to Article 9 of the European Convention on Human Rights on religious freedom, but the Court confined itself to interpreting Article 10 alone. A general conclusion is that the European Court of Human Rights accepts that the concept of religious freedom requires a respect for the religious beliefs of believers and an obligation for others to refrain from expressing ideas that may shock, offend or disturb. The fact that there is no uniform European understanding of the requirements to protect the rights of others in

[6] Bratza (2022), p. 268.

[7] ECHR, I.A. v. Turkey, Application no. 42571/98, 13 September 2005. Kuhn (2019), p. 124.

[8] ECHR, Sekmadienis Ltd. v. Lithuania Application no. 69317/14, 31 January 2018.

relation to attacks on their religious beliefs means that the contracting states have a broader margin of discretion when regulating freedom of expression in relation to issues that may arise to offend personal beliefs in the sphere of morals or religion. However, the Court seems to think that repressive or criminal treatment of these issues, which may result in imprisonment, is not a proportionate and legitimate measure in a democratic society.[9]

In November 2006, Azerbaijani journalist Rafig Tagiyev authored an article published in the newspaper Sanat Gazeti, where Samir Huseynov served as editor-in-chief. The piece, part of a series comparing Western and Eastern values, critiqued the role of religious traditions, with a focus on Islam, in shaping societal norms, including claims that "Europe does not accept Islam" and references to the Prophet Muhammad that some viewed as derogatory. Following complaints from religious organizations, Azerbaijani authorities initiated criminal proceedings under Article 283 of the Criminal Code (incitement to religious hatred). The applicants were detained for over a year, convicted, and sentenced to 3 years' imprisonment. Domestic courts upheld the convictions, deeming the article propagandistic and hostile toward Islam. The European Court of Human Rights, in a unanimous Chamber judgment, found a violation of Article 10 of the European Convention on Human Rights (freedom of expression). The Court acknowledged the interference was prescribed by law and pursued legitimate aims, namely preventing disorder and protecting the rights of others under Article 9, freedom of religion. However, it ruled the convictions disproportionate and unnecessary in a democratic society because the article contributed to public debate on religion's societal role, without inciting violence or hatred, mere offense to religious beliefs does not justify restrictions and the severe sanctions (imprisonment) created a "chilling effect" on journalistic discourse.[10]

The case represents a significant evolution in the Court's jurisprudence on the intersection of freedom of expression and religious sensitivities, particularly in contexts of public debate. Unlike earlier cases such as *Otto-Preminger-Institut v. Austria* or *E.S. v. Austria*, where restrictions were upheld to protect religious peace in majority-faith regions, this judgment prioritizes objective criteria (absence of incitement to hatred or violence) over subjective offense.

The Court's emphasis that "*the fact that some people can be offended in their religious beliefs cannot be a sufficient argument to interfere with the right to freedom of expression as part of a public debate on matters of religion*" marks a robust defense of critical journalism, especially on Islam in non-Western European states. This aligns with the post-Sekmadienis v. Lithuania trend toward proportionality in blasphemy-like restrictions, rejecting criminal penalties for non-abusive critique. Critically, the ruling exposes systemic issues in Azerbaijan, where vague

---

[9] Naskou Perraki (1999), p. 787. See also Kuhn (2019), p. 120.

[10] ECHR, Tagiyev and Huseynov v. Azerbaijan, Application no. 13274/08, 5 December 2019. Tragically, Tagiyev was stabbed to death in 2011 amid unresolved threats, leading to a separate pending Article 2 (right to life) case. ECHR, Tagiyeva v. Azerbaijan, Application no. 31613/12, 7 July 2022.

"incitement to hatred" laws are weaponized against independent media, fostering self-censorship and endangering journalists. It also serves as a cautionary tale on the "chilling effect" of imprisonment, urging states to favor civil remedies over penal sanctions in religious defamation cases. In a broader European context, amid rising populism and online extremism, the decision reinforces pluralism: religious doctrines must tolerate scrutiny, but hate speech remains proscribable. However, its application in diverse cultural settings remains tested, as the margin of appreciation could still allow leeway for states facing genuine risks of unrest. Overall, this unanimous outcome bolsters press freedom advocates, signaling a growing intolerance for disproportionate curbs on debate about religion's public role.

The case of *Tagiyev and Huseynov v. Azerbaijan* underscores the tension between freedom of expression and religious sensitivities, a dynamic further complicated by rising anti-blasphemy extremism in Europe, as analyzed by Herbach and Siampakou in their 2024 study. They trace the escalation of violent responses to perceived blasphemy, from the 2004 murder of Theo van Gogh to recent attacks and threats linked to Quran desecrations and Prophet Muhammad caricatures, driven by groups like Tehreek-e-Labbaik Pakistan (TLP) and the Islamic State, Khorasan Province (ISKP). These actors exploit narratives of Islam under threat, using online propaganda and offline networks to incite violence, as seen in cases targeting individuals like Samuel Paty in France. The study critiques counter-measures like Denmark's 2023 Quran-burning ban for potentially violating freedom of expression under the ECHR, echoing the shift in *Sekmadienis v. Lithuania* toward objective criteria over subjective offense. It advocates for preventive strategies, such as the Netherlands' Cartoon Working Group, and proportionate criminal justice responses that respect human rights, aligning with the European Courts's emphasis on proportionality and the margin of appreciation in navigating these complex issues.[11]

Bouton v. France concerned the criminal conviction of a feminist activist who, during a demonstration inside a church, exposed her bare chest bearing the slogan "344e salope" in protest against the Catholic Church's stance on abortion. The applicant argued that her conviction for sexual exhibition violated her right to freedom of expression under Article 10 of the Convention. The European Court of Human Rights found a violation of Article 10, holding that the domestic courts had failed to strike a fair balance between the applicant's expressive conduct and the protection of religious sensibilities and public order. While acknowledging that the action took place in a religious setting and could be perceived as offensive by believers, the Court emphasized that the performance was a form of political expression aimed at criticizing institutional positions of the Catholic Church rather than an attack on individual believers. The judgment is particularly relevant to the evolving Strasbourg approach to blasphemy-related issues, as it signals a clear reluctance to legitimize restrictions on expression solely on the basis of religious offense, reaffirming that pluralism in a democratic society entails the tolerance of provocative,

[11] Herbach and Siampakou (2024).

critical, and unsettling forms of expression, even when they occur within religious spaces.[12]

References

Bratza N (2022) The 'precious asset': freedom of religion under the European convention on human rights. Ecclesiastical Law J 14:256–271

Kuhn PY (2019) Reforming the approach to racial and religious hate speech under article 10 of the European convention on human rights. Hum Rights Law Rev 19:119–147

Naskou Perraki P (1999) The case law of the European court of human rights on the protection of religious freedom in Greece. EEEurD:785–814. (in Greek)

Venice Commission (2010) Blasphemy, insult and hatred: finding answers in a democratic society, science and technique of democracy, No. 47. Council of Europe Publishing, Strasbourg

Herbach M, Siampakou N (2024) Faith and fury: rising anti-blasphemy extremism in Europe and its legal implications. International Centre for Counter-Terrorism. https://www.icct.nl/publication/faith-and-fury-rising-anti-blasphemy-extremism-europe-and-its-legal-implications

[12] ECHR, Bouton v. France, Application no. 22636/19, 13 October 2022.

Chapter 6
Language Rights

Contents

Language is a key dimension of individual and collective identity. For many people belonging to minorities, their language is one of the main factors of their identification and recognition. However, language, like cultural identity, is not static but evolves over time.[1] Linguistic rights have been linked to issues of a strong political nature and have been used by many institutions and states to promote their strategies in a particular geographical area. In this sense, they can be used as a pretext to protect a national or linguistic minority by destroying or limiting the political power of another ethnic group.[2]

The European Charter for Regional or Minority Languages stipulates that a minority or regional languages are "i*) traditionally used within a given territory of a State by nationals of that State who form a group numerically smaller than the rest of the State's population; and ii) different from the official language(s) of that State*".[3] Under the Framework Convention for the Protection of National Minorities and the Charter for Regional or Minority Languages, language rights could be categorized into (a) educational process rights, which include teaching in the minority

---

[1]Advisory Committee on the Framework Convention for the Protection of National Minorities, Commentary on the Language Rights of Persons belonging to National Minorities under the Framework Convention for the Protection of National Minorities, ACFC/44DOC (2012) 001 rev, Strasbourg, 24 May 2012, p. 6.

[2]See Tsitselikis (1996a, b), p. 59.

[3]The European Charter for Regional or Minority Languages (ECRML) of the Council of Europe, is the only multilateral convention dealing exclusively with the protection of minority languages. Established in 1992, it aims to protect and promote Europe's historic regional and minority languages. The Charter entered into force on 1 August 1998, when 5 countries completed its ratification. Although the Charter does not establish any rights for speakers of regional or minority languages, it is nevertheless useful, in conjunction with the provisions of the Framework Convention for the Protection of National Minorities, to categorize rights corresponding to the linguistic speakers. Ó Riagáin (2001), pp. 34–37; Mancini and de Witte (2008), pp. 250–275.

N. Gaitenidis, *The Rights of Cultural Identity in the Case Law of the European Court of Human Rights*, European Union and its Neighbours in a Globalized World 36, https://doi.org/10.1007/978-3-032-23045-4_6

language and (b) the right to use the language in private and in public, including the use of the minority language before administrative, judicial and political authorities, the media, the right to post signs and to use place names in that language, and the right to set up associations with the purpose of the promotion of the linguistic and cultural identity of the minority group.[4] In addition, the Charter, like all basic human rights conventions, includes a non-discrimination clause on the use of minority languages.[5]

Despite the special importance that is attributed to language as a distinctive part of cultural identity, the European Court of Human Rights has been very reluctant in the recognition of linguistic rights to minorities. In the landmark *Belgian Linguistics* case the Court did not accept the claim that, under Article 8 of the Convention, the language used by children in public education should be chosen by their parents.[6] Similar claims cannot be justified nor guaranteed by Articles 9 or 10 of the Convention.[7]

In this context, the granting of radio and television licenses that involve the expression of culture and identity through the use of minority languages is crucial for minority communities. A monopoly on broadcasting can hinder the exercise of freedom of expression through the media. The European Court of Human Rights has established in its case law that licenses can be denied for various reasons, such as the nature and goals of a proposed station or obligations arising from international law.[8] Nevertheless, the fundamental principle in these cases is that the dissemination of information and ideas should be guided by the principle of pluralism.[9]

The right to use a personal name and patronymic in a minority language and its official recognition is at the "core" of language rights and is closely linked to the personal identity and dignity. The states must guarantee that individuals are free from obstacles or pressure regarding the use and recognition of their names in their own language even in cases in which individuals were forced to change or give up their names. While the provision of Article 11 of the Framework Convention is worded in a way that allows states to apply their special conditions and legal system, they should guarantee a clear legislative framework according to international standards.[10] The Court in several cases has accepted that the arrangement of names falls within the scope of family and private life, if the name of a person represents a

[4] Tsitselikis (1996a, b), p. 216.

[5] European Charter for Regional or Minority Languages, Article 7 and Part III.

[6] Belgian Linguistic Case (Case relating to certain aspects of the laws on the use of languages in education in Belgium), Application Nos. 1474/62, 1677/62, 1691/62, 1769/63, 1994/63, 2126/64, 23 July 1968.

[7] ECHR, Inhabitants of Alsemberg and Beersel v. Belgium, Application No. 1474/62, 26 July 1963.

[8] ECHR, Groppera Radio AG and Others v. Switzerland, Application No. 10890/84, 28 March 1990.

[9] Medda-Windischer (2021), p. 41.

[10] Advisory Committee on the Framework Convention for the Protection of National Minorities, opt. cit., p. 19–20. See also, Coeriel et al. v. the Netherlands, Communication No. 453/1991, UN Doc. CCPR / C / 52 / D / 453/1991.

medium for his identity and a person's bond with his family.[11] In the *Kuharec v. Latvia* case[12] "*the Court recalled that there was no common policy among the states about the recognition and use of personal names, which largely depend on historical, linguistic, religious and cultural factors, and that, as a consequence, states enjoy a broad margin of appreciation regarding the use of an official language or languages in personal documents and other official documents. Under the specific circumstances of the case, in striking a balance between individual rights and state interests, the Court noted that the adaptation of the applicant's name ('Kuharec' instead of 'Kuhareca') and the consequences in her life were minimal. Therefore, by taking a rather conservative approach towards minority rights, the Court declared the change of the applicant's name as not discriminatory and the application inadmissible*". According to the Court "*A language is not in any sense an abstract value. It cannot be divorced from the way it is actually used by its speakers. Consequently, in adopting the national language, the State undertakes, in principle, to guarantee its citizens the right to use that language both to impart and to receive information, without hindrance not only in their private lives, but also in their dealings with public authorities*".[13]

The spelling of surnames and names according to minority languages falls into the scope of Article 8. Nevertheless, the Court adopted one rather restrictive approach in this area, granting a wide margin of appreciation in the states taking into account the existence of historical, linguistic, religious and cultural factors in each country and the absence a common European system.[14] In the case *of Erdagoz v. Turkey,* the applicant requested the correction of the spelling of her name, explaining that her name was "Gozel" and not "Guzel" and the European Court of Human Rights accepted that the negative attitude of the Turkish courts to allow her the use of her name with Kurdish accent is not necessary in a democratic society and has unanimously acknowledged that there has been a violation of Article 8 of the Convention.[15]

In the case of *Kemal Taşkın and Others v. Turkey*, the Court denied that there had been a violation of Article 8 of the European Convention on Human Rights on the ground that the applicants' Turkish names could not be changed to Kurdish because the names they chose contained characters that did not appear in the official Turkish

---

[11] ECHR, Burghartz v. Switzerland, Application No. 16213/90, 22 February 1994.

[12] ECHR, Lidija Kuharec alias Kuhareca v. Latvia, Application No. 71557/01, 7 December 2004. See more at de Varennes and Kuzborska (2015), pp. 977–1023.

[13] Medda-Windischer (2021), p. 39.

[14] ECHR, Mentzen v. Latvia Application No. 71074/01, 7 December 2004, ECHR, Bulgakov v. Ukraine, Application No. 59894/00, 11 September 2007, ECHR, Baylac-Ferrer and Suarez v. France, Application No. 27977/04, 25 September 2008, ECHR, Stjerna v. Finland, Application No. 18131/91, 25 November 1994 and ECHR, Guillot v. France, Application No. 22500/93, 24 October 1996.

[15] ECHR, Erdagoz v. Turkey, Application No. 21890/93, 22 October 1997.

alphabet.[16] Peroni argues that "*At the heart of the applicants' complaints lies an attempt to maintain what they see as central to their cultural identity. The linguistic and cultural attachment to their names is clear from both the applicants' arguments and the historical context of the case*". The European Court disregarded the minority's perspective when balancing the competing interests as the applicants could not prove that their names, if spelled differently, would create obstacles to their personal and social life.[17] This reasoning reflects the Court's tendency to prioritize formal linguistic uniformity over the subjective experience of cultural identity. By requiring proof of concrete social disadvantage, the Court adopts an evidentiary threshold that is difficult to meet in cases where harm is primarily symbolic or identity-based.

In the case *X v. Austria*, the applicant, who belonged to a Slovenian minority but spoke German as her mother tongue, could not express her allegiance to that minority by participating in a linguistinc census. She claimed, citing Article 3 of the European Convention on Human Rights that she had been ill-treated because she had to choose between making a false statement by participating in the census, as her mother tongue was not Slovenian, and denying her faith in the Slovenian minority. The Commission was not persuaded by that argument, considering that the applicant had no obstacle to expressing her allegiance to the minority to which she belonged in other ways than this specific census. As stated in the decision, the Convention does not recognize minority rights as such. While doctrinally consistent, this position reveals a structural limitation of the Convention system, which protects minority members only indirectly, through individual rights, rather than engaging with minority identity as a legal interest in itself. Thus, the protection of its members is limited to the right not to be discriminated in the enjoyment of the rights recognized by the Convention, because they belong to the minority.[18] This approach illustrates the Court's reluctance to conceptualize minority identity as a collective and lived experience. By emphasizing alternative means of expressing affiliation, the Court implicitly treats minority belonging as interchangeable, rather than as context-specific and socially embedded. This indirect protection model helps explain the Court's cautious approach to linguistic claims that do not produce tangible interference with private life or procedural fairness.

In the case *of Podkolzina v. Latvia,* the applicant, who was a member of the Russian minority in Latvia, was excluded from the list of candidates for the Latvian Parliament due to the negative assessment of her language proficiency by the authorities. The Court ruled that there had been a violation of Article 3 of the First Additional Protocol to the European Convention on Human Rights, which concerns the right to free elections, expressing distrust to the objectivity and transparency of

---

[16] ECHR, Kemal Taşkın and Others v. Turkey, Application Nos. 30,206/04, 37,038/04, 43,681/04, 45,376/04, 12,881/05, 28,697/05, 32,797/05, 45,609/05, 2 February 2010.

[17] Peroni (2012), p. 451.

[18] ECHR, X v. Austria, Application No. 8142/1978, 10 October 1979.

the proceedings. However, the Court has observed that the obligation of candidates for national parliaments to have sufficient knowledge of the official language of the State in which they reside is dictated by a legitimate aim which justifies the necessary margin of appreciation for the provision of such conditions by States. The Court even clarified that the Convention does not guarantee the right to use a specific language to communicate with public authorities or to receive information in the language of choice of each citizen, except in the cases of Articles 5 and 6 of the Convention. This judicial interpretation gives states the discretion to regulate at national level the use of the language in administrative proceedings and to act in the name of linguistic homogeneity.[19]

In the case *of Mehmet Nuri Ozen and Others v. Turkey,* it was acknowledged that Article 8 of the European Convention on Human Rights had been violated on the ground that a detainee was not allowed to correspond in his mother tongue, which was Kurdish.[20] Finally, language rights are also protected under Article 10 of the Convention. For example, in the *Ulusoy case and Others v.Turkey* The Court ruled that the ban on the production of a Kurdish-language play at the town hall was a violation of freedom of expression.[21]

According to established case law, judicial authorities are not obligated to provide translation or interpreter assistance if they can determine that the applicant has sufficient knowledge of the official language used in court. The European Court of Human Rights does not automatically grant the free assistance of an interpreter or translator based solely on an individual's membership in a national or linguistic minority.[22] If the national authorities refuse to provide free translation or interpretation in judicial proceedings, the Court will presume the applicant's sufficient knowledge of the official language based on evidence such as their origins, place of birth, and residence. The burden of proof then shifts to the government to demonstrate that the applicant has effective language skills for the proceedings.[23]

More recently in the case of *Ádám and Others v. Romania*, Hungarian-speaking minority members challenged restrictions on using their language in local administrative proceedings and public signage in a Romanian municipality with a significant Hungarian population. The applicants argued that these limitations infringed their linguistic and cultural identity. The European Court of Human Rights found a violation of Article 8 (right to respect for private and family life) in conjunction with Article 14 (prohibition of discrimination), stressing that states have a positive obligation to accommodate minority language use in public life where it forms a core

[19] ECHR, Podkolzina v. Latvia, Application N o. 46,726/99, 9 April 2002.

[20] ECHR, Mehmet Nuri Ozen and Others v. Turkey, Application Nos. 15,672/08, 24,462/08, 27,559/08, 28,302/08, 28,312/08, 34,823/08, 40,738/08, 41,124/08, 43,197/08, 51,938/08 and 58,170/08, 11 January 2011.

[21] ECHR, Ulusoy and Others v.Turkey Application No. 34797/03, 3 May 2007.

[22] ECHR, Kamasinski v. Austria, Application No. 9783/82, 19 December 1989.

[23] Medda-Windischer (2021), p. 40.

part of cultural identity. Nonetheless, the Court granted states a margin of appreciation to balance administrative efficiency with minority rights.[24] Drawing on its earlier jurisprudence under Article 8 concerning personal names and the use of language in private correspondence, the Court acknowledged that the ability to use one's minority language in public life may form a core element of cultural and linguistic identity. While this reasoning signals a gradual evolution in the Court's sensitivity to the identity dimension of language use, it does not amount to a departure from its traditionally cautious approach to linguistic rights. The Court reaffirmed the State's margin of appreciation, allowing limitations justified by administrative efficiency, provided that a fair balance is struck and that minority language use is not rendered illusory. As such, Ádám reflects a contextual and incremental development rather than a general recognition of autonomous linguistic rights.

More recently, the European Court of Human Rights has shifted focus toward broader minority issues, such as Roma discrimination, migrant pushbacks[25] and political participation in geopolitically sensitive contexts.[26] Pure linguistic rights cases remain rare, possibly due to states implementing earlier rulings or a preference for domestic remedies. However, linguistic claims increasingly intersect with identity[27] while contemporary challenges, such as the impact of digital media and globalization, underscore the ongoing relevance of linguistic rights. Streaming platforms and social media can either amplify minority language visibility or marginalize them through algorithmic bias and dominant-language content, necessitating updated legal frameworks to ensure their preservation and promotion in an increasingly digital world.

References

de Varennes F, Kuzborska E (2015) Human rights and a person's name: legal trends and challenges. Hum Rights Q 37(4):977–1023

Mancini S, de Witte B (2008) Language rights as cultural rights: a European perspective. In: Francioni F, Scheinin M (eds) Cultural human rights. Martinus Nijhoff Publishers, Leiden, Boston, pp 247–284

Medda-Windischer R (2021) Religious and linguistic minorities and the European court of human rights: between restrictive measures and concerted solutions. Europa Ethnica 78(1–2):36–47

Peroni L (2012) Erasing Q, W and X, erasing cultural differences. In: Brems E (ed) Diversity and European human rights: rewriting judgments of the ECHR. Cambridge University Press, Cambridge, pp 445–469

Ó Riagáin D (2001) Many tongues but one voice: a personal overview of the role of the European Bureau for Lesser Used Languages in promoting Europe's regional and minority languages. In: O'Reilly C (ed) Language, ethnicity and the state. Palgrave, New York, pp 20–39

[24] ECHR, Ádám and Others v. Romania, Application No. 81114/17, 13 October 2020.

[25] ECHR, C.O.G.G. and Others v. Lithuania, Application No. 17764/22 (pending).

[26] ECHR, Kovačević v. Bosnia and Herzegovina, Application No. 17764/22 (pending).

[27] ECHR, A.M. and Others v. Russia, Application no. 47220/19, 6 July 2021.

Tsitselikis K (1996a) Minority languages and "Minoritization", the law as a regulatory factor. In: Kentro Ellinikis Glossas (ed) "strong"—"weak" languages in the European Union - aspects of linguistic hegemony - proceedings of the conference, pp 213–224. (in Greek)
Tsitselikis K (1996b) The international and European regime for the protection of the linguistic rights of minorities and the Greek legal order. Sakkoulas Athens (in Greek)

Chapter 7
Educational Rights

Contents

The concept of education is defined by the Court in the case of *Campbell and Cosans v. the United Kingdom* as "*the whole process whereby, in any society, adults endeavour to transmit their beliefs, culture and other values to the young*".[1] The right of education is guaranteed in the framework of the European Convention of Fundamental Rights by the Protocol No. 1 to the Convention. Pluralistic societies require the examination of educational rights, in the context of international law, in the light of multiple and sometimes conflicting goals which must be compromised and balanced. The different stakeholders in education (trainees, teachers, parents, minority groups, local, regional and central authorities) have needs and expectations which may differ and are constantly re-evaluated.[2] The right to education is traditionally considered part of the family of economic, social and cultural rights. It is an "empowerment right" which allows individuals, adults and children to participate fully in their communities or society. Education constitutes a necessary condition for enjoyment of many others human rights and freedoms.[3] For example, individuals cannot fully enjoy other economic and social rights, such as right to work without the required education and training. The essential participation in civic life via

---

[1] ECHR, Campbell and Cosans v. the *United Kingdom*, Application No. 7511/73, 23 March 1983.

[2] Advisory Committee on the Framework Convention for the Protection of National Minorities, Commentary on Education under the Framework Convention for the Protection of National Minorities, ACFC / 25DOC (2006) 002, Strasbourg, 2 March 2006, p. 5.

[3] UN Committee on Economic, Social and Cultural Rights, General Comment on the Right to Education (Art. 13), 8 December 1999, 21st sess., UN Doc. E / C.12 / 1999/10 (1999), para. 1.

N. Gaitenidis, *The Rights of Cultural Identity in the Case Law of the European Court of Human Rights*, European Union and its Neighbours in a Globalized World 36, https://doi.org/10.1007/978-3-032-23045-4_7

freedom of expression, freedom of assembly and the exercise of the right to be elected also requires knowledge and skills that can be obtained only through education.[4] At the same time, education is a mechanism that can be used improperly; education can contribute to the increase of social exclusion and strengthen the dominant anti-egalitarian ideologies and values of the nation-state.[5]

The triad-goal of "dignity - cultural identity – diversity" can be detected in several international texts as one of the main goals of education. A person's sense of dignity depends on the acquisition of a "cultural identity", defined as a set of cultural values by which individuals or groups identify, express and desire to be recognized. Cultural identity implies freedoms inherent in the dignity of the individual and combines cultural diversity, memory and work in an ever-evolving process. The right to education is therefore particularly important for ethnic, linguistic and religious minorities as a means of preserving their cultural identity and protecting them from various forms of discrimination.[6]

Most provisions of international human rights law restrict the educational rights of persons belonging to minorities in the provision of equal opportunities in education and the inclusion in the objectives of education of the development of respect for human rights, the spirit of understanding, peace, tolerance, equality and respect for identity, language and cultural values.[7] However, the right to education includes the recognition of parents as the primary caregivers and educators of their children, according to their religious and philosophical beliefs, and states are obliged to respect their beliefs about the way in which they should be educated.[8]

---

[4] EU Network of Independent Experts on Fundamental Rights (2006), p. 141.

[5] Panagiotidis (2005), pp. 132–134.

[6] International law recognizes that education, in addition to being a universal human right, is also a critical area of minority rights, who face adverse situations in order to maintain their identity; the importance of transmitting values and attitudes to minorities through education was recognized by the international community before the establishment of human rights as a universal institution through the Charter of the United Nations. The protection of individual rights is based on the principle of non-discrimination. Thus, the right does not only ensures the simple formal access of every child to education, but also the full development of the human personality. Dieter Beiter (2006), pp. 85–154.

[7] The United Nations Convention on the Rights of the Child clarifies the content of the right to education in Articles 28 and 29. In addition, Article 2 of the First Protocol to the European Convention on Human Rights states that "*No person shall be denied the right to education. In the exercise of any functions which it assumes in relation to education and to teaching, the State shall respect the right of parents to ensure such education and teaching in conformity with their own religious and philosophical convictions*".

[8] The responsibility for the upbringing of the child and for his development belongs primarily to the parents or to their legal guardians. The best interests of the child must be their primary concern, according to Articles 14 and 18 of the UN Convention on the Rights of the Child. A similar provision is found in the Universal Declaration of Human Rights; according to Article 26 para 3 "*Parents have a prior right to choose the kind of education that shall be given to their children*". Also, the International Covenant on Civil and Political Rights, according to which "*The States Parties to the present Covenant undertake to have respect for the liberty of parents and, when applicable, legal guardians to ensure the religious and moral education of their children in conformity with their own convictions*" (Article 18, paa 4). Particular reference should be made to the UNESCO

The dimensions of the right to education concerning cultural identity and the special needs of persons belonging to minorities could be summarized as follows: a) access to education at all levels and to vocational training and continuous training without discrimination, b) freedom of education, c) respect for the freedom of parents to ensure the education and training of their children in accordance with their religious and philosophical beliefs, d) the right to learning and knowledge of culture, history, language and religion of national minorities and of the majority, including the promotion of multicultural and intercultural perspective e) the right to learn and teach in the minority language. The right of persons belonging to minorities to create and to manage their own private educational institutions and training is subjected to the regulations concerning the mandatory education. The educational facilities are subject in the same forms of state supervision, in particular regarding teaching standards. The right of persons belonging to minorities to create and to manage their own private educational institutions does not imply a financial obligation for the state, but does not rule out the possibility of such contribution.[9]

Article 2 of Protocol No. 1 to the European Convention of Human Rights establishes the right to education; According to Garlicki the Article provides that the State would "*assume functions in relation to education and to teaching*" but, in the exercise of those functions, should "*respect the right of parents to ensure such*

Convention against Racial Discrimination in Education, 1960, which deals exclusively with education and which includes the educational rights of minorities. The Convention specifically addresses minorities in Article 5; according to this provision, it is necessary to recognize the right of members of national minorities to pursue their own educational activities, including the maintenance of schools and the use or teaching of their own language provided, however, that (a) understanding of the culture and language of the whole community and participation in the activities is not hindered; (b) national sovereignty is not endangered, (c) the level of education will not be lower than the general level already set or accepted by the competent authorities and (d) attendance at these schools is optional and not compulsory. In addition, the establishment of educational institutions from individuals must be allowed, always in accordance with the minimum standards defined by the State. The Council of Europe Framework Convention for the Protection of National Minorities provides that "*under the education system, the Parties recognize the right of persons belonging to a national minority to establish and manage their own private educational institutions*" without, however, any financial obligation from the states. The Framework Convention further provides for measures, if necessary, in the field of education and research to promote the knowledge of the culture, history, language and religion of national minorities, as well as the majority and training opportunities for teachers, access to school textbooks and the facilitation of contacts between students and teachers from different communities. The Framework Convention attaches particular importance to the learning of a minority language and to the right of every person belonging to a national minority to learn his or her minority language without prejudice to the learning or teaching of the official language. In particular, in areas of significant or traditional settlement of persons belonging to national minorities, when there is sufficient demand, States should ensure that persons belonging to these minorities can learn the minority language or they are educated in this language within their educational system. Council of Europe Framework Convention for the Protection of National Minorities, Articles 12, 13 and 14.

[9] Advisory Committee on the Framework Convention for the Protection of National Minorities, Commentary on Education under the Framework Convention for the Protection of National Minorities, ACFC / 25DOC (2006) 002, Strasbourg, 2 March 2006, p. 13–28. See Stavrinaki (2013), *pp. 693–706.*

education and teaching in conformity with their own religious and philosophical convictions". "*Thus, the State has a right (or – rather – an obligation) to provide public schooling for all children whose parents are not ready to use private schools. At the same time, the State must respect both, the general freedom of religion and conscience and the specific guarantee of that freedom in respect to the operation of the public schools system*".[10]

In the *Sampanis and Others v. Greece* case, Greek nationals of Roma origin were living in Psari, an authorised residential site near Aspropyrgos, Greece. The applicants have appealed to the European Court of Human Rights alleging a violation of Article 2 of Protocol No. 1 and Article 14 of the Convention, claiming that the authorities failed to provide schooling for the their children during the 2004–2005 school year and placed their children in special classes, in an small building next to the main Aspropyrgos primary school building, a measure related to the Roma origin of the children. In addition, on 12 September 2005, at the start of the school year, Roma parents, including the applicants, accompanied their children to school, but at its entrance, many non-Roma parents had gathered and verbally assaulted the Roma and blocked the entrance to the school until the Roma children were transferred to another building. The Court condemned the Greek tactic of segregation of this minority in the school environment, and the episodes of intolerance. The Court ruled that there is a violation of Article 14 together with Article 2 of Protocol No. 1 to the European Convention of Human Rights. The Court also underlined the value of acquiring knowledge as well as integration into society and stressed that special importance should be given to ensuring the enrollment of all school-age children in school, which becomes even more important when children belong to minorities. The Court also stressed that in a democratic society which is based on the principles pluralism, a different treatment, which is based solely or decisively on the ethnic origin of a person, cannot be objectively justified.[11]

In the *Kjeldsen v. Denmark* case,[12] the European Court established, according to Garlicki, four principal rules: (a) the State's obligation to assure access to education includes also a power to decide what kind of public schools system should be established as well as the structure and content of the school curriculum, (b) Application of Article 2 of Protocol No. 1 and, in particular, its "religious guarantee" to the entire educational program thus it is not possible to draw distinction between religious instruction and other subjects, (c) Incorporation of information transmitting religious, philosophical and moral messages in many "non-religious" subjects; as a result the European Convention cannot be interpreted as preventing states from

---

[10] Garlicki L (2015), pp. 321–341.

[11] ECHR, Sampanis and Others v. Greece, Application No. 32526/05, 5 June 2008. The Court also found that the Greek Government had not adduced evidence of the availability of an effective remedy and therefore there had been a violation of Article 13. Stavrinaki (2013), pp. 693–706. *See also, ECHR, D.H. and Others v. the Czech Republic,* Application No. 57325/00, 13 November 2007 and ECHR, Oršuš and Others v. Croatia, Application No. 15766/03, 16 March 2010.

[12] ECHR, Kjeldsen, Busk Madsen and Pedersen v. Denmark, Application nos. 5095/71; 5920/72; 5926/72, 7 December 1976.

imparting through teaching or education information or knowledge of religious or philosophical kind, and (d) Every information that may have religious or philosophical connotations must be conveyed in an objective, critical and pluralistic manner and a failure to observe this requirements transforms legitimate education into a process of indoctrination in violation of parents' rights.[13]

States are therefore free to set minimum standards, for example the school curricula and teaching or discipline methods. Private schools can follow religious, philosophical or pedagogical goals of their choice. However, it is imperative that even private institutions abide by democratic principles. This means that private schools must provide guidance in an objective way, critical and pluralistic, similarly to public institutions. States therefore have an obligation to adjust the public and private schools, so that the fundamental rights and freedoms of all students to be protected. For example, the case of *Campbell and Cosans v. United Kingdom*, was brought by two mothers whose children attended schools at which they were at risk of experiencing corporal punishment; the Court ruled that their right to ensure the education of their children in line with their philosophical convictions (Article 2 of Protocol No. 1 to the Convention) had been breached. The Court decided that as neither child had been subjected to corporal punishment, there had been no violation of Article 3. However, one of the children had been suspended from school when he refused to accept corporal punishment, which, according to the Court constitutes a violation of the child's right to education.[14]

Respect for the freedom of parents to ensure the education and training of their children in accordance with their religious and philosophical beliefs stems from the recognition, under international law, of the parents as the primary caregivers and educators of their children, as well as the obligation to protect the freedom of thought, conscience and religion. The European Court of Human Rights in the *Campell and Cosans* case clarified that the philosophical beliefs should be respected in a democratic society and should not be incompatible with human dignity. In addition, the philosophical beliefs of the parents must not contradict the child's

[13] Garlicki (2015), p. 326.

[14] ECHR, Campbell and Cosans v. United Kingdom, Application No. 7511/76, 25 February 1982. See also the case *Costello-Roberts v. UK,* A seven-year old boy was subjected to corporal punishment by the headmaster of the private boarding school which he attended. The punishment was in line with the school's disciplinary code. The boy and his mother claimed that the boy had suffered degrading treatment and unjustified interference with his right to respect for his private life. However the Court ruled that that in order for the punishment to be "degrading" and in breach of Article 3, the humiliation or debasement involved must attain a particular level of severity and exceed the usual element of humiliation inherent in any punishment. Assessing whether punishment is degrading involves looking at the full circumstances of the case, and there was no evidence here of any severe or long-lasting effects. As such, the punishment could not be considered degrading. In addition, the administration of corporal punishment at school did not amount to a violation of the family's right to private life. ECHR, *Costello-Roberts v.UK,* Application No. 13134/87, 23 February 1993.

fundamental right to education.[15] The Court ruled further in the case *Kjeldsen, Busk Madsen and Pedersen v. Denmark* that the obligation of the state to respect the beliefs of parents is not satisfied merely with the establishment of private schools but the state must ensure respect of parental beliefs throughout the public education program. In this case a group of parents complained that the sexual training in public schools of Denmark violated their beliefs about how their children should be trained.[16] The Court was confronted with similar cases with regard to compulsory ethics classes that offended some parents' religious sentiments,[17] different religious dogmas or philosophical convictions[18] or religious teaching for Christianity in conflict with the philosophical beliefs non Christian parents. The Court's reasoning in all these cases is the same: the State, in fulfilling the functions assumed by it in regard to education and teaching, must ensure that information or knowledge included in the curriculum is conveyed in an objective, critical and pluralistic manner. If this is not the case, the State authorities are under an obligation to grant children full exemption from the lessons in accordance with the parents' religious or philosophical convictions.[19]

In the *Papageorgiou and Others v. Greece* case, the European Court of Human Rights further elucidated the scope of parental rights under Article 2 of Protocol No. 1, reinforcing the principles established in *Campbell and Cosans v. United Kingdom* and *Valsamis v. Greece*. The applicants, parents in Greece, challenged the mandatory Orthodox Christian religious education in public schools, arguing that it conflicted with their philosophical and religious convictions and that the requirement to disclose their beliefs to obtain exemptions violated their privacy (Article 8) and freedom of religion (Article 9). The Court found a violation of Article 2 of Protocol No. 1, ruling that Greece's exemption process was neither accessible nor transparent and that compelling parents to reveal their beliefs imposed an undue burden. The Court emphasized that states must ensure educational content is delivered in an objective, critical, and pluralistic manner and provide exemption mechanisms that respect parental convictions without procedural obstacles.[20] This case adds depth to the chapter's exploration of how states must facilitate exemptions without imposing burdens, aligning with the requirement to respect parental beliefs in a democratic society while ensuring education remains inclusive and non-discriminatory.

The *Osmanoğlu and Kocabaş v. Switzerland* case concerned the applicants' refusal to send their daughters to compulsory school swimming lessons on the

---

[15] ECHR, Campell and Cosans v. the United Kingdom, Application No. 7511/76, 7743/76, 25 February 1982.

[16] ECHR, Kjeldsen, Busk Madsen and Pedersen v. Denmark, Application No. 5095/71, 7 December 1976.

[17] ECHR, Appel-Irrgang v. Germany, Application No. 45216/07, 6 October 2009.

[18] ECHR, Hasan and Eylem Zengin v. Turkey, Application No. 1448/04, 9 October 2007.

[19] ECHR, Folgerø and Others v. Norway, Application No. 15472/02, 29 June 2007. See also, Naskou Peraki and Tzivaras (2021), pp. 199–220.

[20] ECHR, Papageorgiou and Others v. Greece, Applications nos. 4762/18 and 6140/18, 31 October 2019. Brzozowski (2020), pp. 355–360. See also, Roberts (2020), pp. 208–211.

grounds that their beliefs prohibited them from allowing their children to take part in mixed-sex swimming lessons. They alleged that there had been a violation of Article 9 of the Convention because the school refused to exempt their daughters from the swimming lessons. In a unanimous chamber decision, the European Court of Human Rights ruled that states had a wide margin of discretion with regard to the balance between religious freedom and the state's wish to educate pupils according to their tradition and needs. It put emphasis on the fact that the school had shown flexibility by offering to allow the girls to swim in burkinis and to change their clothes in a room with no boys present. It further found that it was important for social integration, particularly for children of foreign origin, that pupils take full part in their education and not be exempted because of their parental background. The Court thus found that the Swiss authorities did not violate the European Convention when they fined the girls' parents, also saying that the fine in this case was proportional to the aim pursued and not an unduly harsh punishment.[21]

In the Valsamis case v. Greece case, the applicants were Jehovah's Witnesses. At the beginning of the school year the parents of the students submitted a written statement according to which their daughters should be excluded from attending religious studies, church services and any other celebration that was contrary to their religious beliefs, such as celebrations of national anniversaries and public parades, as pacifism is a key element of their religion, which forbids any behavior related to war or violence. One month later, the two students were asked to join their classes in a parade to celebrate the national holiday commemorating the 28 of October 1940. The students informed their school principals that their religion did not allow them to participate in the anniversary of a war. The educational authorities rejected their request due to vagueness. When they did not show up at the march they were punished by the teachers' council with expulsion. The European Court of Human Rights had ruled that the mandatory participation of students in parades does not in any way impede the right of parents to advise, enlighten and ultimately guide their children according to their own worldview and their own philosophical and religious beliefs. Furthermore, the Court has no competence to rule on the question of the appropriateness of the educational methods or whether the teaching methods which the applicants consider to be the best are indeed the most appropriate for young people to learn about the history of their country. However, the Court found that the right to an effective remedy had been violated under Article 13 of the European Convention on Human Rights, as the applicants had no legal remedy to challenge the legality of the sentence imposed on the two schoolgirls, or even to challenge it.[22]

A case brought before the European Court of Human Rights had the potential to be a "landmark" in defending secularism in Europe. However, this did not happen as in March 2011 Italy's appeal to the Plenary Session of the Court of Justice

[21] ECHR, Osmanoğlu and Kocabaş v. Switzerland, Application No. 29086/12, 10 January 2017. See also, Gutan (2021), pp. 175–195.

[22] ECHR, Valsamis v. Greece, Application no. 21787/93, 18 December 1996. See. Naskou Perraki (2006), pp. 333–337. Stavrinaki (2013), *pp. 693–706.*

succeeded in reversing the original ruling of the Court of Justice in November 2009. In the *Lautsi case and Others v. Italy*, one parent successfully argued that Italian administrative law requiring the public presence of the Crucified One in any public school room violated parents' right to ensure that their children were educated in accordance with their own religious and philosophical beliefs. In November 2009, seven judges ruled unanimously against Italy. The text of the decision made it clear that this decision complied with the Italian Constitution, which has been secular since 1985. The public presence of religious symbols cannot be justified either by the request of other parents who want a religious education that is consistent with their beliefs or by a forced compromise with Christian-inspired political parties. The state is committed to religious neutrality in public education where attendance is required regardless of religion and should seek to instill critical thinking in students. Italy has exercised its right to appeal the decision to the Plenary Session of the European Court of Human Rights. Apart from the Italian Government, the governments of other European countries, including the Greek and Cypriot ones, as well as the Vatican, also intervened against the decision. The Court, in the second instance, accepted the appeal of the Italian government, ruling that the school environment is under state supervision. Although the state must respect religious freedom, a religious symbol in schools, such as the Crucified One, does not constitute an influence of this magnitude that could affect the psyche of a child or young person. Also, the cross, as a symbol, is a historical element of the Italian state and is under the cultural protection of the government, which must ensure the continuity of the Italian nation. It may, of course, offer a prominent place in the religion of Christianity, but that is not enough to be characterized as having a proselytizing effect. After all, in Italy the other religions are equally recognized and enjoy freedom and tolerance by the official state.[23]

Tamimi remarks that "*In the Lautsi cases, the state's national identity takes a much more explicit and prominent role. Christian tradition is acknowledged as the national Italian religious identity. Moreover, the accommodation of several 'excesses' - from Italy's perspective - of identity is part of the Grand Chamber's argument for allowing the continuation of the state's explicit religious symbolism. Italy's openness toward headscarves, Ramadan festivities and non-Christian religious education are considered a sign that the national identity is not obstructing other manifestations of religion*".[24]

Knowledge of the culture, history, language and religion of minorities is a prerequisite for maintaining the cultural identity of persons belonging to minorities and avoiding forced assimilation. The promotion of this knowledge as well as the knowledge of the culture, history, language and religion of the majority introduces

---

[23] ECHR, Lautsi and Others v. Italy, Application No. 30814/06, 18 March 2011. See also, Naskou Peraki and Tzivaras (2021), pp. 199–220.

[24] Tamimi (2018), p. 294.

an intercultural perspective on the rights of persons belonging to minorities.[25] States apply different methods and structures for teaching minority languages. Among the most common methods and structures found in primary education are: (a) schools where the minority language is dominant and where the majority language is taught only as a subject, (b) schools where minority language is dominant and specific subjects, such as history or geography, are taught using the majority language, (c) schools where the majority language is dominant and where only a few courses are taught in the minority language and (d) bilingual schools where minority and majority languages are at the same level of importance.[26]

In the *Belgian Linguistic Case,* the first to raise cultural rights issues of a minority community, the applicants, French-speaking residentσ of a Flemish province, claimed that the European Convention on Human Rights had been violated because their children had not been granted access to a French-language educational institution. According to the Court, the definition of the language taught in educational institutions is solely a matter for the State's competence; therefore Article 2 of the First Protocol in conjunction with the non-discrimination clause in Article 14 does not guarantee the right of children or parents to be provided with education in the language of their choice. Consequently, the Court did not find a breach of the Convention and the First Additional Protocol, considering that the latter did not recognize linguistic claims and that the specific legal provisions did not unjustifiably disrupt the applicants' private and family life.[27]

However, the position of the Court was different in the case *Cyprus v. Turkey.* In this case, the Court found that there was a violation of this Article on the grounds that the Greek Cypriot residents in the northern part of Cyprus did not have access to Greek-language secondary schools. According to the European Commission, the complete absence of Greek-language secondary schools in the northern part of Cyprus, although the Turkish Cypriot authorities know that all Greek Cypriots in the region prefer to be taught in their own language, is a denial of the essence of the right to education. In addition, the teaching provided in Turkish or English does not meet the needs of these individuals, who have a legitimate desire to maintain their own national and cultural identity. Although Article 2 of the First Additional Protocol guarantees access only to existing educational structures, in this case the requested structures existed in the past, but were abolished by the Turkish Cypriot

[25] The goal is to create a sense of tolerance and dialogue, as mentioned in preamble of Council of Europe Framework Convention for the Protection of National Minorities and Annex II to the Vienna Declaration of leaders States and governments. Vienna Declaration, 9 October 1993.

[26] Advisory Committee on the Framework Convention for the Protection of National Minorities, Commentary on Education under the Framework Convention for the Protection of National Minorities, ACFC/25DOC (2006) 002, Strasbourg, 2 March 2006, pp. 16–17.

[27] Belgian Linguistic Case (Case relating to certain aspects of the laws on the use of languages in education in Belgium), Application Nos. 1474/62, 1677/62, 1691 / 62, 1769 / 63, 1994/63, 2126/64, 23 July 1968.

authorities.[28] In the case Fanrfan Temel and Others v. Turkey, the Court considered that there had been a violation of the Article 2 of the First Protocol due to the suspension of eighteen students from the university for two terms as a disciplinary measure because they had asked the introduction of optional Kurdish language courses to the curriculum.[29]

In *Oršuš and Others v. Croatia*, the Grand Chamber further clarified the limits of permissible differentiation in education involving minority children. The case concerned the placement of Roma pupils in separate classes, officially justified by insufficient knowledge of the Croatian language. While acknowledging that temporary special measures may be legitimate in principle, the Court emphasized that such arrangements must be accompanied by adequate safeguards, regular assessment, and a clear aim of integration. The absence of effective measures to facilitate the pupils' transfer to mainstream classes led the Court to conclude that the separation amounted to indirect discrimination. Accordingly, it found a violation of Article 14 in conjunction with Article 2 of Protocol No. 1.[30] This judgment marks a consolidation of the Court's approach to Roma education, confirming that segregation (whether explicit or disguised as pedagogical differentiation) raises a strong presumption of discrimination incompatible with pluralism in a democratic society.

More recently, the Court was called upon to rule on the restrictions in schools of Transnistria. Specifically, the case concerned the appeal of Moldovan nationals who live in the Moldavian Democracy of Transnistria, a separatist entity that has not yet been recognized by the international community, currently under de facto control of the Russian Federation. The applicants, blaming the authorities of Transnistria (and consequently Moldova) and Russia, claimed that the prohibition of the use of Latin scripts in the field of education, and related harassment of students participating in schools using the Moldovan language is a violation of the right to education under Article 2 of the First Protocol, as well as the Articles 8 and 14 of the European Convention on Human Rights. The Court found that there was a violation of the applicants' right to education. Although the Court recognized the "fundamental importance of primary and secondary education", it noted that the right to education is not unlimited. A state may impose certain restrictions on the exercise of this right, but such restrictions must pursue a legitimate aim. The Court noted that although the closed schools were later reopened, they were located in less convenient locations and with worse equipment. The Court ruled that, as a result of the relocation of schools, parents had to choose between sending their children in degraded facilities or send their children to schools where they would learn a language that is not used outside Transnistria. The Court finally ruled, unanimously, that there was a

[28] ECHR, Cyprus v. Turkey, Application No. 25781/94, 10 May 2001. See also, Naskou Peraki and Tzivaras (2021), pp. 199–220.

[29] ECHR, Fanrfan Temel and Others v. Turkey, Application No. 36458/02, 3 March 2009.

[30] ECHR, Oršuš and Others v. Croatia, Application no. 15766/03, 16 March 2010.

violation of Article 2 of the First Protocol by the Russian Federation but not by the Republic of Moldova.[31]

In conclusion, the state has a serious responsibility to manage fairly the concept of difference in the field of education. The knowledge, preservation and development of the culture, history, language and religion of a minority is a major issue, directly related to the protection of its rights, but also to its very existence, while at the same time the knowledge of the prevailing culture lays the foundations for the consolidation of the principles of tolerance and respect in a pluralistic democratic society. The European Court of Human Rights has shown an insistence on interpreting Article 2 of the First Additional Protocol to the European Convention on Human Rights in a way that does not complicate state education policy or make it “inapplicable”, leaving some minorities vulnerable against formal education policy.[32]

An analysis of the European Court of Human Rights’ jurisprudence reveals a consistent effort to interpret Article 2 of the First Additional Protocol in a manner that preserves the coherence and operability of national education systems. However, this cautious and system-oriented approach has come at a cost. By prioritizing administrative feasibility and state discretion, the Court has often refrained from engaging fully with the substantive impact of educational policies on minority identity. As a result, certain forms of exclusion, assimilation, or indirect discrimination may persist under formally neutral educational frameworks.

From a critical perspective, this jurisprudence reflects the structural limits of a system that protects minority interests primarily through individual rights rather than through a robust recognition of collective educational needs. While recent case law indicates a gradual shift toward substantive equality and positive obligations, the absence of a clearer normative standard on minority education continues to leave vulnerable groups insufficiently protected against the homogenizing effects of state education policies.

References

Brzozowski W (2020) Papageorgiou and others v Greece: exemption from a mandatory course in religion and the art of Reading between the lines. Ecclesiastical Law Journal 22(3):355–360

Dieter BK (2006) The protection of the right to education by international law including a systematic analysis of article 13 of the international covenant on economic, social and cultural rights. Martinus Nijhoff Publishers, Leiden

EU Network of Independent Experts on Fundamental Rights (2006) *Commentary of the Charter of Fundamental Rights*. http://ec.Europe.eu/justice/fundamental-rights/files/networkcommentaryfinal_en.pdf

[31] ECHR, Catan and Others v. Moldova and Russia, Application Nos. 43,370/04, 8252/05, 18,454/06, 19 October 2012.

[32] Naskou Perraki (2006), p. 336–337.

Garlicki L (2015) The Strasbourg court on issues of religion in the public schools system. In: Hermann-Josef Blanke HJ, Villalón PC, Klein T, Ziller J (eds) Common European legal thinking, essays in honour of Albrecht weber. Springer, London, New York, pp 321–341

Gutan B (2021) Cultural rights of migrants - living together in dignity? In: Başak Ç, Bianku L, Motoc J (eds) Migration and the European convention on human rights. Oxford Academic, Oxford, pp 175–195

Naskou Perraki P (2006) Religious Freedom. In: Naskou-Perraki P, Kistakis G (eds) Greek cases in Strasbourg , volume I, 1991–2001. Ant. N. Sakkoulas, Thessaloniki-Athens, pp 321–353. (in Greek)

Naskou Perraki P, Tzivaras I (2021) The right to education. Sakkoulas, Athens-Thessaloniki (in Greek)

Panagiotidis NM (2005) Rights and minorities. Grafis, Alexandroupoli (in Greek)

Roberts CK (2020) The negative aspect of the freedom to manifest religion or belief in the educational context in Greece. Oxford Journal of Law and Religion 9(1):208–211

Stavrinaki T (2013) First protocol, article 2. In: Sicilianos LA (ed) European convention on human rights, interpretation by article. Nomiki Vivliothiki, Athens, pp 693–706. *(in Greek)*

Tamimi Y (2018) Human rights and the excess of identity: legal and theoretical inquiry into the notion of identity in Strasbourgh case law. Soc Leg Stud 27(3):283–298

Chapter 8
Religious and Cultural Practices

Contents

The right to exercise cultural practices and traditions is the most controversial and complex issue regarding the protection of the cultural identity of individuals, especially those who belong to minority cultures. The term "cultural practice" could be defined as the manifestation of elements of a culture or sub-culture, especially concerning the traditional and custom practices of a particular ethnicity or other cultural group. It refers to the traditional practices that have been developed in the context of a specific civilization, in particular those aspects of the civilization that have been practiced since ancient times. Examples of cultural practices under this term are practices related to religious and other spiritual rituals, traditional medical techniques, dietary preferences, ways of housing and residence, child-rearing practices, family relationships etc. Cultural practices related to individuals' religious beliefs include, in addition to formal rituals, practices related to clothing, holidays, use of religious symbols, dietary requirements and use of other substances, family relationships, marriage and divorce, the arrangements for the disposal of the dead etc.[1]

[1] Article 5 para 1 of the Council of Europe Framework Convention for the Protection of National Minorities provides that "*The Parties undertake to promote the conditions necessary for persons belonging to national minorities to maintain and develop their culture and to preserve the essential elements of their identity, namely their religion, language, traditions and cultural heritage*". The Article appears to be inspired by Article 27 of the International Covenant on Civil and Political Rights, according to which "I*n those States in which ethnic, religious or linguistic minorities exist, persons belonging to such minorities shall not be denied the right, in community with the other members of their group, to enjoy their own culture, to profess and practice their own religion, or to use their own language*".

N. Gaitenidis, *The Rights of Cultural Identity in the Case Law of the European Court of Human Rights*, European Union and its Neighbours in a Globalized World 36, https://doi.org/10.1007/978-3-032-23045-4_8

In the context of the Council of Europe and the European Convention on Human Rights, where the rights of people belonging to minorities are interpreted not as special minority rights, but are fully integrated into human rights,[2] Article 9 of the Convention is considered of particular importance; while the Article provides protection of the freedom of religion, its scope is much wider and applies to all personal, philosophical, moral beliefs. It extends to ideas, philosophical beliefs of all kinds, and the individual's own way of personal and social perception of life. For example, a philosophical idea, such as pacifism, falls under the scope of the Article 9 of the Convention. The personal beliefs are more than simple opinions; they are ideas that have reached one certain level of persuasiveness, seriousness, coherence and importance.[3] In this sense, atheism[4] and strict veganism[5] are value systems protected by Article 9 of the Convention. Freedom of thought, conscience and religion, as guaranteed by the Article 9 of the Convention, constitutes a highly important right for persons belonging to minorities in order to preserve their identity, as it protects the manifestation of these beliefs in both the private and in public life, regarding worship, education, practices and ceremonies. Worship is the most obvious form of manifestation of religious beliefs. Access to places of worship and the restrictions placed in the ability of the faithful to take part in events of worship could raise the need for the protection under Article 9.[6]

In the *Izzettin Dogan and Others v. Turkey* case, where the Court reaffirmed that religion is a crucial aspect of believers' identity. The case involved a complaint about the non-recognition of the Alevi faith as a distinct religious denomination from the majority Sunni Islam.[7] While the Court ruled that the religious freedom of the Alevis was violated, it did not consider the impact of this misrecognition on their religious identity. Instead, the Court based the violation primarily on the State's failure to maintain neutrality and impartiality towards the Alevi faith.[8]

In addition, the state has a positive obligation to prevent attacks on worshippers by followers of another religious affiliation. In the case *Members of the Gldani Congregation of the Jehovah's Witnesses and Others v. Georgia,* 96 applicants were attacked, humiliated and severely beaten during their congregation's meeting on account of their religious beliefs. The applicants were subsequently confronted with total indifference and a failure to act on the part of the authorities, who, on account of the applicants' adherence to a religious community perceived them as a threat to Christian orthodoxy and took no action in respect of their complaints. The Court considered that, through their inactivity, the relevant authorities failed in their duty

---

[2] Christopoulos (2002), p. 189. See also, Petty (2016), pp. 807–893.

[3] ECHR, *Arrowsmith v. United Kingdom,* Application No. 7050/75, **Comm. Rep. 1978.**

[4] ECHR, Angelini v. Sweden, Application No. 10491/83, December 3, 1986.

[5] ECHR, CW v. the United Kingdom, Application No.18187/91, 10 February 1993.

[6] ECHR, Cyprus v. Turkey [GC], Application no. 25781/94, 10 May 2001.

[7] ECHR, Izzettin Dogan and Others v. Turkey, Application no. 62649/10, 26 April 2016.

[8] Tamimi (2018), p. 290.

to take the necessary measures to ensure that the applicants could exercise freely their rights to freedom of religion.[9]

Special attention has been attributed in the activities of so-called "sects" and "cults".[10] The European Court of Human Rights considered the issue of new religious movements in the *Fédération chrétienne des témoins de Jéhovah de France v. France*. The Court observed that the French legislation aimed at criminal and preventive action against heretical movements that violate human rights and fundamental freedoms. The Court clarified that it is not possible to rule on the legislation and examine its compatibility with the Convention *in abstracto*. However, it provided some guidelines: while it refrained from defining the content of the term "heresy" (sect), it noted that to the extent that the legislation provided for their dissolution, such a measure should be invoked only by the courts and under certain conditions, such as the existence of final convictions for the sect in question or its leaders, for reasons that are exhaustively enumerated.[11]

The right in conscientious objection in military service, which is recognized from the Article 10 para 2 of the Charter of Fundamental Rights of the European Union, does not meet a corresponding recognition in European Convention on Human Rights. In 2000, the European Court of Human Rights avoided to provide an answer to the question whether sanctions for conscientious objections can be infringing the right to freedom of thought, consciousness and religion as guaranteed by the Article 9 of the Convention.[12]

Based on the Article 9, the Court dealt with interesting topics that are related to the role of the state in religious matters. For example, in the *Manoussakis and others*

---

[9] ECHR, Members of the Gldani Congregation of the Jehovah's Witnesses and Others v. Georgia, Application No. 71156/01, 3 May 2007.

[10] European Parliament, 29 February 1996, Resolution on cults in Europe; and Council of Europe, Parliamentary Assembly, Recommendation 1412, Illegal activities of sects, 22 June 1999. EU Network of Independent Experts on Fundamental Rights (2006), *p. 112*. Human Rights Committee, General Comment 22, Article 18 (1993), CCPR/C/21/Rev.1/Add.4.

[11] ECHR, Fédération chrétienne des témoins de Jéhova de France v. France, Application no. 53430/99, 6 November 2001.

[12] ECHR, Thlimmenos v. Greece, Application No. 34369/97, 6 April 2000. The UN Human Rights Commission accepted this right already in 1993. Human Rights Committee, General Comment 22, Article 18 (1993), CCPR / C /21/ Rev. 1/ Add. 4. Similarly, the Commission has recognized everyone's right to conscientious objection in military service as a legal exercise of the right to freedom of thought, conscience and religion. UN Commission on Human Rights, Resolution 2002/45 of 23 April 2002. In 2001, the European Committee of Social Rights considered a case where the duration of the alternative service was not equal to military service. The Commission found that this extra duration was excessive. ECSR, Quaker Council for European Affairs v. Greece (coll. Compl. No. 8/2000), 25 April 2001. Regarding the case law of the European Court of Human Rights Bratza mentions that "*in Ülke v. Turkey, and again in Taştan v. Turkey, the prohibition against ill-treatment in Article 3 of the ECHR was invoked by the Court, which found that the repeated use of prosecution and imprisonment for a refusal to serve in the armed forces and the requirement that a 78-year-old man should perform such service amounted to degrading treatment*". Bratza (2012), pp. 256–271. See cases ECHR, Ülke v. Turkey, Application no. 39437/98, 24 January 2006 and ECHR, Taştan v. Turkey, Application no. 63748/00, 4 March 2008.

v. Greece case, the Court underlined that states have limited margin of appreciation regarding the sensitive relationship between the state and religions.[13] The case concerned the criminal conviction of Jehovah's Witnesses for operating a place of worship without first applying for an administrative permit.[14] In the *Serif v. Greece* case, the Court pointed out that the role of the state is not to remove the tension by eliminating pluralism, but to apply all the necessary measures to ensure that the various religious communities tolerate each other.[15]

8.1 Reasonable Accommodations

The European Court of Human Rights has also dealt with the special nutritional needs of people belonging to minorities. The case of *Chaa're Shalom ve Tsedek v. France* is of particular relevance. The case concerned the refusal of the authorities to grant to the applicants a license for a special form of ritual slaughter, subject to strict religious rules, in order to prepare special meat (glatt). The Court held that ritual slaughter constituted a rite of passage and was therefore protected by Article 9 of the Convention. According to the Court, there would be an interference with Article 9 only if it were impossible for ultra-Orthodox Jews to obtain meat derived from animals slaughtered according to their religious prescriptions. In fact, the applicants could obtain such meat from various butchers in Belgium. In this respect, the Court concluded that the refusal of the authorization did not constitute a breach of Article 9, in conjunction with Article 14 on non-discriminatory treatment, because the difference in treatment between the applicant's organization and a similar organization (ACIP) which had obtained a license, had a limited scope and pursued the legitimate aim of avoiding the proliferation of associations that carry out the particular process of ritual slaughter of animals.[16]

---

[13] ECHR, Manoussakis and others v. Greece, Application no. 18748/91, 26 September 1996.

[14] See in detail, Naskou Perraki (2006), pp. 327–332.

[15] ECHR, Serif v. Greece, Application no. 38178/97, 14 December 1999.

[16] ECHR, Chaa're Shalom ve Tsedek v. France, Application no. 27417/95, 27 June 2000. See more at Donders (2010), p. 28. The derogation from the obligation to stun in cases of slaughter in slaughterhouses in the context of religious practices has been also established by the Directive 93/119/EC of the European Union. It could be argued that the derogations in question provided by the Directive meet the requirements of Article 13 of the Treaty on the Functioning of the European Union which provides that "*In formulating and implementing the Union's agriculture, fisheries, transport, internal market, research and technological development and space policies, the Union and the Member States shall, since animals are sentient beings, pay full regard to the welfare requirements of animals, while respecting the legislative or administrative provisions and customs of the Member States relating in particular to religious rites, cultural traditions and regional heritage*". **Council Directive 93/119/EC of 22 December 1993 on the protection of animals during their slaughter and/or killing,** OJ L 340 of 31.12.1993, pp. 21–34. See also **Council Regulation (EC) No 1099/2009 of 24 September 2009 on the protection of animals at the time of killing (Text with EEA relevance), OJ L 303, 18.11.2009, p. 1–30**.

In the *Jacobski v. Poland* case, a Buddhist prisoner asked to be served meat-free meals to be able to follow the religious dietary rules required by Mahayana Buddhism. The prison authorities provided him with a 'PK diet'—which is a diet that contains no pork—but did not provide him with a complete meat-free diet. The applicant complained about a violation of his freedom of religion. The Court ruled that the applicant's decision to adhere to a strict vegetarian diet can be considered to be inspired from his religion and was not of absurd nature. Consequently, the denial of prison authorities to provide him a vegetarian diet falls into the scope of the Article 9 of the Convention.[17] Similarly, with the decision in the case of *Vartic v. Romania*, the European Court of Human Rights underlined that the dietary restrictions as a religiously motivated act includes a positive obligation for the state to take reasonable and appropriate measures to safeguard the applicant's rights under Article 9. The Court observed that the requested by the applicant meals do not need a special process of preparation nor did he require special food in a way that would result in a disruption to the management of the prison or any reduction in the quality of the meals, since indeed a diet without animal products was already available to prisoners who observed the requirements of the Christian Orthodox fasting period. Consequently, the Court held that the authorities had failed to strike a fair balance between the interests of the prison authorities and those of the applicant, namely his right to manifest his religion and found that there is a violation of Article 9 of the European Convention on Human Rights.[18]

The wording used by the Court in the above cases, especially the reference to the positive obligation of the state to take reasonable and appropriate measures, is a worthy reference to the concept of "reasonable accommodations". Reasonable accommodation could be defined as an adjustment made in a system to accommodate a proven need for an individual. As the European Network of Legal Experts in the Non-discrimination field notes "*In both the United States and Canada, the concept of reasonable accommodation first emerged in equality law as a means of handling religious diversity. It was then applied to other grounds of discrimination, most notably disability, but also, at least in Canada, to ethnic origin, age, family status, gender and pregnancy. In the European Union, the evolution of anti-discrimination law is following a different path: an explicit duty of reasonable accommodation was for the first time established by the Employment Equality Directive*[19] *but only with respect to disability. Nonetheless, the question of whether a right to reasonable accommodation can be derived from the prohibition of (indirect) discrimination based on other grounds laid down by the different equality directives (the Race Equality Directive with respect to race and ethnicity,*[20] *the*

[17] ECHR, Jacobski v. Poland, Application no. 18429/06, 7 March 2011. See more at Chaib (2016), p. 56.

[18] ECHR, Vartic v. Romania, Application no. 14150/08, 7 January 2014.

[19] Council Directive 2000/78/EC of 27 November 2000 establishing a general framework for equal treatment in employment and occupation, OJ L 303, 2.12.2000, p. 16–22.

[20] Council Directive 2000/43/EC of 29 June 2000 implementing the principle of equal treatment between persons irrespective of racial or ethnic origin, OJ L 180, 19.7.2000, p. 22–26.

Employment Equality Directive with respect to age or religion and belief, the Goods and Services Equality Directive[21] *and the Framework Gender Equality Directive*[22] *with respect to gender and pregnancy), or, alternatively, whether such a right should be recognized in future European legislation, is becoming increasingly salient*".[23] The Parliamentary Assembly of the Council of Europe has decided that "*The reasonable accommodation of religious beliefs and practices constitutes a pragmatic means of ensuring the effective and full enjoyment of freedom of religion. When it is applied in a spirit of tolerance, this concept allows all religious groups to live in harmony in the respect and acceptance of their diversity*".[24]

Regarding the case law of the European Court of Human Rights, the Network observes that "*On a number of occasions, the institutions interpreting the European Convention on Human Rights have had to deal with cases in which a demand similar to a request for reasonable accommodation for religious reasons was at issue. For a long time these institutions have not looked favourably at the recognition of a "duty of reasonable accommodation" whether solely on grounds of freedom of religion (Article 9 of the Convention) or on grounds of Article 9 read in conjunction with Article 14 which prohibits discrimination with respect to any of the rights and freedoms guaranteed by the Convention. In the context of Article 9, this concept could nevertheless find support in the criterion of proportionality, which determines the compatibility of a measure impairing freedom of religion with the Convention. Article 9 § 2 provides that a restriction on religious freedom is only permitted if it is prescribed by law and is necessary in a democratic society to achieve one of the legitimate aims listed in the same provision, the concept of "necessary in a democratic society" has been interpreted by the Court as implying the requirement of proportionality between the means used and the ends envisaged. In a number of cases, the Court has held that the proportional character of a measure entails that amongst the various means of achieving a certain end the authorities should opt for those least impairing rights and freedoms. Accordingly, one could argue that if a provision that is justified by a legitimate objective impairs the religious freedom of certain individuals and that an accommodation would allow the avoidance of such an impairment without at the same time compromising the intended aim, this second solution should be favoured because it represents the less restrictive solution to achieve the objective*".[25]

---

[21] Council Directive 2004/113/EC of 13 December 2004 implementing the principle of equal treatment between men and women in the access to and supply of goods and services, OJ L 373, 21.12.2004, p. 37–43.

[22] Directive 2006/54/EC of the European Parliament and of the Council of 5 July 2006 on the implementation of the principle of equal opportunities and equal treatment of men and women in matters of employment and occupation (recast), OJ L 204, 26.7.2006, p. 23–36.

[23] Bribosia et al. (2013), p. 5.

[24] Parliamentary Assembly, Resolution 2036 (2015) Final version, Tackling intolerance and discrimination in Europe with a special focus on Christians, Article 2.

[25] Bribosia et al. (2013), p. 22.

For example, in the case of *Gatis Kovalkovs v. Latvia*, a Latvian prisoner attached to the Hare Krishna movement claimed that his right to freedom of religion had been violated and that he had been discriminated against on the basis of his religion. He claimed that he has been ridiculed by his fellow prisoners and by the prison staff and that his religious duties were restricted in his cell, as he was unable to read religious texts and pray in his cell. His incense sticks were also confiscated by a prison guard. The Court considered whether a fair balance had been achieved between the conflicting interests at stake, finding that the applicant's claims were religiously inspired and not unreasonable. It held that the interference with the applicant's right did not completely prevent him from manifesting his religion. According to the Court, the obligation to pray, read religious texts and meditate in the presence of others is an almost unavoidable hardship in prisons, but it does not contradict the essence of freedom of religion. Relying mainly on the argument that the applicant did not make use of the opportunity granted to him to pray in another room, the Court decided that the interference with the applicant's right was not disproportionate. The Court also noted that burning incense sticks usually creates a strong smell that is not pleasant for everyone and could be disturbing to other prisoners. Finally, the Court concluded that limiting the list of items permitted to be stored in prisoners' cells that are not essentially necessary for the manifestation of the prisoners' religious beliefs is not a disproportionate restriction to protect the rights and freedoms of others.[26]

Vavřička and Others v. the Czech Republic concerned the compatibility with the Convention of a statutory duty to vaccinate children against certain diseases as a precondition for access to preschool education. The applicants argued that compulsory vaccination violated their right to respect for private life under Article 8 and, implicitly, their philosophical convictions regarding bodily integrity and child-rearing. The Grand Chamber accepted that the interference fell within the scope of Article 8 and acknowledged that opposition to vaccination could be rooted in deeply held philosophical beliefs. Nevertheless, the Court found no violation, emphasizing the legitimate aims pursued by the state, namely the protection of public health and the rights of others, particularly vulnerable individuals who could not be vaccinated. Central to the Court's reasoning was the concept of social solidarity: the duty to vaccinate was framed as a proportionate means of ensuring collective protection in a democratic society, especially in the context of scientific consensus and public health policy.[27]

From an analytical perspective, *Vavřička* illustrates the Court's post-2020 tendency to prioritize collective interests and social cohesion over individual belief-based practices, even where such practices form part of a coherent philosophical worldview. Although the case did not formally turn on Article 9, its reasoning is highly relevant to the protection of cultural and religious practices, as it confirms

---

[26] ECHR, Gatis Kovalkovs v. Latvia, Application no. 35021/05, 31 January 2012.

[27] ECHR, Vavřička and Others v. the Czech Republic, Applications nos. 47,621/13 and 5 others, 8 April 2021.

that the Court remains reluctant to require extensive accommodation where individual convictions conflict with broadly defined public interests. The judgment reinforces the view that pluralism under the Convention is not unlimited and that belief-based practices (whether religious or philosophical) may legitimately be restricted when the Court considers them incompatible with social solidarity and the effective functioning of public policy.[28]

Le Mailloux v. France addressed a complaint by an applicant who claimed that his opposition to vaccination constituted a protected belief under Article 9 of the Convention. The applicant argued that measures taken against him for refusing vaccination interfered with his freedom of thought, conscience, and religion. The Court declared the application inadmissible, holding that the applicant's views did not attain the required level of cogency, seriousness, cohesion, and importance to qualify as a "belief" within the meaning of Article 9. In particular, the Court found that the applicant's arguments were largely based on personal opinions and distrust of medical authorities rather than on a structured and consistent belief system deserving Convention protection.[29]

The decision in *Le Mailloux* is significant because it confirms the Court's continued role as a gatekeeper of protected beliefs under Article 9. By maintaining a high threshold for the recognition of beliefs, the Court effectively limits the scope of protection for non-mainstream, dissenting, or counter-cultural practices that challenge dominant scientific or social paradigms. This restrictive approach aligns with earlier jurisprudence distinguishing "essential" from "non-essential" manifestations of belief and reinforces the structural difficulty faced by minority or unconventional belief systems in obtaining recognition under the Convention framework.

Taken together, this line of case law suggests that while the European Court of Human Rights continues to resist the recognition of an explicit and autonomous duty of reasonable accommodation under Article 9, it has progressively integrated accommodation-based reasoning through the language of proportionality, positive obligations, and fair balance. As several commentators have observed, the Court increasingly examines whether state authorities could have achieved their legitimate aims through less restrictive means, particularly where the requested accommodation does not impose excessive burdens or fundamentally disrupt institutional functioning.[30] Nevertheless, this implicit accommodation logic remains uneven and highly context-dependent. Where individual religious or philosophical practices conflict with broadly defined public interests, the Court has shown a consistent tendency to privilege collective considerations and social cohesion over the protection of minority or non-dominant belief systems. As a result, the absence of a clearly articulated duty of reasonable accommodation under Article 9 continues to limit the Convention's capacity to address structural disadvantages affecting minorities, leaving accommodation largely contingent on judicial discretion rather than grounded in a stable and predictable normative standard.

---

[28] Nugraha et al. (2022), pp. 579–585. doi:10.1017/ajil.2022.36.

[29] ECHR, Le Mailloux v. France, Application no. 18108/20, 5 November 2020.

[30] Ouald Chaib (2012), pp. 33–58.

8.2 Essential and "Unnecessary" Manifestations

One of the most controversial aspects of the Court's Article 9 jurisprudence lies in its assessment of which religious manifestations deserve protection. When assessing the legitimacy of religious manifestations, the European Court of Human Rights distinguishes between "normal and recognized manifestations" of religion and manifestations without strong coherence. The Court's approach has led to a distinction between "proper" manifestations of religion and acts merely inspired or influenced by religion. In some cases, the Court has, implicitly or expressly, required full conformity with religious orders or doctrines in order to consider some practices as "manifestations" of religion for the purposes of Article 9. The dependence of a religious manifestation on compliance with institutional or recorded commands or practices, limits the scope of the protection not including the "experiential part of religion", i.e. the actual experience of religious people beyond institutionally defined beliefs and practices.[31] For example, in the case *X. v. the United Kingdom,* 1981, a Muslim teacher went to Court because he was forced to resign from his job as he was not allowed to take a few hours off work on Fridays to attend prayer at a nearby mosque. One of the main issues that arose was whether this specific form of manifestation of religion was "required" by Islam and therefore constitutes a "necessary part" of his religious practice. The Commission found that the applicant did not prove convincingly that he was obliged by Islam to ignore his contractual obligations.[32] In another case, *X. v. the United Kingdom*, of 1974, the Commission similarly held that a Buddhist prisoner, managed to prove that the communication with others Buddhists was an important part of religious practice, but failed to prove that publishing articles in a religious magazine was a necessary part of this practice.[33] More recently, the Court held that the placing of a memorial stone incorporating a photograph on the grave is not a "requirement" of the applicant's religion, despite the fact that the religion permits the placing of a photograph, and therefore the act does not fall within the protection of Article 9 of the Convention.[34] On the other hand, in the case *D. v. France,* the Commission held that, unlike previous cases where the applicants sought to engage in practices that seemingly are not required from religions, Article 9 did not protect the applicant because he wanted to participate in an act that is considered "contrary" to the requirements of his religion, that is, not to deliver the divorce document (get) to his ex-wife, according to the custom of Jewish law.[35] It was noted by the Court that the applicant would seem to be at variance on this point with the religious leaders under whose authority he claims to

[31] Peroni (2014), pp. 671–672.

[32] ECHR, X. v. the United Kingdom, Application no. 7215/75, November 5, 1981.

[33] ECHR, X. v. the United Kingdom, Application no. 5270/72, 20 December 1974.

[34] ECHR, Jones v. the United Kingdom, Application no. 42639/04, 13 September 2005.

[35] ECHR, D. v. France, Application no. 10180/82, 6 December 1983.

be acting.[36] In *Gough v. The United Kingdom,*[37] the applicant adhered to a strong belief in the inoffensiveness of the human body, which he expressed by waking naked on the countryside. The Court held that he had not shown that his beliefs met the necessary requirements of cogency, seriousness, cohesion and importance to fall within the scope of Article 9 of the Convention.[38] In *W v. The United Kingdom,*[39] involving a vegan prisoner who refused to work in the prison print shop, the British government claimed that the applicant had acted inconsistently by failing to mention his vegan beliefs in disciplinary prison proceedings. However, it was concluded that this negligence could not be held against the applicant as she had expressly invoked the requirements of her vegan beliefs in written complaints to the prison authorities before the disciplinary proceedings.[40]

The approach adopted by the Court (and the Commission), in cases like the aforementioned has been criticized for placing in a disadvantageous position those religious people who don't accept every dogmatic order of one particular religion or who believe that their religion imposes further demands on them. In addition, this approach does not take into consideration the fact that some religions define a set of mandatory practices but also encourage their members to prove their piety by participating in religious activities beyond those considered mandatory.[41] Even in cases where a particular practice is considered to be an essential part of a religion, the Court often has recognized the legitimacy of state interventions in the form prohibitions or restrictions. For example, in the *Mann case Singh v. France,* which concerned the authorities' refusal to renew a Sikh man's driver's license because of his reluctance to remove his turban for a photograph, the Court held that Sikh faith compels to wear the turban in all circumstances and it is considered non only a manifestation at the core of their religion, but also an integral part of their identity. However, it decided that the restriction of the applicant's religious freedom was justified and necessary to protect public security.[42]

The Court's distinction between "essential" and "non-essential" manifestations of religion has attracted sustained criticism for its normative and methodological implications. By conditioning Article 9 protection on conformity with institutional doctrines, officially recognized practices, or demonstrable religious obligation, the Court risks privileging hierarchical and orthodox interpretations of religion over lived, experiential, and individualized forms of belief. As commentators have observed, this approach places individuals who dissent from dominant interpretations within their own religious communities, or who understand religious commitment as dynamic rather than prescriptive, at a structural disadvantage (Peroni 2014;

[36] Wolff (2021), p. 274.

[37] ECHR, Gough v. The United Kingdom, Application no. 49327/11, 28 October 2014.

[38] Wolff (2021), p. 269.

[39] ECHR, W v. The United Kingdom, Application No. 11095/84, 7 March 1989.

[40] Wolff (2021), p. 281.

[41] Peroni L., opt. cit., p. 675.

[42] ECHR, Mann Singh v. France Application no. 24479/07, 13 November 2008.

Wolff 2021).[43] Moreover, the insistence on identifying mandatory practices fails to reflect the internal diversity of many religious traditions, where optional or supererogatory acts may nonetheless carry profound spiritual significance.

From a broader perspective, this jurisprudence reveals the Court's persistent unease with adjudicating the authenticity of belief while simultaneously engaging in precisely such assessments. Although the Court formally disclaims any role in defining religion, its practice of filtering protected manifestations through tests of necessity, coherence, and doctrinal consistency effectively positions it as an arbiter of religious legitimacy. This tension is particularly problematic for minority and non-traditional belief systems, whose practices may be more vulnerable to being classified as "inessential" or merely inspired by religion. Even where a practice is acknowledged as central to religious identity, as in cases concerning religious dress or symbols, the Court has frequently accepted far-reaching state restrictions in the name of public security, neutrality, or social order, thereby reinforcing a model of religious freedom that remains largely conditional and deferential to state interests (Bratza 2012; Brems 2020).[44]

References

Bratza N (2012) The 'precious asset': freedom of religion under the European convention on human rights. Ecclesiastical Law J 14:256–271

Bribosia E, Rorive I, Waddington L (2013) Reasonable accommodation beyond disability in Europe?. European network of legal experts in the non-discrimination field. European Commission, Directorate-General for Justice, Belgium. https://tandis.odihr.pl/bitstream/20.500.12389/21768/1/07881.pdf

Chaib SO (2016) Religious accommodation in the workplace: improving the legal reasoning of the European court of human rights. In: Foblets MC, Katayoun Alidadi K (eds) A test of faith? Religious diversity and accommodation in the European workplace. Routledge, New York, pp 33–58

Christopoulos DK (2002) Otherness as a power relation, Aspects of the Greek, Balkan and European experience, Series: Minority Group Research Center: Series of Studies Series Leader: Tsitselikis K, Christopoulos DK. Kritiki, Athens (in Greek)

Donders Y (2010) Do cultural diversity and human rights make a good match? Int Social Sci J 61(199):15–35

EU Network of Independent Experts on Fundamental Rights (2006) Commentary of the Charter of Fundamental Rights. http://ec.Europe.eu/justice/fundamental-rights/files/networkcommentaryfinal_en.pdf

Naskou Perraki P (2006) Religious freedom. In: Naskou-Perraki P, Kistakis G (eds) Greek cases in Strasbourg, volume I, 1991–2001. Ant. N. Sakkoulas, Thessaloniki-Athens, pp 321–353. (in Greek)

Nugraha IY, Regules JM, Vavřička VM, Others v. (2022) The Czech Republic. Am J Int Law 116(3):579–585. https://doi.org/10.1017/ajil.2022.36

[43] Wolff (2021), pp. 259–286.

[44] Bratza (2012), pp. 256–271.

Peroni L (2014) The European court of human rights and intragroup religious diversity: a critical review. Chi-Kent Law Rev:663–687

Petty AR (2016) Religion, conscience, and belief in the European court of human rights, 48, vol 802. George Washington Int Law Rev, pp 807–893

Ouald Chaib S (2012) Religious accomodation in the workplace: improving the legal reasoning of the European court of human rights. In: Alidadi K, Foblets MC, Vrielink J (eds) A test of faith? Religious diversity and accommodation in the European workplace. Ashgate, pp 33–58

Tamimi Y (2018) Human rights and the excess of identity: legal and theoretical inquiry into the notion of identity in Strasbourgh case law. Soc Leg Stud 27(3):283–298

Wolff T (2021) True believers?—sincerity and article 9 of the European convention on human rights. Eur Const Law Rev 17(2):259–286

Chapter 9
Collective Dimensions of Freedom of Religion

Contents

Freedom of religion, as a universal human right, can be nullified unless complemented by the collective dimension of the right of religious groups to organize.[1] The European Court of Human Rights recognized that religious communities traditionally and universally exist in the sense of organized structures and follow the rules that are often authenticated as being of divine origin. Religious ceremonies have their meaning and sacred value for the believers if they have been conducted by the priests empowered for that purpose in compliance with these rules. When therefore made organizational issues of the religious community, Article 9 of the European Convention on Human Rights must be interpreted in the light of Article 11, which ensures the associative life against unjustified state interference. The study of the European Court of Human Rights case law highlights two basic principles underlying the collective aspect of religious freedom, namely the principle of autonomy and the principle of neutrality.[2]

[1] Dinstein (1992), pp. 145–169; Vagias (2019), p. 500.

[2] ECHR, Hasan and Chaush v.Bulgaria, Application no. 30985/96, 26 October 2000.

N. Gaitenidis, *The Rights of Cultural Identity in the Case Law of the European Court of Human Rights*, European Union and its Neighbours in a Globalized World 36, https://doi.org/10.1007/978-3-032-23045-4_9

9.1 The Principle of Autonomy

The autonomy of religious communities is indispensable in order to ensure pluralism in a democratic society and thus it is an issue at the very heart of the protection of Article 9. According to the case law of the Court, a church or religious institution can exercise on behalf of his followers, the rights guaranteed by Article 9 of the Convention.[3] The European Court held unanimously that the government intervention in the organizational structure of a religious community, such as intervention in the selection of religious leaders or the refusal to grant legal recognition to a religious community, violates this right.[4] According to Bratza, the principle of autonomy is manifested in three main areas, namely a) the internal organization of the religious community, including the selection of its leaders, b) the grant or refusal of official recognition to certain faiths in national law and c) the regulation by the state of places of worship. For example, as Bratza remarks "*the Court's case law has frequently involved the intervention by the state in internal disputes within a religious community. In the Hasan and Chaush case itself, following a dispute within the Bulgarian Muslim community as to who should be its national leader, the Government's intervention effectively to replace the applicant who had been elected to the office with another, previous holder of the post was held to be in violation of Article 9, the intervention being found to have been arbitrary and based on legal provisions that allowed an unfettered discretion to the executive. Violations have been found even where the aim of the intervention was one of avoiding intra-faith conflict, the Court emphasising that the existence of tensions within a divided religious community is one of the 'unavoidable consequences of pluralism' and that the role of the authorities in such circumstances is not to intervene to remove the cause of tension by eliminating pluralism but to ensure that the competing groups tolerate each other*".[5]

According to the principle of autonomy, a state cannot compel a religious community to accept new members or expel existing ones.[6] In this respect, Article 9 of the Convention does not guarantee a "right to opposition" within a religious organization. In case of disagreement between one religious community and its members

[3] ECHR, Chaa're Shalom ve Tsedek v. France, Application no. 27417/95, 27 June 2000.

[4] ECHR, Serif v. Greece, Application no. 38178/97, 14 March 2000, ECHR, Hasan and Chaush v Bulgaria, Application no. 30985/96, 26 October 2000, ECHR, Supreme Holy Council of the Muslim Community v. Bulgaria, Application no. 39023/97, 16 March 2005, ECHR, Metropolitan Church of Bessarabia and ors v Moldova. Application no. 45701/99, 27 March 2002, ECHR, Religionsgemeinschaft der Zeugen Jehovas and Ors v Austria, Application no. 40825/98, 31 October 2008.

[5] Bratza (2022), pp. 256–271. See also the case ECHR, Hasan and Chaush v Bulgaria, Application no. 30985/96, 26 October 2000.

[6] ECHR, Svyato-Mykhaylivska Parafiya v. Ukraine, Application no. 77703/01, 14 June 2007.

on the subjects of doctrine or the organization, the religious freedom of the individual is guaranteed through the freedom to withdraw and exit the community.[7]

An important aspect of the principle of autonomy of religious communities is manifested in the area of labor law, especially in the choice of workers with specific criteria for a religious community. Questions arise as to whether organizations and institutions with religious are entitled to practices that would otherwise be prohibited by the equality legislation. The prevailing view, which seems to be adopted by the European Court of Human Rights is that an entity based on a strong religious ethos, has the right to require its staff to comply with its moral code as in the case of *Rommelfanger v the Federal Republic of Germany* which concerned the termination of the employment of a doctor by a Catholic hospital due to his expressed beliefs on pregnancy termination and his opposition to the Church's manifested dogma on abortion.[8]

The Court had also the occasion to rule on that question in its judgment delivered on 23 September 2010. In the case *Obst v. Germany*, the applicant, director of the Public Relations Department of the Mormon Church, was dismissed without notice for adultery, which was a typical violation clause of his contract. He alleged a violation of Article 8 of the Convention, which guarantees the right to respect for private life. The Court held that there was no violation of Article 8 since, the special nature of the professional requirements imposed on the applicant relied on the fact that the employer's ethos was based on religion or belief.[9] In contrast, in *Schüth v. Germany*, the Court came to a different conclusion, holding that while it is accepted that, under the European Convention on Human Rights, in case of an employer whose ethos is based on religion or a philosophical belief may impose special duties of loyalty on its employees, a decision of dismissal based on a breach of these duties cannot be subject to limited judicial review by the competent national court, without taking into account the nature of the position in question and without properly weighing the conflicting interests, in accordance with the principle of proportionality.[10]

In *Lombardi Vallauri v. Italy*, the Council of the Law Faculty of the Sacro Cuore Catholic University of Milan refused to consider a job application by a lecturer who had taught philosophy of law there for more than twenty years on annual renewable contracts, on the ground that the Congregation for Catholic Education (a body of the Holy See) had not given its approval and instead had simply noted that certain statements by the applicant were "clearly at variance with Catholic doctrine". The Court observed that the Faculty Council had not informed the applicant, or made an assessment, of the extent to which the allegedly unorthodox opinions he was accused of holding were reflected in his teaching activities, or of how they might affect the

[7] ECHR, Holy Synod of the Bulgarian Orthodox Church (Metropolitan Innocence) and Others, Applications nos. 412/03 and 35,677/04, 5 June 2009, ECHR, Karlsson v. Sweden, Application no. 12356/86, decision of the Commission, 8 September 1988.

[8] ECHR, *Rommelfanger v* the Federal Republic of Germany, Application No. 12242/86, 6 September 1989.

[9] ECHR, Obst v. Germany, Application no. 425/03, 23 September 2010.

[10] ECHR, Schüth v. Germany, Application no.1620/03, 23 September 2010.

university's interest in providing an education based on its own religious beliefs. Therefore, the Court concluded that the university's interest in providing an education based on Catholic doctrine could not extend so far as to impair the very essence of the procedural safeguards inherent in Article 10.[11]

The case *Fernández Martínez v. Spain* concerned a conflict between the applicant's right to respect for privacy and the collective dimension of the right to freedom of religion of the Catholic Church. The applicant, a priest employed in a Catholic school, had expressed his support for "voluntary celibacy" of Catholic priests and had made a civil marriage, resulting in the decision by the School not to renew his employment contract. The Court ruled that the requirements of the principles of religious freedom and neutrality do not allow the further examination of the necessity and proportionality of the decision of non-renewal of the employment contract and the role of the Court is limited to verifying that the fundamental principles of the rule of law and the dignity of the applicant are not violated.[12] This view seems to support an "organic" conception of the workplace or education according to which those employed in a teaching institution within a religious community fulfill a higher spiritual mode. The European Court of Human Rights, in *Fernández Martínez v. Spain,* seems to move away from the logic of an *ad hoc balancing of the conflicting interests arising from the principle of the autonomy of religious communities and individual rights, which applied in the aforementioned,* and to adopt the theory of "ministerial exception".[13] The possibility of establishment of the *Fernández Martínez v. Spain* as a jurisprudential doctrine carries the risk of excluding many people from the protection against discrimination in labor, causing dilemmas about the necessity of said restriction of individual freedom in favor of the autonomy of religious communities. The establishment of a clear dividing line between the collective autonomy of religious communities and individual freedom is a rather difficult task and a complex process and often leads to contradictory conclusions, as well as controversial jurisprudential findings.[14]

[11] ECHR, Lombardi Vallauri v. Italy Application no. 39128/05, 20 October 2010.

[12] ECHR, Fernández Martínez v. Spain, Requête no 56030/07, 15 mai 2012.

[13] This seems similar to the approach of the Supreme Court of the United States. The Ministerial exception is a legal doctrine in the United States intended to protect freedom of religion by exempting religious institutions from employment discrimination laws. Lund (2011), pp. 1–72; Seglow (2011), pp. 52–64.

[14] Cismas (2014), pp. 146–150. The principle of autonomy of religious communities is also ensured in the framework of the European Union. For example, Directive 93/104/EC **concerning certain aspects of the organization of working time** provides for the possibility of derogations from the general principles established for workers for churches and religious communities. In addition, the Directive 2000/78/EC establishing a general framework for equal treatment in employment and occupation, provides that in the case of occupational activities within churches and other public or private organizations the ethos of which is based on religion or belief, a difference of treatment based on a person's religion or belief shall not constitute discrimination where, by reason of the nature of these activities or of the context in which they are carried out, a person's religion or belief constitute a genuine, legitimate and justified occupational requirement, having regard to the organization's ethos. This difference of treatment shall be implemented taking account of Member States' constitutional provisions and principles, as well as the general principles of Community

Tothpal and Szabo v. Romania concerned state interference in an internal dispute within a Protestant religious community, following a schism that resulted in competing claims to ecclesiastical authority. The applicants, ministers belonging to a faction not recognized by the state-supported church leadership, complained that their criminal convictions for "impersonation" violated their freedom of religion under Article 9 of the Convention. The European Court of Human Rights found a violation, holding that the domestic authorities had failed to respect the autonomy of the religious community by effectively taking sides in an internal theological and organizational dispute. The Court reiterated that, in matters of religious doctrine, leadership, and internal organization, the role of the state must be strictly neutral and impartial, and that civil authorities are not competent to determine which faction within a religious community represents the "true" or "legitimate" interpretation of the faith.[15]

The case is particularly significant for the protection of minority and intragroup religious diversity. The judgment marks a clear reaffirmation of the principle that religious freedom under Article 9 extends not only to protection against external interference but also to safeguarding pluralism within religious communities themselves. Unlike earlier case law that tended to privilege officially recognized religious bodies, the Court acknowledged that internal dissent and fragmentation are inherent features of religious life in democratic societies. The case thus signals a cautious but meaningful shift away from state-backed homogenization of religious identity, emphasizing that misrecognition and selective endorsement of religious authority can themselves constitute a violation of freedom of religion. At the same time, the judgment remains grounded in institutional autonomy rather than individual accommodation, illustrating once again the Court's preference for structural

law, and should not justify discrimination on another ground. See, Council Directive 93/104/EC of 23 November 1993 concerning certain aspects of the organization of working time, OJ L 307, 13.12.1993 p. 18–24. Also, Council Directive 2000/78/EC of 27 November 2000 establishing a general framework for equal treatment in employment and occupation, OJ L 303, 2.12.2000, p. 16–22. The Court of the European Union in the IR v JQ case, which concerned the dismissal of a Catholic doctor from a managerial position by a Catholic hospital due to his remarriage after a divorce, found that the decision of a Church or other organisation the ethos of which is based on religion or belief and which manages a hospital (in the form of a private limited company) to subject its employees performing managerial duties to a requirement to act in good faith and with loyalty to that ethos that differs according to the faith or lack of faith of such employees must be amenable to effective judicial review. Thus, the Court concluded that adherence to the notion of marriage advocated by the Catholic Church does not appear to be necessary for the promotion of IR's ethos due to the importance of the occupational activities carried out by JQ, namely the provision of medical advice and care in a hospital setting and the management of the internal medicine department which he headed. Therefore, that does not appear to be a genuine requirement of that occupational activity. Judgment of the Court (Grand Chamber) of 11 September 2018, IR v JQ, C-68/17, ECLI:EU:C:2018:696.

[15] ECHR, Tothpal and Szabo v. Romania, Application nos. 28,617/13 and 50,919/13, 19 February 2019.

neutrality over a more robust engagement with the lived experience of minority believers.[16]

The principle of autonomy of religious communities occupies a central place in the Court's interpretation of Article 9, functioning as both a safeguard of pluralism and a limit on state interference in matters of doctrine, leadership, and internal organization. The Court's case law demonstrates a consistent commitment to protecting institutional religious autonomy against arbitrary or partisan state intervention, particularly where misrecognition or enforced uniformity threatens intragroup diversity. At the same time, this emphasis on collective autonomy has generated persistent tensions with individual rights, especially in the fields of employment, education, and internal dissent. While recent judgments reaffirm the importance of neutrality and pluralism within religious communities, they also reveal the Court's reluctance to articulate clear criteria for reconciling institutional autonomy with individual dignity and equality, leaving this balance largely dependent on contextual assessments and judicial discretion.

9.2 The Principle of Neutrality

The principle of neutrality means respect for different beliefs as a primary obligation of the state, which cannot make value judgments regarding religious beliefs or their means of expression. The European Court of Human Rights ruled that a state cannot depict a religious group in a derogatory or defamatory manner.[17] However, one state may characterize a religion as "heresy", even if this definition involves a pejorative importance, when it seeks to provide evidence to contribute to the dialogue of a democratic society and to draw attention to the risks arising from the groups usually characterized as "sects".[18] In addition, the principle of neutrality does not imply that a religious practice or a religious community completely escapes the control of the state or the judicial authorities. For example, in the case *Raëlien Suisse v Switzerland*, the European Court of Human Rights found that the State did not violate the freedom of expression and religious freedom of the applicant through banning posters of their organization, which was probably expressing beliefs apologetic pedophilia.[19] Similarly, the European Court of Human Rights declared that it was accepted for a state to run an information campaign which highlighted the dangers to young people of becoming associated with a particular religious movement.[20] As Evans notes "*Whilst such information might be considered merely*

[16] Bauer (2020).

[17] ECHR, Leela Förderkreis EV and Others v. Germany, Application no. 58911/00, November 6, 2008.

[18] Gatti (2019), p. 142.

[19] ECHR, Raëlien Suisse v. Switzerland, Application no. 16354/06, 13 July 2012.

[20] ECHR, Leela Förderkreis e.V. and Others v. Germany, Application No. 58911/00, 6 November 2008.

'informational', not 'coercive'-and it is of course well established that a state may not seek to coerce a person into changing their religion or belief-, the idea that the state cannot have views concerning various forms of belief, and act on them, is, then, simply not true".[21]

On several occasions, the European Court of Human Rights has dealt with national regulations regarding the registration of religious entities. The Court has recognized that states have the right to verify if a movement or association of persons exercises, for the pursuit of religious purposes, activities which are harmful to their followers.[22] However, when registration is required, the law must identify the substantive criteria which will determine whether a religious movement or organization will be registered. The absence of specific criteria, calls into question the "prescribed by law" refusal required by Article 9 of the Convention. In addition, procedural guarantees must be foreseen, to avoid any arbitrary exercise of power.[23] The European Court of Human Rights ruled that the imposition of a ten-year waiting period for the recognition of a "religious society" (Religionsgesellschaft) which halted the provision of a series of privileges, such as the right to teach religion to public schools constituted a violation of Article 9 of the Convention by the authorities. The Court decided that Article 9 imposes the obligation of the state authorities to remain neutral during the exercise of their duties and therefore when a state establishes a framework for the award of legal personality to religious groups, all religious groups must have a fair opportunity to apply without discrimination.[24]

Similarly, in the case *Savezcrkava "Riječ života" and Others v. Croatia, t*he applicants were three Reformist churches which are registered as religious communities under Croatian law. Having been entered in the register of religious communities in Croatia in 2003, the applicants submitted requests in order to conclude an agreement with the Government of Croatia which would regulate their relations with the State and allow them certain privileges, including the ability to (i) provide religious education in public schools and nurseries, (ii) provide pastoral care to their members in medical and social-welfare institutions, and prisons and penitentiaries, and (iii) perform religious marriages with the effects of a civil marriage. These requests were refused on the basis that the applicants did not satisfy the criteria set out in the Instruction issued by the government in December 2004 as they had not been present in Croatia since 6 April 1941, and the number of their adherents did not exceed 6000. The Government also claimed that pursuant to the 2004 Health Care Act and the 1999 Enforcement of Prison Sentences Act, members of the applicants' churches still had the right to receive pastoral care in medical and social-welfare institutions as well as in prisons and penitentiaries. The Court reiterated that the

[21] *Evans* (2017*), p*. 90.

[22] ECHR, Manoussakis a.o. v. Greece, Application no. 18748/91, 26 September 1996.

[23] ECHR, *Hasan and Chaush* v. *Bulgaria,* Application no. 30985/96, 26 October 2000, ECHR, *Metropolitan Church Of Bessarabia And Others* v. *Moldova,* Application no. 45701/99, 27 February 2002.

[24] ECHR, Religionsgemeinschaft der Zeugen Jehovahs and Others v. Austria, Application no. 40825/98, 31 July 2008.

imposition of criteria which a religious community that already had legal personality had to satisfy in order to obtain special privileges raised delicate questions, "*as the State had a duty to remain neutral and impartial in exercising its regulatory power in the sphere of religious freedom and in its relations with different religions, denominations and beliefs*". As the government of Croatia had been unable to provide any meaningful explanation as to why some religious communities satisfied the criteria of belonging to "the European cultural circle" whereas others, including the applicants, did not, the Court found that such distinction without "objective and reasonable justification" constituted a violation of Article 14 in conjunction with Article 9.[25]

In another case, the applicants alleged that, as members of the Evangelical Baptist Church and unlike Spaniards of the Catholic faith, they were unable when completing their income-tax returns to allocate part of their income tax directly for the financial support of their own Church. They considered that the difference in treatment amounted to unlawful discrimination contrary to Articles 14 and 9 of the Convention. The Court declared their application inadmissible, and noted that "*the conclusion of agreements between the State and a particular Church establishing a special tax regime in favour of the latter does not, in principle, contravene the requirements of Articles 9 and 14 of the Convention, provided that there is an objective and reasonable justification for the difference in treatment and that similar agreements may be entered into by other churches wishing to do so*".[26]

Finally, the state must not take action which obstructs the normal operation of a religious community. Consequently, an excessive tax that could seriously disturb the internal organization and function of a religious community, constitutes an intervention in the exercise of the rights that derive from the Article 9 and may be a violation, if the Court deems it to be disproportionate.[27] As Sajó and Uitz comment, "*State authorities insisting on architectural specifications tailored for traditional religions appear as though they abuse their regulatory powers over unwanted religious minorities*".[28]

In conclusion, the principle of state neutrality, as developed in the Court's jurisprudence under Article 9, operates less as a requirement of complete abstention from engagement with religion than as a demand for impartiality, consistency, and procedural fairness. While the Court accepts that states may regulate, monitor, and even critically assess religious movements in order to protect public order and vulnerable individuals, it has consistently emphasized that such intervention must not translate into value judgments favoring dominant religions or disadvantaging minority faiths. The case law on registration, recognition, and access to privileges reveals

---

[25] ECHR, avezcrkava "Riječživota" and Others v. Croatia, Application no. 7798/08, 9 December 2010. See also, ECHR, Religionsgemeinschaft der Zeugen Jehovas and Others v. Austria, Application no. 40825/98, 31 July 2008.

[26] ECHR, Alujer Fernández and Caballero García v. Spain, Application no. 53072/99, 14 June 2001.

[27] ECHR, Association Les Témoins de Jéhovah v. France, Application no. 8916/05, 30 June 2011. See also, Garay (2008), pp. 185–190.

[28] Sajó and Uitz (2020), p. 303.

that neutrality is breached not by differentiation as such, but by arbitrariness, lack of objective justification, and the selective application of regulatory criteria. In practice, however, the broad margin of appreciation afforded to states in this sensitive area risks legitimizing structural inequalities, particularly where historical, cultural, or numerical factors implicitly shape regulatory frameworks. The principle of neutrality thus remains an essential but fragile safeguard, whose effectiveness ultimately depends on the Court's willingness to scrutinize not only formal equality, but also the substantive impact of state policies on religious pluralism.

References

Bauer N (2020) Neutralité de l'État et dissensions ecclésiales : réflexions à partir d'un arrêt récent de la Cour européenne, Revue du droit des religions. http://journals.openedition.org/rdr/1127

Bratza N (2022) The 'precious asset': freedom of religion under the European convention on human rights. Ecclesiastical Law J 14:256–271

Cismas I (2014) Religious actors and international law. Oxford University Press, Oxford

Dinstein Y (1992) Freedom of religion and religious minorities. In: Dinstein Y (ed) The protection of minorities and human rights. Martinus Nijhoff Publishers, Leiden, pp 145–169

Evans M (2017) The freedom of religion or belief in the ECHR since Kokkinakis: or quoting Kokkinakis. Religion Human Rights 12:83–98

Garay A (2008) Association les Témoins de Jéhovah versus France the jurisprudence of the European court of human rights on religious activities and taxation issues. Religion & Human Rights 3(2):185–190

Gatti M (2019) Autonomy of religious organisations in the European convention of human rights and European Union law. In: Rossi LS, Di Federico G (eds) Fundamental rights in Europe and China. Regional identities and universalism. Editoriale Scientifica, Napoli, pp 132–153

Lund CC (2011) In Defense of the ministerial exception. North Carolina Law Rev 90:1–72

Sajó A, Uitz R (2020) Individual religious freedom under the European convention of human rights. In: Mancini S (ed) Constitutions and religion. Edward Elgar Publishing, pp 286–306

Seglow J (2011) Theories of religious exemptions. In: Calder G, Ceva E (eds) Diversity of Europe, dilemmas of differential treatment in theory and practice. Routledge, London, pp 52–64

Vagias M (2019) Freedom of thought, conscience and religion. In: Naskou Perraki P (ed) Human rights, international and regional protection. Sakkoulas, Athens, pp 493–501. (in Greek)

Chapter 10
Private and Family Life as a Cultural Practice

Contents

Apart from practices linked to the religious identity, the way of life of a minority has been recognized by the European Court of Human Rights to be part of a person's identity, protected by Article 8 of the European Convention on Human Rights as part of private and family life. For example in *Mikulic' v. Croatia* the European Court had affirmed that "private life, includes a person's physical and psychological integrity and can sometimes embrace aspects of an individual's physical and social identity".[1] In several cases concerning Roma rights, among which *Aksu v. Turkey,* the Court held that an affront to ethnic identity can also fall within the scope of private life.[2] Moreover, in *Putistin v. Ukraine*,[3] the Court accepted that the reputation of an ancestor could in some circumstances affect a person's private life and identity, and thus might engage Article 8 of the Convention.[4]

Article 8 of the Convention protects those who do not wish to disclose their nationality, as well as their religious and philosophical beliefs to school authorities.[5] Regarding negative stereotypes associated with ethnic groups, they constitute an interference with the right to identity, but must be weighed against the freedom of expression, as guaranteed in Article 10 of the Convention. In this context, the European Court of Human Rights ruled that the reference to stereotypical

[1] ECHR, Mikulic' v. Croatia, Application No. 53176/99, 7 February 2002.

[2] For example, ECHR, Aksu v. Turkey, Applications Nos. 4149/04 and 41,029/04, 15 March 2012 and ECHR, Peringek v. Switzerland, Application No. 27510/08, 15 October 2015.

[3] ECHR, Putistin v. Ukraine, Application No. 16882/03, 21 November 2013.

[4] Tamimi (2018), pp. 288–289.

[5] ECHR, Folgerø and Others v. Norway, Application No. 15472/02, 29 June 2007.

N. Gaitenidis, *The Rights of Cultural Identity in the Case Law of the European Court of Human Rights*, European Union and its Neighbours in a Globalized World 36, https://doi.org/10.1007/978-3-032-23045-4_10

descriptions of Roma in a Turkish book falls under freedom of expression, but acknowledged that it would be preferable for the characterization to be labeled as "derogatory" or "offensive".[6]

Recent scholarship has increasingly emphasized that Article 8 has evolved into one of the Convention's most flexible provisions for the protection of cultural identity, precisely because of its open-ended reference to "private life." As Panagopoulou-Koutnatzi notes, the Court has progressively detached Article 8 from a narrow understanding of intimacy, allowing it to encompass social identity, memory, belonging, and culturally shaped ways of living, even where no physical intrusion occurs. This interpretative elasticity explains why claims linked to ethnic affiliation, family traditions, naming practices, housing patterns, and collective memory have been examined under Article 8 rather than through an autonomous right to cultural identity. At the same time, scholars underline that this expansion has occurred primarily at the level of recognition, while the Court remains hesitant to derive concrete positive obligations for states from this broader conception of private life.[7]

Regarding the settlement of Roma persons Donders notes that "*The right to housing is firmly established in international human rights law. It is explicitly protected in treaties on economic, social and cultural rights and it is part of the right to respect for private life, family life and home as included in treaties on civil and political rights. Together with the general principles of equality and non-discrimination they form the legal basis of the protection of the specific way of housing of Roma, gypsies and travellers. As such, it forms a good example of the indivisibility and interdependence of all human rights, irrespective of their nature and no matter to which category they belong*".[8]

When examining cases concerning the way of life and identity of minorities, in most cases Roma and travelling/nomadic populations, extensive reference is made to the Framework Convention for the Protection of National Minorities[9] in order to limit the discretion of states in this field and to allow cultural diversity by preserving different ways of life and culture. By virtue of the Article 8, the Court was confronted with a lot cases concerning the families of the Roma in the United Kingdom and the refusal of the authorities to allow the setting up of their caravans to a specific

[6] ECHR, Aksu v. Turkey, Applications Nos. 4149/04 and 41,029/04, 15 March 2012. See, Panagopoulou Koutnatzi (2021), p. 432.

[7] Donders (2016), p. 23.

[8] Donders (2016), p. 23.

[9] It should be noted that due to the absence of a universally accepted definition of the term "minority," several states have made interpretative statements, either defining what they consider as a minority or specifying particular groups to which the Framework Convention applies. Furthermore, the Framework Convention does not have binding character, meaning that it cannot be appealed to a court in order to ensure its implementation. The Framework Convention guarantees a range of rights (such as the right to self-identification, linguistic rights, educational rights, etc.) as well as a series of obligations for individuals belonging to minorities (such as the obligation to respect internal legislation, respect the rights of others, adhere to international standards, and have knowledge of the official language of the state). Grammatikas (2019), p. 112. See also, Telalian (2002), pp. 117–136.

piece of land. The Court did not find violation of the Article 8 in those cases, mainly because the European Convention does not include so extensive positive obligations for the state to allow the granting a specific choice of residential house.[10]

The case of *Buckley v. the United Kingdom* is the first relevant case concerning the negative response by British local authorities to the installation of caravans in a certain area. The Court rejected the application for a violation of Article 8, considering that the competent state authorities have the discretion when applying the Convention, to balance the individual interest against the general interest. Regarding the refusal to settle in the residence proposed by the authorities, the Court emphasized that Article 8 does not allow individuals to choose their place of residence at the expense of the general interest.[11]

In *Chapman v. the United Kingdom,* the applicant, a Gypsy, alleged a violation of her right to private life as she was refused the permission to station caravans on her land. As stated in the Court' decision, "*The Court considers that the applicant's occupation of her caravan is an integral part of her ethnic identity as a Gypsy, reflecting the long tradition of that minority of following a travelling lifestyle*". The Court also stated that "*Although the fact of belonging to a minority with a traditional lifestyle different from that of the majority does not confer an immunity from general laws intended to safeguard the assets of the community as a whole, such as the environment, it may have an incidence on the manner in which such laws are to be implemented*" as well as "*As intimated in Buckley, the vulnerable position of Gypsies as a minority means that some special consideration should be given to their needs and their different lifestyle*". However, the Court found no violation of Article 8 as the interference pursued the legitimate aim of protecting the "rights of others" through the preservation of the environment.[12]

The judgment in the *Chapman* case was delivered in conjunction with other four cases involving Gypsies against the United Kingdom[13] which concerned the denial of the government to provide building permits for gypsy families. Despite the fact that the circumstances of the cases are slightly different, the Court in all cases came to the same conclusion. Those cases are particularly interesting for the protection of cultural identity, because the Court established a remarkable correlation between the traditional way of life of the gypsies and respect of private life. Invoking international and European acts for minorities, the Court noted that there is an emerging international consensus "*recognizing the special needs of minorities and an obligation to protect their security, identity and lifestyle, not only for the purpose of safeguarding the interests of the minorities themselves but to preserve a cultural*

[10] Donders (2010), p. 28.

[11] ECHR, Buckley v. the United Kingdom, Application No. 20348/92, 7 February 1992. See also, Farget (2012), pp. 291–316.

[12] ECHR, Chapman v. the United Kingdom, Application No. 27238/95, 18 January 2001.

[13] ECHR, Beard v. the United Kingdom, Application No. 24882/94, 18 January 2001, ECHR, Coster v. the United Kingdom, Application No. 24876/94, 18 January 2001, ECHR, Lee v. the United Kingdom, Application No. 25289/94, 18 January 2001, and ECHR, Jane Smith v. the United Kingdom, Application No. 25154/94, 18 January 2001.

diversity of value to the whole community". However, the Court continued stating that a definitive agreement between states for which action would be desirable in a given situation does not yet exist. The Court pointed out that the complexity and sensitivity of issues related to the policies of balancing the interests of the general population, especially regarding the protection of the environment, and the interests of a minority renders the role of the European Court exclusively supervisory. This statement highlights the limitations of the Court, which does not seem willing to impose positive obligations to the states.[14]

As Donders points out "*With regard to the special treatment of gypsies in relation to non-discrimination, the Court adopted a rather curious view. On the one hand, the Court emphasized the special position minorities may have in policy-making. On the other hand, the Court argued that, if gypsies had been treated differently from other citizens, this would be in conflict with non-discrimination. As stated above and confirmed by the European Court itself, non-discrimination not only implies that equal cases should be treated equally but also that different situations should be treated differently. In some cases, cultural communities may need special measures to protect their (cultural) interests*".[15]

As Donders comments, the Court attempted to demonstrate a growing consensus in Europe regarding the treatment of minorities and their unique role in policy-making. However, the Court also argued that if gypsies were treated differently from other citizens, it would violate Article 14. Case law and doctrine have made it clear that non-discrimination means treating equal cases equally, but also recognizing that different situations require different treatment. The situation of gypsies, particularly in planning policies, is distinct from that of other citizens, and therefore they may require special measures to protect their interests. The Court acknowledged this in the *Yordanova v. Bulgaria* case,[16] where it stated that Article 14 was applicable and rejected the argument that tailored approaches for the Roma community would discriminate against the majority population. The Court found it contradictory that the State had special programs for Roma inclusion based on their underprivileged status, yet claimed that giving them "privileged treatment" would discriminate against the majority. Essentially, the Court dismissed its own argument

[14] Donders (2010), p. 29. It is pointed out in the academic literature that "There have been a number of important developments in this area. In 1998 the European Commission against Racism and Intolerance issued a General Policy Recommendation (No. 3) combating Racism and Intolerance against Roma/Gypsies. The Organisation for Security and Co-operation in Europe (OSCE) issued its "Report on the Situation of Roma and Sinti in the OSCE Area" (2000) and following that an "OSCE Action Plan on Improving the Situation of Roma and Sinti within the OSCE area" (2003). The Framework Convention for the Protection of National Minorities by the Council of Europe binds the signatory states to submit a report to the Council of Europe containing "full information on the legislative and other measures taken to give effect to the principles set out in this framework Convention" (Article 25). All these developments point to a consensus among European states regarding the special needs of minority groups". Ringelheim (2012), pp. 426–444.

[15] Donders (2010), p. 29.

[16] ECHR, Yordanova and Others v. Bulgaria, Application No. 25446/06, 24 April 2012.

from the *Chapman* case in the *Yordanova* case. However, the Court did not need to rule on Article 14 in this instance, as it had already found a violation of Article 8.[17]

Taken together, these judgments illustrate the Court's willingness to acknowledge cultural identity in principle while deferring, in practice, to national planning policies through a broad margin of appreciation. Notably, developments in the Court's post-2020 jurisprudence have not significantly altered this cautious approach to cultural identity claims under Article 8. As recent analyses observe, while the Court continues to acknowledge that minority ways of life fall within the scope of private and family life, it has refrained from revisiting the core reasoning of *Chapman* in cases concerning housing, settlement, or land-use policies affecting cultural minorities.[18] This relative jurisprudential stagnation suggests that the Court regards questions of spatial planning and minority lifestyles as areas requiring a particularly wide margin of appreciation, despite the growing international consensus on the need to protect cultural diversity. The absence of new landmark judgments in this field thus reinforces the structural limits of Article 8 as a tool for advancing substantive cultural pluralism.[19]

More recent doctrinal commentary has highlighted that the Court's gradual shift toward acknowledging vulnerability and structural disadvantage, as reflected in *Yordanova*, remains insufficiently theorized within its Article 8 analysis. As Ringelheim argues, the Court continues to oscillate between an individualistic conception of harm and a contextual recognition of group disadvantage, without fully integrating a structural discrimination framework into its reasoning. This tension is particularly visible in cases involving Roma communities, where cultural practices are inseparable from long-standing patterns of exclusion. While Article 14 has occasionally served as a corrective lens, its potential to address systemic inequalities remains underutilized when detached from a robust conception of positive obligations under Article 8.[20]

The Court applied these principles in a case concerning the effects of Roma traditional marriage. The man and woman were Spanish nationals belonging to the Roma community. At a time when, under Spanish law, the only state-recognized form of marriage was a Catholic ceremony, the couple married according to Roma rites. The couple did not take advantage of a subsequent change to Spanish law to enter into a civil marriage. When the man died, the woman applied for a survivor's pension, but was refused on the ground that the Roma marriage had not been registered. The woman complained that the refusal to grant her a survivor's pension amounts to discrimination under European Convention on Human Rights, under Article 14 combined with Article 1 of Protocol 1, concerning property, and also argued that the failure of the Spanish authorities to recognize Roma marriage as having any civil effect was discriminatory, under Article 14 in conjunction with

[17] Donders (2016), p. 8.

[18] Farget (2012), pp. 291–316.

[19] Ringelheim (2010).

[20] Farget (2012), pp. 291–316.

Article 12, the right to marry. The Court held that the refusal to grant a survivor's pension to a member of the Roma community, following the death of a Roma to whom she had been married according to the community's special rites, for 19 years, amounted to a violation of Article 14 of the Convention in conjunction with Article 1 of Protocol 1. The Court took into account the fact that the applicant belonged to a community within which the validity of marriage, according to its ceremonies and traditions, had never been challenged or considered contrary to public order by the government. The Court stated that the power of a community's culturally defined collective beliefs cannot be ignored and pointed out that it is necessary to emphasize the importance of the beliefs that the applicant derives from her participation in the Roma community, a community that has its own values that are well established and deeply rooted in Spanish society.[21] In the specific case "*the reasoning used by the Court is merely based on a general perception of discrimination, with little relevance given to the ethnic background of the applicant. This case offered a useful opportunity to develop clearer and more ambitious arguments, with the objective of advancing and defending a diversity or minority approach beyond the individual case by broadening the scope of what we understand about discrimination, and by detecting discrimination in the Spanish State's refusal to recognise Roma traditional marriage, unlike other religious forms of marriage practised by other minorities*".[22] The case represented a missed opportunity for the Court to articulate a more robust minority-sensitive conception of discrimination, capable of addressing structural exclusion rather than merely individual disadvantage.

Subsequent academic reassessments of *Muñoz Díaz v. Spain* confirm that the judgment reflects a broader pattern in the Court's minority jurisprudence: the tendency to resolve culturally sensitive cases through narrow individual-rights reasoning rather than through an explicit engagement with collective identity and legal pluralism.[23] By framing the violation primarily in terms of unequal treatment in social security law, the Court avoided addressing the deeper issue of symbolic recognition of minority family structures, thereby limiting the judgment's transformative potential for minority protection beyond the individual applicant.

In conclusion, the Court's jurisprudence under Article 8 demonstrates an increasing willingness to recognize cultural identity and minority ways of life as integral components of private and family life. However, this recognition has remained largely symbolic where it has not been accompanied by corresponding positive obligations or a consistent application of substantive equality. While later judgments such as *Yordanova v. Bulgaria* indicate a more nuanced understanding of vulnerability and structural disadvantage, the Court continues to approach cultural diversity with caution, privileging state discretion in areas such as housing, planning, and family law. As a result, the protection of minority cultural practices under Article 8

[21] ECHR, Muñoz Díaz v. Spain, Application No. 49151/07, 8 December 2009.

[22] Ruiz Vieytez (2012), p. 416.

[23] Ruiz Vieytez (2024).

remains contingent, uneven, and heavily dependent on contextual balancing rather than grounded in a clear normative commitment to cultural pluralism.

References

Donders Y (2010) Do cultural diversity and human rights make a good match? Int Soc Sci J 61(199):15–35

Donders Y (2016) Protecting the home and adequate housing: living in caravan or trailer as human right. Int Human Rights Law Rev 5(1):1–25

Farget D (2012) Defining Roma identity in the European court of human rights. Int J Minority Group Rights 19(3):291–316

Grammatikas V (2019) International protection of minorities. In: Naskou Perraki P (ed) Human rights, international and regional protection. Sakkoulas, Athens, pp 109–120. (in Greek)

Panagopoulou Koutnatzi F (2021) Article 8. In: Sarmas I, Kontiadis X, Anthopoulos C (eds) ECHR, interpretation by article. Sakkoulas, Athes—Thessaloniki, pp 423–463. (in Greek)

Ringelheim J (2010) Minority rights in a time of multiculturalism—the evolving scope of the framework convention on the protection of National Minorities. Hum Rights Law Rev 10(1):99–128. https://doi.org/10.1093/hrlr/ngp038

Ringelheim J (2012) Chapman redux: the European court of human rights and Roma traditional lifestyle. In: Brems E (ed) Diversity and European human rights: rewriting judgments of the ECHR. Cambridge University Press, Cambridge, pp 426–444

Ruiz Vieytez E (2012) Minority marriage and discrimination: redrafting Muñoz Díaz v. Spain. In: Brems E (ed) Diversity and European human rights: rewriting judgments of the ECHR. Cambridge University Press, Cambridge, pp 401–425

Ruiz Vieytez E (2024) Religious diversity, minorities and human rights: gaps and overlaps in legal protection. Religion 15(1). https://doi.org/10.3390/REL15010087

Tamimi Y (2018) Human Rights and the Excess of Identity: Legal and Theoretical Inquiry into the Notion of Identity in Strasbourgh Case Law. Social & Legal Studies, 27(3):283–298

Telalian M (2002) European framework convention for the protection of National Minorities and its personal scope of application. In: Affredsson G, Stavropoulou M (eds) Justice pending: indigenous peoples and other good causes, essays in honour of Erica-Irene a. Daes. Martinus Nijhoff Publishers, The Hague, pp 117–136

Chapter 11
Participation in Public Life

Contents

The right of persons with diverse cultural background is considered necessary so that, those persons are promoted in all areas of economic, social, political and cultural life and in order to promote their interests and values and contribute to the emergence of an integrated and pluralistic society based on tolerance and dialogue.[1] Effective participation is also vital for strengthening social cohesion and prevent social exclusion and tensions between different groups.[2]

The right to effective participation in public life implies that persons belonging to minorities have the right, in the same way as other members of the society, to form, join or even leave any association they wish, including educational or religious institutions, and other associations related to cultural, linguistic or religious identity. The right of association of persons belonging to minorities extends both nationally and internationally. Their right to form or participate in associations can only be restricted by law, and the restrictions can only be the same that apply to associations of the majority. In addition "*The right to contacts has three facets, permitting intra-minority contacts, inter-minority contacts, and transfrontier contacts. The right to intra-minority contacts is inherent in the right of association. Inter minority contacts make it possible for persons belonging to minorities to share experience and information and to develop a common minority platform within the*

[1] Economic and Social Council, UN Sub-Commission on the Promotion and Protection of Human Rights, Commentary Of The Working Group On Minorities To The United Nations Declaration On The Rights Of Persons Belonging To National Or Ethnic, Religious And Linguistic Minorities, E/CN.4/Sub.2/AC.5/2005/2, 4 April 2005, para 35.

[2] Advisory Committee on the Framework Convention for the Protection of National Minorities, para 9 The term "public life" should be interpreted in a broad sense, as in the case of Article 1 of the International Convention on the Elimination of All Forms of Racial Discrimination. It includes political, social, economic and cultural life, free elections, exercising public office and power as well as participation in other political and administrative sectors. Participation can be secured in many ways, including the establishment of minority associations, being member of other associations etc.

N. Gaitenidis, *The Rights of Cultural Identity in the Case Law of the European Court of Human Rights*, European Union and its Neighbours in a Globalized World 36, https://doi.org/10.1007/978-3-032-23045-4_11

State. The right to transfrontier contacts constitutes the major innovation of the Declaration, and serves in part to overcome some of the negative consequences of the often unavoidable division of ethnic groups by international frontiers. Such contacts must be free, but also peaceful".[3]

Regarding the right to participate in the political, social, economic and cultural life, the European Court of Human Rights mainly relies on the interpretation of Article 11 of the European Convention on Human Rights on freedom of assembly and association. For example, the European Court of Human Rights examined the refusal of the Turkish authorities to allow the movement of a Cypriot of Turkish origin from the northern/occupied part of Cyprus to the southern part of Cyprus in order to participate in meetings between the two communities. The Court rejected Turkey's objection that the appeal concerned the application of Article 2 of Protocol 4 on freedom of movement and examined the case in the light of Article 11, ruling that the right in question was the freedom of assembly. Thus, the authorities must refrain from applying unreasonable, indirect restrictions to this right.[4] In addition, the Court held that the mere participation in a peaceful demonstration may not be subject to restriction and therefore may not give rise to disciplinary punishment, as long as the person concerned did not participate or commit any reprehensible act.[5]

The European Court of human Rights determined that cultural organisations set up to preserve and develop a minority culture and traditions are, in principle, protected under Article 11 of the European Convention of Fundamental Rights. In this respect, the Court held that "*the existence of minorities and different cultures in a country is a historical fact that a democratic society has to tolerate and even protect and support according to the principles of international law*".[6] It should be noted that, the ECHR has made clear that only "peaceful" forms of association and assembly are protected by the European Convention of Human Rights. The key element in the Court's assessment is the means deployed to achieve this, which must be democratic and exclude any use of violence. Also, any change that is proposed or

[3] Economic and Social Council, UN Sub-Commission on the Promotion and Protection of Human Rights, Commentary Of The Working Group On Minorities To The United Nations Declaration On The Rights Of Persons Belonging To National Or Ethnic, Religious And Linguistic Minorities, E/CN.4/Sub.2/AC.5/2005/2, 4 April 2005, para 51–52. See also, Kastanas (2017), pp. 536–540.

[4] ECHR, Djavit An v. Turkey, Application No. 20652/92, 20 February 2003.

[5] ECHR, Ezelin v. France, Application No. 11800/85, 26 April 1991. In this case the Court had to assess the simple participation of a lawyer in a demonstration, in protest of two court decisions by which supporters of the independence of Guadeloupe had been condemned. The applicant, a lawyer, was sentenced to a minor disciplinary penalty, because he did not keep the necessary distances in the face of the insulting and abusive expressions of the demonstrators and refused to give a relevant statement. The Court considered that "*that the freedom to take part in a peaceful assembly – in this instance a demonstration that had not been prohibited – is of such importance that it cannot be restricted in any way, even for an avocat, so long as the person concerned does not himself commit any reprehensible act on such an occasion*".

[6] ECHR, Sidiropoulos and others v. Greece, Application No. 26695/95, 10 July 1998.

advocated must be compatible with fundamental democratic principles.[7] For example, the Court examined the refusal of national authorities to register an organization on the ground that their real intention was to circumvent the provisions of the electoral law, thus they were trying to shed state sovereignty.[8] In the *Gorzelik and others v. Poland* case, the Court dealt with an appeal against the Polish courts' refusal to register an association with the name "Union of People of Silesian Nationality". The Court held that there was an interference with the right of association, which, however, was aimed at the legitimate aim of preserving order and the rights of third parties, which was also provided for by Polish law. As for the necessity of the intervention, the Court ruled that although pluralism and tolerance are characteristics of every democratic society and freedom of assembly is very important for minorities, this right is not unlimited and cannot justify the establishment of a union that endanger the institutions of the state or the rights and freedoms of others. The recognition of this union could mobilize electoral aspirations which are incompatible with the institutions of Poland. In particular, the organization, due to its name and because of the purposes listed in its statute, sought to circumvent the provisions of the electoral law or other acts that grant specific rights to national minorities, claiming the recognition of the Silesians as a national minority.[9] Therefore, the refusal of the registration was necessary in a democratic society.[10]

Similarly, in the *Refah Partisi and others v. Turkey* the Court held that the dissolution of a political party which advocated the implementation of the Shariah law did not constitute a violation of the Convention, since Shariah is not compatible with the Convention and undermined the basic democratic structures of the State. In this context, the pursuit of power by totalitarian movements or parties cannot be tolerated. Therefore, the preemptive dissolution of a party may constitute a pressing

---

[7] ECHR, Refah Partisi (Prosperity Party) and Others v.Turkey, Applications nos. 41,340/98, 41,342/98, 41,343/98 and 41,344/98, 13 February 2003.

[8] ECHR, Gorzelik and others v. Poland, Application no. 44158/98, 17 February 2004.

[9] According to Encyclopedia Britannica "*Silesia (Śląsk) is a historical region located today in the southwestern part of Poland. It was originally a province of Poland that came into the possession of the Bohemian Crown in 1335. In 1526 it passed to the House of Habsburg and, with the Treaty of Berlin, to Prussia in 1742. After the First World War, the Treaty of Versailles of 1919 provided for a referendum which would determine whether Upper Silesia would remain German or unite with Poland. The results of* the *referendum, in 1921, were favorable for Germany except for the* eastern Department her Upper Silesia. After armed uprising in 1922, the League of Nations agreed on the division of the territory. Thus, most of the industrial zone, passed to Poland. In the wake of the Pact of Munich of 1938, most geographical part of the Czech Silesia was divided between Germany and of Poland. *After the German occupation of Poland in 1939, the whole of Silesia was* attached by Germany. *After the Second World War the pre-1938 status of the border between Poland and Czechoslovakia was restored. The western border of Poland, however, reached as far as the Oder and Lusatian Neisse rivers. Thus, all of German Silesia, west of the Lusatian River Neisse, was incorporated into Poland while only a small part of Lower Silesia, west of the Neisse River, remained in the former East Germany, in the Land of Saxony*". Britannica (2023), para 1.

[10] ECHR, Gorzelik and others v. Poland, Application no. 44158/98, 17 February 2004.

social need if there are already indications of an imminent danger to constitutional democracy.[11]

In another case concerning the Kurdish minority in Turkey, the Court was more cautious in mentioning the right to identity of the minority. The Court found a violation of Article 11 of the European Convention of Human Right due to the dissolution of a Communist political party.[12] The contentious element in this case is that it involves a minority with its own national identity within a nation. The Court explicitly referred to the political program of the party, which advocates for the participation of groups with their own national identity in politics.[13]

Regarding the political participation of individuals belonging to linguistic minorities, the European Court has ruled[14] that imposing restrictive language requirements for candidates running in elections violates their right to effectively participate in public affairs.[15]

The Strasbourg's Court case *United Macedonian Organization Ilinden and others v. Bulgaria* is of particular interest. The United Macedonian Organization Ilinden (UMO Ilinden) was founded on April 14 1990. The goals of the organization, according to its statute and its program, were to "unite all Macedonians of Bulgaria in regional and cultural base" and achieve "the recognition of the Macedonian minority in Bulgaria". The same year the Organization had requested its registration but was not accepted by the competent courts, according to which the goals of the union turn against the unity of the nation, the organization supports national and ethnic hatred, and was dangerous for her territorial integrity of Bulgaria, since it includes the "political development of Macedonia" and the "united, independent Macedonian State".[16] Another attempt to register the union was not accepted in 1998–1999.[17]

Subsequently, Umo Ilinden-Pirin was established on 28 February 1998, as a political party, with some of its founders being members of the previous organization. Although the party was founded in 1998, it was finally registered at the Municipal Court of Sofia on February 12, 1999, after making some necessary changes to its statute. After only a short time, sixty-one members of the Bulgarian parliament asked the Bulgarian Constitutional Court to declare Umo Ilinden-Pirin unconstitutional. According to the members of the parliament who called for the party to be declared unconstitutional, the ultimate goal of the party was an

[11] ECHR, Refah Partisi and others v. Turkey Application nos. 41,344/98, 41,342/98, 41,343/98 and 41,344/98, 13 February 2003.

[12] ECHR, The United Communist Party of Turkey and Others v. Turkey, Application No. 19392/92, 30 January 1998.

[13] Tamimi (2018), p. 292.

[14] ECHR, Podkolzina v. Latvia, Application No. 46726/99, 9 April 2002.

[15] Medda-Windischer (2021), p. 40.

[16] ECHR, Stankov and the United Macedonian Organization Ilinden v. Bulgaria, Application nos. 29,221/95 and 29,225/95.

[17] ECHR, The United Macedonian Organization Ilinden and Others v. Bulgaria, Application no. 59491/00, 9 September 2004.

independent Macedonian state, formed through the secession of "Pirin Macedonia" from Bulgaria. The party, according to the conclusions of the Constitutional Court of Bulgaria, had requested the full cultural, political and economic autonomy of the "Macedonian" minority, the withdrawal of Bulgarian troops from the region, the creation of a Macedonian Orthodox Church, independent of the Bulgarian Orthodox Church, and the recognition of the unique folk art, culture, traditions, and individuality of the "Macedonian" people. The party printed a map of "Macedonia" which included the lands belonging to Bulgaria and Greece and also issued a memorandum calling the situation of "Macedonians" in Bulgaria a modern genocide. The Constitutional Court issued its decision on February 29, 2000, which declared the party unconstitutional.

Umo Ilinden-Pirin, sought redress in the European Court of Human Rights, arguing that neither its activities nor the activities of its leaders and members incited hostility towards a democratic form of government, and that the territorial integrity of a state was open to discussion as any other matter of public concern, since no call for the use of force was made. According to the European Court of Human Rights, the Constitutional Court of Bulgaria did not examine whether the party's statutes and program of action were compatible with the country's Constitution, but relied mainly on certain statements and activities of its party leaders and members, both before and after the party's establishment (rallies, speeches, press conferences, letters or maps). In the view of the European Court of Human Rights, elements of exaggeration and provocation included in the party's statements and speeches of its leaders, do not automatically translate into an imperative social, democratic need for the party's exclusion from political life, through dissolution. For this reason, The Court considered that the intervention in Article 11 of the European Convention on Human Rights was not necessary in a democratic society.[18]

The cases of *Sidiropoulos and others v. Greece* and *Ouranio Toxo and others v. Greece* sparked a large amount of controversy in Greece. The facts of the first case begin in 1990 when the six applicants, all Greek citizens, decided to establish an association in Florina called "Stegi Makedonikou Politismou" (House of Macedonian Culture). The aims of the association, according to article 2 of the statute submitted to the Court of First Instance of Florina, were (a) the cultural, educational and artistic development of the members and the population of Florina in general as well as the development of a spirit of cooperation, solidarity and love among them, (b) cultural decentralization and the protection of artistic and cultural manifestations and traditions and generally the preservation and development of popular culture and (c) the protection of the natural and cultural environment of the region. In June 1990, the Civil Court of First Instance denied the request on the grounds that the true objective of the association was not the one stated in article 2 of the statute, but the promotion of the idea of the existence of a "Macedonian minority" in Greece which comes against the national interest of Greece and

[18] ECHR, The *United Macedonian Organization Ilinden—PIRIN and Others v. Bulgaria,* Application no. 59489/00, 20 October 2005.

therefore against the law.[19] Then the court of Thessaloniki rejected the appeal.[20] Both the European Commission and the Court unanimously concluded that there was a violation of the Convention due to the unjustified extent of the preventive control that had been exercised in Greece. In the report drawn up by the Commission, it was emphasized that even if it is assumed that the true purpose of establishing the union was to promote the idea that there is an oppressed "Macedonian minority" in Greece, it could not be considered a necessary reason to justify the restriction of freedom of association within a democratic society.[21] In addition, according to the Commission, the margin of appreciation of the states is always accompanied by a European supervision, even in matters of national security.[22] Thus, the Commission unanimously decided that there was a violation of Article 11 of the European Convention on Human Rights and referred the case to the Court. The Court noted that the purposes of the Association named "Stegi Makedonikou Politismou", as stated in its statutes, aim exclusively at the preservation and development of the folk culture of the Florina region. These purposes appear to the Court to be perfectly legitimate. It is permissible for the inhabitants of a region of a state to create associations in order to promote, for historical as well as economic reasons, the particularities of that region. Even if it is assumed that the founders of the association have a minority consciousness, the final text of the Copenhagen Conference on the human dimension of the CSCE (chapter IV) of 29 June 1990 and the Charter of Paris for a new Europe of 21 November 1990,[23] which Greece has signed, allow them to create associations to preserve their cultural and spiritual heritage.[24] As the Court observed, national integrity, national security and public order are not threatened by the activities of an organization which intends to promote the local culture of an area, even if it intends to promote the culture of a minority. The existence of minorities and different cultures in a country is a historical fact that a democratic society must tolerate, even protect and support, according to the principles of international law. The Court also took into account that the Greek legislation did not provide for a regime of preventive control of the establishment of non-profit associations. Although it did not rule out that the association could, after its formation, engage in activities incompatible with its objectives, it found that the national authorities treated this

---

[19] Commission Report, Application No. 26695/95. See Christopoulos (2002), p. 182.

[20] The court of appeals referred in a series to titles of Greek and foreign language literature, to the presence of some of the founders at the conference of the human dimension of the Conference on Security and Cooperation in Europe (CSCE) in 1990, where they questioned the Hellenic character of Macedonia, and to a newspaper article, according to which the founders of the union participated in a conspiracy against Greece driven by a "Slavic directive". An appeal was also brought to the Supreme Court and was rejected. Christopoulos (2006), pp. 376–377.

[21] Commission Report, Application No. 26695/95.

[22] Christopoulos (2002), pp. 184–185.

[23] See more at Tavernier (1994), p. 27.

[24] ECHR, Sidiropoulos and others v. Greece, Application No. 26695/95, 10 July 1998. See Christopoulos (2002), p. 188.

possibility as a certainty which could only be refuted by specific acts which the association did not have the time to commit.[25]

In the second case, the applicants were the political party "Ouranio toxo" (Rainbow), founded in 1994, and two Greek members of its political secretariat. The declared goals of the party were, among other things, the defense of the "Macedonian minority" living in Greece. The party has been regularly participating in elections since 1994. In September 1995, the party acquired its offices in Florina. A sign was put up with the party's name in two languages. It included the word "vino-zito", written in the "Slavic alphabet", which means "rainbow", but was also the slogan of the forces that had sought to occupy Florina during the Macedonian civil war. On September 12, 1995, priests from the church of Florina called the people to take part in a "demonstration of protest against the enemies of Greece who shamefully wave signs with anti-Greek inscriptions". The next day the city council published a notice of protest in the local press, and the prosecutor ordered the removal of the sign on the grounds that writing the party's name could provoke the local population. On September 13, 1995, police officers removed the sign without explanation to the applicants, who attempted to install new ones. That same evening, according to the applicants, they were insulted and threatened by a crowd gathered outside the party premises, which included the mayor, and a number of people entered the premises and harassed those inside, demanding that they take down the sign, which the applicants did. According to the applicants, they called the police station but were told that there were no police officers available. The prosecutor took no action against those who took part in the events but criminal proceedings were initiated against party officials for provoking the local population. The applicants were acquitted in September 1998. In December 1995, the applicants filed a lawsuit against those responsible for the events and requested to participate in the proceedings as a political party. However, due to lack of evidence, the proceedings were terminated. The applicants then appealed to the Supreme Court. Their application was rejected on January 30, 2003. The applicants complained about the delay in the proceedings by the prosecution and the violation of the right of association, claiming a violation of Articles 6 and 11 of the European Convention on Human Rights. The European Court of Human Rights noted that the national proceedings lasted more than seven years which does not conform to the concept of "reasonable time" required for the administration of justice. Thus, there has been a violation of Article 6 para 1, on the right to a fair trial. In addition, the Court noted that "Ouranio Toxo" was a legally established party, with one of its goals being the defense of the "Macedonian minority" living in Greece. The posting of a sign on the front of its premises with the name of the party written in "Macedonian language" cannot be considered reprehensible or constitute a direct threat to public order. The Court could accept that the use of the term "vino-zito" had provoked aggressive feelings among the local population. In addition, the danger of provoking hostilities within the community by the public use of political terms is not sufficient to justify limiting

[25] Christopoulos (2006), p. 379.

freedom of association. Regarding the behavior of the authorities, the Court noted that the city council had incited the people of the city to protest against the applicants and some of its members took part in the protest events. In this way, the spread of hatred in a section of the population against the applicants was facilitated. The role of state authorities was to defend and promote the fundamental values of a democratic system, such as pluralism, tolerance and social cohesion. In this case the local authorities should promote a compromise solution, rather than encouraging aggressive behaviors. Regarding the conduct of the police, the Court ruled that it could have foreseen the risk of violence and the risk of violations of the right of association. The state had to take adequate measures to repel or control the violence. The Greek government did not provide an explanation for the lack of police officers, given that events were predictable. Furthermore, in cases of violation of the right of association by individuals (not the state), the competent authorities have a duty to take adequate investigative measures. Based on the above, the Court ruled that the Greek authorities, by their acts and omissions, violated Article 11 of the European Convention on Human Rights.[26]

The European Court of Human Rights found violations of Article 11 of the European Convention by Greece regarding the Muslim minority of Thrace. The case of *Bekir-Ousta and others v. Greece* came before the Court of Strasbourg following the rejection by the Greek courts of the request of the applicants for the judicial recognition of their association with the name "Youth Association of the Minority of South Evros". The judicial refusal to register the association was based on mere suspicion about its real intentions to represent a religious or ethnic minority. The European Court of Human Rights ruled that even assuming that the true aim of an association is to spread the idea that there is an ethnic minority whose rights are not fully respected, that alone does not amount to a threat to democratic society, especially when there is nothing in the articles of association to suggest that its members advocate the use of violence or antidemocratic or anti-constitutional methods. Had the association been registered, the national judiciary would not have been powerless, since it could have ordered its dissolution if it was pursuing illegitimate aims and objective that were not included in the statute of the association, or if its functioning proved to be contrary to law, morality or public order. In addition, the Court declared that the pursuit of purposes such as the protection of intellectual and cultural heritage, the search for national identity and the manifestation of minority consciousness, which are aspects of the freedom of association, through the establishment of a union, serves pluralism and the democratic functioning of a society and should not be considered as an offence to public order. The Court stated that the existence and coexistence of minorities and different cultures in a state is a historical fact, which, according to the principles of international law, a democratic state should respect and protect. According to the Court, the conclusions of the Greek courts regarding the threat to territorial integrity and public order were essentially based on legally indifferent, non-binding and selective readings of reality. The

[26] ECHR, Ouranio Toxo and others v. Greece, Application No. 74989/01, 20 October 2005.

Greek courts relied on a simple suspicion as to the intention of the union, while such a thing would only be proven through the manifestation of anti-democratic and unconstitutional actions in practice.[27]

More recently, the European Court of Human Rights reaffirmed this line of jurisprudence in *Sagir and Others v. Greece*, concerning the refusal of the Greek authorities to register a cultural association of Turkish women in the Prefecture of Xanthi. In its judgment of 24 June 2025, the Court found a violation of Article 11 of the Convention, holding that the denial of legal personality was based on speculative concerns regarding the association's alleged aims rather than on concrete evidence of unlawful or anti-democratic activity. The Court reiterated that the ability of individuals belonging to minorities to organize formally in order to express cultural identity, preserve traditions, and manifest minority consciousness constitutes a core aspect of freedom of association and serves the principles of pluralism and democratic society. Mere reference to minority identity or cultural affiliation cannot, in itself, justify restrictions on Article 11 rights, and preventive measures based on suspicion exceed the state's margin of appreciation.[28]

Similarly, the European Court of Human Rights ruled that Greece violated Article 11 of the European Convention of Human Rights in the cases *Emin and others v. Greece* and *Tourkiki Enosi Xanthis and Others v. Greece.* In both cases, the national courts rejected the registration of associations on the grounds that their names were misleading about the origin of their members with the intention to spread Turkish ideals in Greece and the recognition of a Turkish minority on the Greek territory. In both cases the Court ruled that the fact that a union invoked minority consciousness cannot in itself justify an intervention in the exercise of the right of Article 11 of the European Convention on Human Rights. The right of everyone to express, within the framework of legality, their beliefs about their national identity cannot automatically constitute a threat to public order and the territorial integrity of a country, since, indeed, the essence of democracy lies in its ability to resolve problems in an open dialogue. In a democratic society, which is founded on the rule of law, political ideas that challenge the established order and whose realization is supported by peaceful means should be able to be expressed through the exercise of freedom of association. Therefore, the Court concluded that the competent Greek authorities exceeded their margin of appreciation and that the dissolutions of the unions in question were not necessary in a democratic society. Thus, there was a violation of Article 11 of the European Convention on Human Rights.[29]

Freedom of assembly may be exercised in various ways. In the *Cisse v. France*, one group of foreigners without documents of legal permanent residence, decided to take collective action in order to draw the attention of the authorities to the

---

[27] ECHR, Bekir-Ousta and others v. Greece, Application No. 35151/05, 11 October 2007. See more, Tsolakou (2010), pp. 1–4.

[28] ECHR, Sagir and Others v. Greece, Application no. 34724/18, 24 June 2025.

[29] ECHR, Emin and others v. Greece, Application No. 34144/05, 27 March 2008. Tourkiki Enosi Xanthis and others v. Greece, Application No. 26698/05, 27 March 2008.

difficulties of reviewing their residence status. Their action peaked with their decision to occupy one church, where they stayed for 2 months. Their presence in the church was not opposed by the priest or the local council, while the various religious ceremonies continued without hindrance. Consequently, the Court ruled that the forced evacuation of the church amounted to an interference with the freedom of peaceful assembly.[30]

The European Court of Human Rights has made clear that only "peaceful" forms of assembly are protected by Article 11 of the European Convention on Human Rights and does not protect demonstrations whose organizers and participants have violent intentions, or advocate the propagation of violence and rejection of democracy with a potential damaging impact. However, the fact that a team requires the autonomy or the secession of a part of a territory, thus demanding fundamental constitutional and territorial changes, cannot automatically justify the ban of the gathering.[31]

In its judgment in the case of *Incal v. Turkey* the Court found that the mere fact that a message read out at a commemorative ceremony to a group of people—which already considerably restricted its potential impact on national security, public order or territorial integrity—contained words such as "resistance", "struggle" and "liberation", did not necessarily mean that it constituted an incitement to violence, armed resistance or an uprising. The European Court of Human Rights found that the conviction of the applicant, for participating in the preparation of a political leaflet containing criticism of the Turkish government's actions against Kurdish street traders and stall keepers violated his right under Article 10 and 6 of the European Convention on Human Rights.[32]

The European Court of Human Rights favors the coexistence of many and multiple cultures and collectivities in a democratic and pluralistic society, even when their members claim to express their minority identity. The Court considers the coexistence of minority collectivities to be dangerous for the national consciousness and internal order only when they manifest themselves violently by not respecting the principle of a legal order or when organized ethnic groups claim electoral privileges, i.e. attempt to undermine the sovereign elements of the state.[33] In this light, according to the Court, cultural pluralism is the condition for political and social pluralism, for the interaction of persons and groups and finally for social cohesion through the expansion and flexibility of the already secured rights.[34]

Freedom of the association protects the organizations, those who wish to assemble as well as those who do not wish to participate in an assembly. Even though it is not stated explicitly in the European Convention Human Rights Article 11 includes

---

[30] ECHR, Cisse v. France, Application No. 51346/99, 9 April 2002.

[31] ECHR, *Stankov* and the United Macedonian Organization Ilinden *v*. Bulgaria, Application nos. 29,221/95 and 29,225/95, 2 October 2001.

[32] ECHR, Incal v. Turkey, Application No. 22678/93, 9 June 1998.

[33] ECHR, Gorzelik and others v. Poland, Application No. 44158/98, 20 December 2001. See Tsolakou (2010), p. 11.

[34] Tsolakou (2010), p. 12.

the right not to join a union.[35] For example, in the case *Chassagnou et autres v. France*, the Court noticed that a person cannot enjoy the right to freedom of association, if in fact the freedom of action or choice is either non-existent or reduced to a level with no practical value. The case concerned a French law (Loi Verdeille) which obliged owners of property of a certain size to become members of approved hunting associations and to cede hunting rights to them. The Court held that the obligation by the law for the landowners to join a union, which is fundamentally opposite to their beliefs and the obligation to participate despite the incompatibility with their beliefs, is disproportionate to the public interest. The Court held that there was an interference with the right to use property as there was no provision available for those ethically opposed to hunting practices. Therefore, this interference of Article 1 of Protocol No. 1 was held not to be justified or reasonable. Furthermore, there was an unjustified discrimination, because large landowners, as opposed to small landowners, did have the right to object to transferring hunting rights.[36]

Based on the above, it can be concluded that the European Convention on Human Rights protects the unhindered right to participate in political, social, economic and cultural life, even in cases that question the current form of democratic organization of the State, as long as their purpose and the means used for its realization are consistent with the rules and principles of democracy. However, in the formation of the judge's arguments, the reference to the protection of the rights of persons belonging to minorities represents a secondary legal reasoning which does not establish, but only assists in the justification and the reasoning of the European Court of Human Rights. The Court consciously avoids evaluative considerations regarding minority issues and as a result the violations found are not specific to minority rights.[37]

In conclusion, the Court's Article 11 jurisprudence demonstrates that effective participation in public life (through associations, assemblies, political parties, and cultural organisations) forms a central mechanism for expressing and preserving cultural identity in a democratic society. Strasbourg repeatedly affirms that pluralism, tolerance, and social cohesion require the state to protect peaceful minority expression, including the pursuit of cultural heritage, minority consciousness, and transfrontier contacts. At the same time, the case law reveals a persistent structural limitation: minority protection is rarely articulated as an autonomous concern, but rather emerges indirectly through general guarantees of association and assembly, with states retaining wide discretion where authorities invoke public order, national security, or constitutional integrity. The result is a model of protection that is powerful in preventing overt suppression of peaceful minority organisation, yet uneven in addressing the deeper dynamics of misrecognition and structural exclusion—leaving the effective enjoyment of participation rights heavily dependent on contextual balancing and the quality of domestic democratic safeguards.

[35] *EU Network of Independent Experts on Fundamental Rights (*2006*),* p. 131.

[36] ECHR, Chassagnou ao v. France, Application No. 25088/94, 29 April 1999.

[37] Christopoulos (2002), p. 191.

References

Christopoulos DK (2002) Otherness as a power relation, aspects of the Greek, Balkan and European experience, series: minority group research Center: series of studies series leader: Tsitselikis K, Christopoulos D. Kritiki, Athens (in Greek)

Christopoulos DK (2006) The right to self-determination. In: Naskou-Perraki P, Kistakis G (eds) The Greek cases in Strasbourg, volume I, 1991–2001. Ant. N. Sakkoulas, Thessaloniki Athens, pp 369–379. (in Greek)

Encyclopedia Britannica (2023) The Editors of Encyclopaedia. "Silesia summary". https://www.britannica.com/summary/Silesia

EU Network of Independent Experts on Fundamental Rights (2006) Commentary of the Charter of Fundamental Rights. http://ec.Europe.eu/justice/fundamental-rights/files/networkcommentaryfinal_en.pdf

Kastanas H (2017) Article 11. In: Sisilianos LA, European convention on human rights, interpretation by article, 2nd edn. Nomiki Vivliothiki, Athens, pp 519–554. (in Greek)

Medda-Windischer R (2021) Religious and linguistic minorities and the European court of human rights: between restrictive measures and concerted solutions. Europa Ethnica 78(1–2):36–47

Tamimi Y (2018) Human rights and the excess of identity: legal and theoretical inquiry into the notion of identity in Strasbourg case law. Soc Leg Stud 27(3):283–298

Tavernier P (1994) Minorités et facteur de tensions en Europe. In: Grigoriou P (ed) Questions de minorités en Europe. Presses Interuniversitaires Européennes, Bruxelles, pp 17–33

Tsolakou T (2010) Commentary on the ECtHR decision of 11.10.2007, Bekir Ousta and others v. Greece. Aristovoulos Manesis Group, pp 1–12. (in Greek). http://constitutionalism.gr/site/wp-content/mgdata/pdf/9tsolakoubekir2752010.pdf

Chapter 12
Right to Exercise Traditional Economic Activities

Contents

Culture is manifested by many forms, such as in a certain way life which is related with the use of the earth's resources, especially in the case of indigenous peoples. This right may include traditional economic activities, such as fishing or hunting, and the right to live in regions which are protected by law. The exercise of these rights may require positive legal protection by the state.[1] Although the Court has accepted that traditional economic activities may fall within the scope of Article 8, it has consistently refrained from deriving meaningful positive obligations or robust protection for indigenous ways of life.

The matter did not escape the jurisdiction of the European Court of Human Rights. For example, in *G and E v. Norway*, two members of the Sami community appealed for alleged infringement of the Article 8 due to a proposed hydroelectric project which would result in a part of the traditional hunting and shepherd land falling under water. The Commission accepted that those traditional economic practices could be are part of the private and family life, protected by Article 8 of the Convention. However, it concluded that "The submersion of a very small area of land because of the construction of a hydroelectric plant, in a vast region populated by shepherds, hunters and fishermen, does not constitute an interference with the population's private life. Even if there were interference, it would be justified as being necessary, particularly for the economic well-being of the country".[2]

[1] UN Human Rights Committee (HRC), CCPR General Comment No. 23: Article 27 (Rights of Minorities), 8 April 1994, CCPR/C/21/Rev.1/Add.5, par. 7.

[2] ECHR, G and E v. Norway, *Application no. 9278/81 and 9415/81,* 3 October *1983. See also, Kovács (*2016*), pp. 781–806.*

N. Gaitenidis, *The Rights of Cultural Identity in the Case Law of the European Court of Human Rights*, European Union and its Neighbours in a Globalized World 36, https://doi.org/10.1007/978-3-032-23045-4_12

In the *Johtti Sapmelaccat Ry and others v. Finland* case, members of the Sami people of Finland complained that the amendment of law on fishing (law of 1997), which made fishing conditional on land ownership, violated their right in peaceful enjoyment of their private life as well as the property rights of Sami people who were not landowners but exercised the activity of hunting which was inherent to the Sami culture and way of life. In addition, the law for fishing expanded the fishing rights to all inhabitants of the area, regardless of their status as indigenous[3] or non-indigenous, weakening the legal status of Sami with no land property and resulting in their fishing rights deprived from constitutional protection. Also, the imposition of fees for the granting of a permit for fishing in the area had changed from being granted on a per-household basis, increasing claimants' costs. Therefore, according to the applicants, their rights under Article 8 of the Convention had been breached. The European Court of Human Rights accepted the claim that fishing is an economic practice, part of the private and family life, but found no violation in this particular case. According to the Court "*The said amendment, however, does not seem to have changed the substance of the earlier regulation of the relevant fishing rights, apart from the technical difference that the traditional fishing rights were recognized on the level of a parliamentary enactment instead of a governmental decree. The only material alteration was that these rights are now applied to the Sámi Home District as a whole and not only to the municipality of residence. This in itself can hardly imply a "weakening" of the applicants' legal status. Besides, it is not clear whether even this provision meant a real change as compared to the earlier situation, rather than a clarification of the law*". Furthermore, it considered that one of the applicants, a non-governmental organization, could not be considered a victim of a violation of Article 8 and thus had no *locus standi* in the Court.[4]

In *Hingitaq 53 and Others v. Denmark*, 428 individuals from the Thule District in Greenland, and Hingitaq 53, a group that represents the interests of relocated Inughuit (the Thule Tribe), complained that they had been deprived of their

[3] Having a historical continuity with pre-colonial societies that developed in their territories, indigenous communities, peoples, and nations consider themselves distinct from other sectors of society that currently prevail in these territories. They are currently non-dominant sectors of society and are determined to maintain the development and transmission of their ancestral lands and their ethnicity as the basis for the continuation of their existence as peoples, in accordance with their own cultural standards, social institutions, and legal systems. The characterization of a group as a "minority" or "indigenous people" has significant consequences in international law, despite the similar characteristics often attributed to these two categories of groups, such as numerical inferiority, social isolation, cultural and linguistic distinctiveness, and geographical concentration. The primary legal distinction between the rights of indigenous peoples and minorities in contemporary international law concerns internal self-determination, which is the right of a group to self-govern within a recognized geographic area without state interference, though in some form of cooperation with state authorities, as in any federal governance system. While some minorities enjoy limited self-governance, either de facto or according to national legislation, only indigenous peoples are currently recognized as having the right to political identity and self-governance based on international law. Daes (2008), p. 18.

[4] ECHR, *Johtti Sapmelaccat Ry. and others* v. *Finland, Application no. 42969/98,* 18 January 2005. See more at Cittadino (2019), pp. 264–334.

homeland and hunting territories and denied the opportunity to use, enjoy and control their land, as a consequence of their forced relocation following the establishment of a US Air Base. However, the European Court of Human Rights declared the complaint manifestly ill-founded as a compensation was given by the Danish courts for the eviction and loss of hunting rights.[5]

As *Kovács* notes, the cases that touch upon indigenous issues brought before the European Court of Human Rights (and the European Commission)[6] clearly highlight a longstanding issue: there has been a lack of substantive rulings on matters concerning indigenous peoples by these tribunals. They mostly pertain to decisions on admissibility, with the Court dismissing each case on procedural grounds despite mentioning the merits of the claims made by indigenous peoples in several instances. The development of the Court's jurisprudence on indigenous peoples is arguably hindered by sociological and demographic factors. For indigenous or tribal groups, their relatively small numbers and remote location on the fringes of Europe have prevented them from gaining significant attention within the broader European consciousness. It is expected that the non-binding United Nations Declaration on the Rights of Indigenous Peoples will positively influence the jurisprudence in Strasbourg, compelling the Court to establish an independent interpretation of property rights specifically for indigenous peoples.[7]

The Court's preference for examining traditional economic activities under Article 8 rather than under Article 1 of Protocol No. 1 is legally and conceptually significant. While property rights might appear more directly applicable to claims concerning land use, hunting, or fishing, Article 8 enables the Court to frame such activities as expressions of private life, cultural identity, and social belonging rather than merely proprietary entitlements. This framing has been observed to produce highly deferential scrutiny, as Article 8 has rarely yielded robust positive obligations in cases involving land, natural resources, or conflicting public interests, contributing instead to a proportionality analysis that places weight on state regulation and development imperatives. In relation to cultural practices, a purely individualistic property lens often fails to capture the collective and intergenerational dimensions that underlie traditional economic activities, making Article 8 a more plausible but still constrained vehicle for protection.[8]

This jurisprudential restraint reflects broader structural limits within the Convention system. Indigenous and traditional peoples' claims challenge deeply embedded assumptions about individualised land ownership, sovereign control over

[5] ECHR, Hingitaq 53 and Others v. Denmark, *Application no. 18584/04, 12 January 2006.*

[6] For example, ECHR, Halvar FROM v. Sweden, 4 March 1998 Application No. 34776/97, ECHR, Johtti Sapmelaccat R Y and Others v. Finland, Application no. 42969/98, 18 January 2005, ECHR, The Muonio Saami Village v. Sweden, Application no. 28222/95, 15 February 2000, ECHR, Handolsdalen Sami Village and Others v. Sweden, Application No. 39013/04, 30 March 2010, ECHR, Chagos Islanders v. United Kingdom, Application No. 35622/04. 11 December 2012. See *Kovács (*2016*), pp. 785–795.*

[7] *Kovács (*2016*), pp. 785–795.*

[8] Lenzerini (2016), pp. 127–141; Otis and Laurent (2013), pp. 156–180.

natural resources, and the prioritisation of economic development, assumptions mirrored in domestic legal systems and, by extension, in Strasbourg's reasoning. Consequently, the Court has hesitated to elaborate an autonomous doctrine for indigenous or community-based rights, instead disposing of such cases through narrow admissibility reasoning or deferential proportionality review.[9] This pattern is less a reflection of doctrinal incoherence than of a structural commitment within the Convention to *state discretion* in economic and environmental regulation.[10]

References

Daes EIA (2008) Indigenous peoples, keepers of our past—custodians of our future. IWGIA, Copenhagen

Kovács P (2016) Indigenous issues under the European convention of human rights, reflected in an inter-American Mirror. George Washington Int Law Rev 48(4):781–806

Cittadino F (2019) Incorporating indigenous rights in the international regime on biodiversity protection: access, benefit-sharing and conservation in indigenous lands. Brill, Leiden

Otis G, Laurent A (2013) Indigenous land claims in Europe: the European court of human rights and the decolonization of property. Arctic Rev Law Politics 4(2):156–180

Lenzerini F (2016) Cultural identity, human rights, and repatriation of cultural heritage of indigenous peoples. Brown J World Aff 23(1):127–141

Pentassuglia G (2011) Towards a jurisprudential articulation of indigenous land rights. Eur J Int Law 22(1):165–202

[9] Otis and Laurent (2013), pp. 156–180.

[10] In contrast, other regional human rights systems have developed more explicit frameworks recognising indigenous peoples' land and resource rights as integral to cultural survival. The Inter-American Court of Human Rights, for example, has recognised collective land rights and traditional resource uses as protected elements of the right to property and to cultural identity, linking dispossession directly to human rights violations. The absence of a comparable jurisprudential architecture in Strasbourg underscores the limited capacity of the European Convention, as currently interpreted, to address cultural practices inseparable from land, resources, and traditional lifeways. Pentassuglia (2011), pp. 165–202.

Chapter 13
Right to Cultural Heritage

Contents

Cultural heritage is a concept which is always perceived to have a positive value. Its preservation is generally considered as a common good from which all mankind benefits. Both individual and communal cultural identities are formed via tangible cultural objects and intangible cultural performances.[1] However, conflicts have arisen regarding the right of minorities to define and manage their cultural heritage as well as their cultural property.[2]

The term "cultural heritage" includes tangible culture, such as buildings, monuments, landscapes, books, works of art and documents, intangible culture, such as folklore, traditions, language and knowledge, and natural heritage, which includes important cultural landscapes and biodiversity. The concept reflects the dynamic character of a good which has been developed, manufactured or created, interpreted and reinterpreted in history and transmitted among generations. Therefore it connects the past, the present and the future, since it includes goods which were

[1] A recent illustration of the European Court of Human Rights' approach to cultural heritage is provided by *The J. Paul Getty Trust and Others v. Italy*. The case concerned the recovery by the Italian authorities of the ancient bronze statue known as the *Victorious Youth*, held by the J. Paul Getty Museum, and the applicants' complaint under Article 1 of Protocol No. 1 alleging an unjustified interference with their property rights. The Court found no violation of the Convention, holding that the protection of cultural heritage constitutes a legitimate public interest capable of justifying restrictions on property rights. It emphasized the wide margin of appreciation afforded to states in identifying, preserving, and recovering cultural objects regarded as part of their national heritage. Importantly, the Court did not recognize a free-standing right to cultural heritage but treated heritage protection as a collective interest pursued through existing Convention guarantees, thereby reaffirming the derivative and contextual nature of cultural heritage protection under the ECHR framework. ECHR, The J. Paul Getty Trust and Others v. Italy, Application no. 35271/19, 2 May 2024. Zaręba (2025), pp. 207–222.

[2] Silverman and Ruggles (2007), pp. 5–6.

N. Gaitenidis, *The Rights of Cultural Identity in the Case Law of the European Court of Human Rights*, European Union and its Neighbours in a Globalized World 36, https://doi.org/10.1007/978-3-032-23045-4_13

passed on by past generations and are considered of such significant value today that individuals and communities wish to pass them on to future generations.[3]

A large number of international acts are adopted for the protection of cultural heritage in time of peace or in time of war, for example conventions concerning international humanitarian law, international criminal law etc. with the first attempts at codification dating back to the nineteenth century.[4] The Convention of the Council of Europe on the Value of Cultural Heritage for Society, or otherwise the Faro Convention of 2007, defines the cultural heritage as "*a group of resources inherited from the past which people identify, independently of ownership, as a reflection and expression of their constantly evolving values, beliefs, knowledge and traditions. It includes all aspects of the environment resulting from the interaction between people and places through time*".[5] The Faro Convention openly adopts a human rights approach to cultural heritage. It recognizes for example that everyone, alone or collectively, has the right to benefit from the cultural heritage and to contribute towards its enrichment and the right of everyone to participate in the process of recognition, study, interpretation, protection, preservation and presentation of cultural heritage. Finally, it refers to the right of access to cultural heritage. It is worth noting that the Convention calls for States to encourage reflection on the ethics and methods of presentation of the cultural heritage, as well as respect for diversity of interpretations.[6]

---

[3] **Human Rights Council,** Report of the independent expert in the field of cultural rights, Farida Shaheed, A/HRC/17/38, 21/03/2011, para. 4–5.

[4] In addition to a series of declarations and recommendations, UNESCO member states have adopted the Convention for the Protection of the World Cultural and Natural Heritage of 1972, the Convention for the Protection of the Underwater Cultural Heritage of 2001, the Convention for the Protection of Intangible Cultural Heritage of 2003 etc. See Vrdoljak (2011), pp. 250–302.

[5] Council of Europe Framework Convention on the Value of Cultural Heritage for Society, Faro, 2005, Article 2. It should be noted that cultural heritage does not only refer to those elements which give pride to communities and to humanity, but includes elements which reflect the dark side of humanity, the memory of which should be passed on to future generations but in a different way. **Human Rights Council,** Report of the independent expert in the field of cultural rights, Farida Shaheed, A/HRC/17/38, 21/03/2011, para. 8 and 20.

[6] Council of Europe Framework Convention on the Value of Cultural Heritage for Society, Articles 4, 5, 7 and 12. Human rights and cultural heritage also intersect in the field of property rights, both as material property as well as intellectual property, such as memory, traditional knowledge etc. Some communities express reasonable concerns regarding procurement, dissemination and utilization of "traditional knowledge" and issues related to the illegal or commercial use of knowledge, images, stories etc. Intellectual property rights are generally manifested as individual rights, while the concept of cultural heritage has to do mainly with the community. This implies that the "creator" is not possible several times to be detected, perhaps because is lost in history, or cultural heritage is the result of a collective effort based on tradition. Traditional knowledge refers to knowledge held by specific indigenous and traditional communities and shared by many sections of society in a particular region or country. Traditional knowledge includes "intangible values" and the conservation of cultural heritage is indeed of prime importance in all its forms including social, religious, cultural values and aesthetic value of the landscape. Given the fact that three-quarters of the world's population depend on herbal traditional medicines and due to biopiracy there are strong reasons to protect traditional knowledge, especially when linked to genetic resources of economic

Many acts of international law underline the important role of individuals and communities, including indigenous peoples for the protection and respect of cultural heritage. As Xanthaki observes, indigenous art is widely abused and traditional knowledge is ignored or used without the groups' consent. Historical injustices, such as the brutal removal of indigenous children from their families, have severed their connection to their heritage, especially intangible heritage. In addition, transnational corporations consistently ignore indigenous spiritual spaces and indigenous communities of their natural heritage. Also, tourism, often encouraged by states, lacks the necessary cultural sensitivity and commercializes sites that are important to indigenous people. Finally, the destruction or theft of cultural objects should also be mentioned. In other cases, the art and sacred relics of indigenous peoples are used without the knowledge or permission of the creator or community. Many cultural artifacts as well as human remains of ancestors are kept in museums and institutions after they were removed from sites without the permission of the indigenous peoples. Indigenous peoples seek the return of these items as a sign of respect for their cultural traditions and practices.[7]

The cultural and spiritual heritage of indigenous peoples includes the traditional practices, knowledge and ways of life that are unique to a people. The custodians of the cultural and intellectual property of indigenous peoples are determined by the customs, laws and practices of the community and may be individuals, a tribe or the people as a whole. The heritage of indigenous peoples includes: (a) language, art, music, dance, song and ceremony, (b) agricultural, technical and ecological knowledge and practices (c) spirituality, sacred sites and human remains ancestors and (d) the recording and documentation of the above.[8]

The right to access and enjoy cultural heritage involves an individual and a collective dimension. However, it is possible to recognize different forms of access and enjoyment, taking into account the diverse interests of individuals and groups, according to their relationship to specific cultural heritage. In this light, the following should be distinguished: (a) the "original beneficiaries" or the "source" communities, i.e. the communities that consider themselves the custodians and "owners" of a particular cultural heritage, the people who keep living cultural heritage and have assumed responsibility for its preservation, (b) individuals and communities, including local communities, who consider a particular cultural heritage an integral part of community life, but cannot actively participate in its maintenance, (c) scientists and artists and (d) the general public gaining access to the cultural heritage of others.[9]

---

value to the industry. Prott (2002), pp. 7–12. European Parliament resolution of 15 January 2013 on development aspects of intellectual property rights in genetic resources: implications for poverty reduction in developing countries (2012/2135(INI)), para. 16–17.

[7] Xanthaki (2010), pp. 3–10.

[8] Human Rights Council, Promotion and protection of the rights of indigenous peoples with respect to their cultural heritage, A/HRC/30/53, para. 4–5.

[9] **Human Rights Council,** Report of the independent expert in the field of cultural rights, Farida Shaheed, A/HRC/17/38, 21/03/2011, para. 60–62.

Given that much of the cultural heritage has a religious complexion, the right to freedom of thought, conscience and religion is very important combined with the right of access and enjoyment of cultural heritage, as it protects access in religious places and monuments and exercise of religious practices.[10] Denying access to religious places is a direct violation of religious freedom. In this context, the state must take positive measures to end any adverse action, such as the assistance of religious communities in the return of goods that have been illegally taken and the possibility of legal action and a fair trial.[11] However, this dimension of religious freedom is not absolute either. For example, in the *Juma Mosque Congregation and others v. Azerbaijan case*, the European Court of Human Rights ruled that the European Convention does not legitimize claims of religious communities to claim a place of worship from public authorities even if its religious use have been accepted for a long time.[12]

Vandalism of cultural monuments, such as architectural monuments and archaeological sites, may take place as a result of disturbance, greed, politics protest, religious intolerance, poverty etc.[13] Religious freedom and the prohibition of destruction of cultural property of specific groups is linked to the principle of non-discrimination, as states must ensure the full protection of religious sites and symbols without discrimination. The responsibility of the state for the protection of religious sites is extended to acts of non-state entities, as the obligation to take preventive and repressive measures especially in cases of deliberate attack.[14] The European Court of Human Rights has recognized that actions related to the exercise of religious freedom and especially the preservation of religious goods, buildings and archives have also historical value and social benefits apart from their strict religious significance, therefore the state maintains a significant margin of appreciation regarding managing their funding.[15] As noted by the research literature, a significant obstacle to judicial protection is the inability of claimants to prove that they are victims of a violation, as for example in the case of claims against Switzerland for the construction of minarets.[16]

---

[10] The construction and maintenance of places of worship as well as the use of ritual objects and symbols are an integral part of respecting religion. **Human Rights Committee, General Comment 22, Article 18 (Forty-eighth session, 1993). Compilation of General Comments and General Recommendations Adopted by Human Rights Treaty Bodies, UN Doc. HRI/GEN/1/Rev.1 at 35 (1994), para 4.** Papaioannou (2013), pp. 285–286.

[11] See more details in Papaioannou (2013), pp. 285–286.

[12] ECHR, *Juma Mosque Congregation and others v.* Azerbaijan, Application no. 15405/04, 8 January 2013. See Papaioannou (2013), p. 286. See also, ECHR, Griechische Kirchengemeinde München und Bayern eV v. Germany, Application no. 52336/99, 18 September 2007.

[13] Silverman and Ruggles (2007), p. 15.

[14] See detailed documentation in Papaioannou (2013), pp. 287–288.

[15] ECHR, *Bruno v. Sweden,* Application no. 32196/96, 28 August 2001. Papaioannou (2013), p. 288.

[16] ECHR, Ouardiri v. Switzerland, Application no. 65840/09 28 June 2011, and ECHR, Ligue des Musulmans de Suisse and Others v. Switzerland, Application no. 66274/09, 8 July 2011.

The importance of the above case lies in the finding that the principle of religious neutrality of the state does not imply that religion is absolutely necessary to be eradicated from the public sphere, especially when it is part of the constitutional tradition and heritage of a state and does not compel citizens to discriminate, as for example in the case of *Buscarini and Others v. San Marino* where it was judged that the mandatory religious oath to the Gospels as a condition for assuming the parliamentary position violates their right under Article 9 of the Convention. The Court, despite what was proposed by the Government, which pointed out the inextricable ties between the state and religion, ruled that it is a limitation of the right to religious freedom not necessary for a democratic society.[17]

Finally, it is worth mentioning that the European Court of Human Rights has awarded few cases concerning the difficult combination of the individual right to property and the public interest in the preservation of cultural goods. In most of these cases, the Court has not gone beyond a strict application of the provisions of Protocol I regarding the protection of the individual right of every natural or legal person to the peaceful enjoyment of their property.[18] For example, the case *Fener Rum Patrikligi (Ecumenical Patriarchate) v. Turkey*, where the Court found unfounded the government's argument that the state's intervention in the right to property is justified due to the lack of measures on the part of the Patriarchate to protect a building of historical value.[19]

The examination of the case law of the European Court of Human Rights demonstrates that the right to cultural heritage is not recognized as an autonomous right under the European Convention on Human Rights. Instead, it functions primarily as a derivative and relational right, protected through the interpretation and interaction of established Convention rights, notably the right to respect for private and family life (Article 8), freedom of thought, conscience and religion (Article 9), freedom of expression and association (Articles 10 and 11), the prohibition of discrimination (Article 14), and the right to property (Article 1 of Protocol No. 1). At the same time, the Court's jurisprudence reveals an increasing sensitivity to the collective dimension of cultural heritage, particularly where cultural, religious, or historical goods are central to the identity and continuity of a community, as illustrated in cases concerning places of worship, religious symbols, and historically significant property. While individuals remain the formal rights-holders before the Court, cultural heritage claims frequently reflect collective interests, and state obligations increasingly encompass positive duties of protection, preservation, and non--discriminatory access. In this sense, the right to cultural heritage may be understood as an emerging collective interest with indirect justiciability, whose protection depends on the Court's evolving interpretation of existing rights rather than on the recognition of a free-standing entitlement. This approach preserves the coherence of

[17] ECHR, Buscarini and Others v. San Marino, Application No. 24645/94, 18 February 1999.

[18] For example Beyeler v. Italy, Application no. 33202/96, 5 January 2000 and Sud Fondi Srl v. Italy, Application no. 75909/01, 20 January 2009. Francioni (2011), p. 12.

[19] ECHR, Fener Rum Patrikligi (Ecumenical Patriarchate) v. Turkey, Application no. 75909/01, 15 June 2010. See, Papaioannou (2013), p. 301.

the Convention system while allowing cultural heritage to be safeguarded as a living element of democratic pluralism and social identity.

References

Francioni F (2011) The human dimension of international cultural heritage law: an introduction. Eur J Int Law 22(1):9–16

Papaioannou M (2013) The protection of cultural property in Public International Law, in search of the human dimension, Doctoral Dissertation, Panteion University, Department of International and European Studies, Athens (in Greek)

Prott L (2002) Individual or collective rights for cultural heritage in the information society? Museum Int Heritage issues in the information society 2 LIV(4):7–12

Silverman H, Ruggles F (2007) Cultural heritage and human rights. In: Silverman H, Ruggles F (eds) Cultural heritage and human rights. Springer, London, pp 5–22

Vrdoljak AF (2011) Cultural heritage in human rights and humanitarian law. In: Oh B-N (ed) International human rights and humanitarian law. Oxford University Press, Oxford, pp 250–302

Xanthaki A (2010) Multiculturalism and International Law: Discussing Universal Standards. Human Rights Quartely 32(1): 21–48

Zaręba S (2025) The Getty trust case: human rights, property issues, and cultural heritage protection. Santander Art Culture Law Rev:207–222

Part II
Human Rights as Restrictions to Cultural Identity

Chapter 14
Protecting the Individual Against Cultural Practices of the Group

Contents

As noted above, human rights related to cultural identity may be weakened or even nullified if they are understood exclusively as collective entitlements. In such cases, restrictions or violations of human rights may arise from norms imposed by the group on its own members, most often in the form of limitations on individual liberty justified in the name of group cohesion, solidarity, or cultural survival.[1] This tension brings into focus the problem of so-called *"minorities within minorities"*, namely individuals or sub-groups who do not fully conform to the dominant norms of a minority community. Frequently, such individuals seek protection from the state against cultural or religious practices they perceive as oppressive, while other members of the same group defend those practices as essential to the preservation of their cultural identity.[2]

[1] Kymlicka (1995), pp. 34–46.

[2] Mahajan (2005), pp. 190–200. Dealing with the problems of minorities within minorities has been the subject of extensive research in political science. For example, Will Kymlicka divides minority rights into "external protections" and "internal restrictions." The first category includes those rights that concern the protection of minorities from the influences of the prevailing culture. They mainly concern the relations between the different minority and majority groups. These rights are intended to limit the vulnerability of this group and its collective cultural identity to the decisions of external groups or the wider society. The second category concerns rules imposed by the group during intra-minority relations, without taking into account individual will. Most often they take the form of restrictions on the freedom of the individual in order to ensure the solidarity of the group. These rules raise the risk of individual oppression and the maintenance of violent and authoritarian regimes, as they can be used to support violent, dominant and authoritarian value

N. Gaitenidis, *The Rights of Cultural Identity in the Case Law of the European Court of Human Rights*, European Union and its Neighbours in a Globalized World 36, https://doi.org/10.1007/978-3-032-23045-4_14

Lajeunesse argues that cultural rights remain fragmented, weakly justiciable, and subordinated to civil and political rights in international law. This structural weakness means that when cultural identity is protected primarily as a collective interest, the law lacks effective tools to address internal power asymmetries within groups. As a result, individuals experiencing oppression from within their own cultural or religious community often fall into a protection gap.[3]

In the context of religious communities and institutions, this tension is further complicated by the principle of religious autonomy, which limits state interference in matters concerning the internal organization of a religious body and its relationship with its members. The European Court of Human Rights has consistently held that, under this principle, a state may not compel a religious community to accept new members or to exclude existing ones.[4] Consequently, Article 9 of the European Convention on Human Rights does not guarantee a right to dissent or object within a religious body. In cases of disagreement concerning religious doctrine or organizational matters, the individual's freedom of religion is generally understood to be exercised through the freedom to leave the community. While this approach safeguards institutional autonomy, it also exposes the limits of Convention protection for individuals who remain formally within a religious group but contest certain internal norms or practices.[5]

A landmark judgment addressing the protection of individuals against culturally or religiously imposed norms is *Molla Sali v. Greece*. The case concerned the mandatory application of Islamic law to members of the Muslim minority of Western Thrace in matters of family and inheritance. The applicant, a Greek national residing in Komotini, was deprived of three quarters of her inheritance after Greek courts invalidated her late husband's will—drawn up in accordance with Greek civil law—and applied Islamic inheritance rules instead. In its Grand Chamber judgment of 19 December 2018, the Court found a violation of Article 14 of the Convention, taken in conjunction with Article 1 of Protocol No. 1, holding that the applicant had suffered discrimination on grounds of religion.[6]

The Court emphasized that when a state establishes a special legal status for religious communities, it must ensure that the conditions governing the exercise of

---

systems. For example, several minority groups are trying to protect their identity from women's independence movements in order not to threaten their traditional role within the group. Therefore, the purpose of group rights should be to protect only the first category, and in no case should individual freedoms be restricted by internal minority restrictions. In a modern liberal legal order, "internal constraints" are forbidden because they are contrary to the principle of free development of personality. Kymlicka (1995), pp. 152–172; Grote (2008), pp. 224–228.

[3] Lajeunesse (2025), pp. 1–3.

[4] ECHR, Svyato-Mykhaylivska Parafiya v. Ukraine, Application no. 77703/01, 14 June 2007.

[5] ECHR, Karlsson v. Sweden, Application no. 12356/86, 8 September 1988, ECHR, Spetz and Others v. Sweden, Application no. 20402/92, 12 October 1994, ECHR, Williamson v. the United Kingdom, Application no. 27008/95, 17 May 1995, ECHR, Holy Synod of the Bulgarian Orthodox Church (Metropolitan Inokentiy) and Others v. *Bulgaria,* Application nos. 412/03 and 35,677/04, 22 January 2009.

[6] Regarding the status of the Muslin minority in Greece, see Tsitselikis (2012), pp. 97–118.

the resulting rights are applied in a non-discriminatory manner. Crucially, it held that denying members of a religious minority the right to choose the application of ordinary civil law in their private legal relations constitutes not only discriminatory treatment, but also a violation of a fundamental principle of minority protection: the right to self-identification and self-determination. The mandatory application of a religious legal regime, particularly where it produces adverse consequences for individuals who neither sought nor consented to it, was found to be incompatible with the Convention. The Court thus concluded that the compulsory application of Islamic law in this context violated the European Convention on Human Rights.[7]

As Askitis observes, the significance of *Molla Sali* lies in its nuanced interpretation of religious freedom. Respect for the religious freedom of a minority does not require the state to introduce or maintain legal arrangements based on that religion. Where such arrangements are voluntarily established, they must nevertheless comply with the principle of non-discrimination. Religious conscience cannot be understood as entailing an automatic waiver of rights guaranteed by international human rights instruments. Accordingly, the state may not impose a separate legal regime in the name of minority protection without the express and individual consent of the persons concerned. The collective construction of minority identity does not automatically prevail over individual choice; rather, the claim to equal treatment grounded in human dignity precedes minority affiliation.[8]

This approach is further illuminated by the contrast between *Molla Sali* and *Refah Partisi and Others v. Turkey*. While in *Refah Partisi* the Court held that certain interpretations of Sharia were incompatible with the fundamental values of the Convention, in *Molla Sali* it deliberately avoided a broad civilizational or normative judgment on Islamic law as such. As noted by Iakovidis and McDonough, the Court adopted a more cautious and context-sensitive approach, acknowledging the complexity of modern identities in Europe and the pluralistic realities of contemporary societies. The foundational principle emerging from the judgment is that no individual may be compelled, against their will, to be subject to a legal regime devised ostensibly for their protection. The principle of self-identification, particularly its negative dimension, namely the right not to be treated as a member of a minority, thus emerges as a cornerstone of minority protection under the Convention and operates as a decisive safeguard against intra-group coercion.[9]

Cultural protection becomes harmful when it is imposed rather than chosen. Lajeunesse argues that cultural identity must be understood as relational and voluntary, not as a status that automatically overrides individual autonomy. Cultural

[7] ECHR, Molla Sali v. Greece, Application no. 20452/14, 19 December 2018.

[8] Askitis (2020), para 11. It should be noted that the European Court had already assessed Shari'a as incompatible with the European Convention on Human Rights in the case ECHR, Refah Partisi (Prosperity Party) and Others v.Turkey, Applications nos. 41,340/98, 41,342/98, 41,343/98 and 41,344/98, 13 February 2003.

[9] Iakovidis and McDonough (2019), pp. 427–446.

regimes that presume consent, especially in family law, inheritance, or religious norms, risk producing epistemic and legal coercion.[10]

14.1 Controversial Cultural and Religious Practices

Every culture produces definitive values which are unique. Some values become laws which determine the rights and the obligations within each state. Sometimes these laws are defined by the international human rights acts which have been created through international consultation and consent. At the same time, international human rights, including cultural rights, are carried out within the cultural reality of each society. Culture thus constitutes the framework within which cultural rights are interpreted and exercised. In many societies, cultural traditions acquire the character of customary law, understood as an established system of norms that has emerged from collective ways of life and has been transmitted across generations.[11] In many cases, cultural traditions take on the character of customary law, that is, of an established system of rules that had emerged from the way of life and mirrors people's desires and remained in the memories of every generation.[12]

Cultural and religious traditions, morals and customary practices are behaviors passed down from generation to generation, which are observed in every social group, functioning largely as a component of group cohesion and continuity. However, apart from this positive dimension, some of these practices constitute, due to their harmful nature, cases of brutal violation of the fundamental rights and freedoms of specific members of the groups that adopt them,[13] for example scarring, genital mutilation, honor killings etc.[14] At the same time, several texts of international law include "safety nets" so that cultural practices that violate human rights are not tolerated. This exclusion is clearly reflected in several core international instruments. Article 5 of the Convention on the Elimination of All Forms of Discrimination against Women obliges States Parties to modify social and cultural patterns that perpetuate gender-based stereotypes or the perceived inferiority of women, and to ensure that the best interests of the child are a primary consideration in family education. Similarly, the Convention on the Rights of the Child requires States to take effective and appropriate measures to abolish traditional practices

[10] Lajeunesse (2025), pp. 12–14.

[11] Stamatopoulou (2007), p. 18.

[12] Bekker (1989), p . 11.

[13] UN Office of the High Commissioner for Human Rights, Fact Sheet No. 23, Harmful Traditional Practices Affecting the Health of Women and Children, August 1995, No. 23, available at: http://www.unhcr.org/refworld/docid/479477410.html

[14] Okin (1999), pp. 9–15. Okin argues that group rights that oppress women should not be allowed on the grounds that they are fundamental to minority cultures whose existence may otherwise be threatened. See also, Papadopoulou (2010), pp. 397–418.

prejudicial to children's health.[15] The Declaration on the Rights of Persons Belonging to National or Ethnic, Religious and Linguistic Minorities further clarifies that the exercise of minority cultural rights does not extend to practices that violate national law or international human rights standards, nor may such rights prejudice the enjoyment of universally recognized human rights and fundamental freedoms by others.[16]

The jurisprudence of the European Court of Human Rights confirms that cultural or religious practices which clearly conflict with international human rights norms cannot, under any circumstances, be justified. This position is particularly evident in the Court's case law under Article 3 of the European Convention on Human Rights, which prohibits torture and inhuman or degrading treatment in absolute terms. For example in *Jabari v. Turkey*, the European Court of Human Rights found that deportation to Iran would constitute a violation of Article 3 due to the application of Islamic criminal law.[17] Someone can come across the inadmissibility decision in the case of *Collins and Akaziebie v. Sweden*, where the applicant, a Nigerian woman from Delta State, sought asylum in Sweden when she was 25 years old and pregnant, on the ground that she wanted to avoid being submitted to female genital mutilation (FGM). Swedish authorities dismissed the claim as unbelievable but reiterated that forced genital mutilation falls within the meaning of "inhuman or degrading treatment". The appeal also failed due to lack of credibility. The European Court of Human Rights held that "*it is not in dispute that subjecting a woman to female genital mutilation amounts to ill-treatment contrary to Article 3 of the Convention*".[18]

---

[15] Convention on the Rights of the Child, 1989, Article 24 par. 3.

[16] Declaration on the Rights of Persons Belonging to National or Ethnic, Religious and Linguistic Minorities, Article 4 par 2. and Article 8 par 2. In addition, the UN Committee on Economic, Social and Cultural Rights has systematically and actively addressed cultural practices that violate human rights, criticizing practices that violate human rights, and encouraging the implementation of policies, laws, and educational programs to address such practices. A systematic review of the Commission's reports reveals that the Commission considers the following types of policies and practices to violate women's human rights: rape and other forms of domestic violence, female genital mutilation of women, discrimination in inheritance law or property, discrimination in education such as high levels of illiteracy, early marriage, forced widow marriages with deceased husband's brother, bride kidnapping, honor killings, polygamy, sexual harassment, discrimination in the workplace, and the general culture of superiority of men over women. Stamatopoulou (2007), pp. 25–26. Several more practices can be identified, such as the preference for male children, which includes practices such as infanticide or neglect of the female child within the family, the force- feeding of women, the imposition of inhumane and degrading punishments on female "offenders" of cultural and religious norms, such as wearing trousers or extramarital sex, imposing inhuman and degrading punishments on female victims of crimes, for example rape. These practices take place either at the level of family and society or, in some states, at institutional level. UN Office of the High Commissioner for Human Rights, Fact Sheet No. 23, Harmful Traditional Practices Affecting the Health of Women and Children, August 1995, No. 23.

[17] ECHR, Jabari v. Turkey, Application No. 40035/98, 11 July 2000.

[18] ECHR, Collins and Akaziebie v. Sweden, Application No. 23944/05, 8 March 2007 and ECHR, Omeredo v. Austria, Application No. 8969/10, 20 September 2011. Judicial recognition of genital mutilation as a determinant for the provision of asylum has been implemented in many European states and was strengthened by the Resolution of the European Parliament, which requested from

It is evident that the European Court of Human Rights considers that cultural practices that are clearly in conflict with international human rights norms cannot, under any circumstances be justified.

Cultural practices that are not tolerated or are considered harmful to human dignity are not only associated with minority religions or cultures but are also found in mainstream cultures. In 2000, the European Court of Human Rights rejected unanimously an appeal by individuals associated with Christian private schools in the UK, who claimed that the ban on corporal punishment of students in private schools breached parents' rights to freedom of religion and family life.[19] Previous decisions during of the 1980s and at the beginning of the 1990s they condemned the school physical punishment, first in public schools and later in private in the United Kingdom.[20] According to the Court the right to private or family life or freedom of religion cannot be used as arguments to reject the prohibition of corporal punishment. Former decisions, during the 1980s and the 1990s condemned school corporal punishment, in public and private schools in UK. According to the Court, neither the right to private life nor freedom of religion could justify corporal punishment of students.[21]

Article 17 of the European Convention of Human Rights is considered to be a useful sufficient to protect individuals from misuse of the rights guaranteed in the Convention and may induce harmful effects on individuals or the society as a whole. According to Article 17 "*Nothing in [the] Convention may be interpreted as implying for any State, group or person any right to engage in any activity or perform any act aimed at the destruction of any of the rights and freedoms set forth herein or at their limitation to a greater extent than is provided for in the Convention*".[22] The case *Hizb Ut-Tahrir v. Germany*, concerned the ban on activities of an Islamist association for advocating the use of violence in order to destroy the State of Israel, banish or kill its inhabitants and overthrow the governments of Islamic States. In the Court's view, the applicant association employed the Convention rights for ends that were clearly contrary to the values of the Convention, notably the commitment to the peaceful settlement of international conflicts and to the sanctity of human life.[23]

From a normative perspective, the protection of cultural and religious diversity cannot be understood as requiring unconditional deference to all practices carried out in the name of culture or tradition. While cultural identity constitutes an

---

the member states to recognize the right to asylum of women and of girls at risk to suffer genital mutilation. European Parliament resolution on female genital mutilation (2001/2035(INI)).

[19] European Court of Human Rights, Corporal punishment, available at: http://www.coe.int/t/dg3/children/corporalpunishment/cplegaltexts_EN.asp.

[20] ECHR, Campbell and Cosans v. the *United Kingdom*, Application No. 7511/73, 23 March 1983, ECHR, Costello-Roberts v. the *United Kingdom*, Application No. 13134/87, 25 March 1993.

[21] ECHR, Seven Individuals v. Sweden, Application No. 8811/79, 13 May 1982, Philip Williamson and Others v. the *United Kingdom*, Application No. 55211/00, September 2000.

[22] European Court on Human Rights, Guide on Article 17 of the European Convention on Human Rights, 2022, available at: https://www.echr.coe.int/Documents/Guide_Art_17_ENG.pdf.

[23] ECHR, Hizb Ut-Tahrir v. Germany, Application No. 31098/08, 19 July 2012.

essential dimension of human dignity and social belonging, it cannot serve as a shield for practices that undermine the fundamental rights of individuals, particularly those in positions of structural vulnerability. In my view, the legitimacy of cultural accommodation depends not only on respect for group autonomy, but also on the presence of genuine individual consent, equality, and the possibility of dissent without coercion. Human rights law performs a crucial corrective function in this context: it affirms that cultural traditions must evolve in dialogue with universal standards of dignity, rather than operate as immutable systems insulated from scrutiny. The challenge for democratic societies is therefore not to choose between cultural pluralism and human rights protection, but to ensure that cultural diversity is preserved in a manner that empowers individuals, safeguards their autonomy, and prevents the reproduction of harm within cultural communities.

14.2 The "European Family" of States

A paradigmatic example of a traditional cultural practice that the European Court of Human Rights has deemed incompatible with the Convention is found in the 1978 *Tyrer* case. The case dealt with judicial corporal punishment, which was still applied on the Isle of Man. According to the Court, the very nature of judicial corporal punishment itself involves physical violence imposed by a human being to another; in this case violence ordered by the judicial authorities and carried out by the police authorities. Thus, although the applicant did not suffer any severe or long-lasting damage, his punishment constitutes an attack on Article 3 of the Convention namely the protection of the dignity and physical integrity of the individual. According to the Court's reasoning the Isle of Man is historically, geographically and culturally included in the European family of nations and must be regarded as sharing the common heritage of political traditions, ideals, freedom and the rule of law. The Court further noted that the prohibition in Article 3 is absolute and states cannot derogate even in time of war or other public emergency threatening the life of the nation. The Court in this case did not take into account either the cultural traditions or the public acceptance of judicial corporal punishment by the local community.[24]

The Court's rejection of judicial corporal punishment cannot be understood merely as a condemnation of a particular penal practice, but rather as a broader assertion of European normative identity. The authors show that the Court's invocation of the "European family of nations" functioned as a doctrinal device to deny cultural or local exceptionalism in relation to Article 3 ECHR. By emphasizing that the Isle of Man was historically, geographically, and culturally part of Europe, the Court foreclosed reliance on local tradition or popular support as justificatory factors, thereby reinforcing the idea that certain minimum standards of human dignity

---

[24] ECHR, Tyrer v. the *United Kingdom*, Application No. 5856/72, 25 April 1978. Brems (2010), opt. Cit., p. 663–716.

apply uniformly within the European legal space. The Convention was explicitly characterized as a “living instrument” whose meaning must be assessed in light of present-day conditions rather than historical intentions or local practices. The Court’s assessment of what constitutes “degrading punishment” was informed by developments and commonly accepted standards across Council of Europe member states, rather than by the cultural attitudes prevailing within the Isle of Man itself.[25]

The judgment is emblematic of the Court’s approach to cultural justifications for practices that undermine human dignity. By refusing to accord weight to cultural tradition or societal acceptance, the Court affirmed that membership in the European human rights system entails adherence to minimum, non-negotiable standards of treatment. The concept of a shared European heritage thus operates not as a vehicle for cultural relativism, but as a normative benchmark that constrains the scope of permissible cultural practices and reinforces the primacy of human dignity within the Convention framework. In this sense, *Tyrer* exemplifies the Court’s firm stance that cultural identity, whether majority or minority-based, is constrained by non-derogable standards of human dignity within the European human rights system.

References

Askitis A (2020) Molla Sali (ECHR): Greece's "velvet condemnation" for the application of sharia to the inheritance disputes of Greek Muslims, (in Greek). https://www.constitutionalism.gr/molla-salli-edda

Bekker JC (1989) Seymour's customary law in southern Africa, 5th edn. Juta & Co. Ltd, Cape Town

Brems E (2010) Human rights as a framework for negotiating/protecting cultural differences: an exploration in the case-law of the European court of human rights. In: Foblets MC, Gaudreault-DesBiens JF, Renteln AD (eds) Cultural diversity and the law: state responses from around the world; proceedings of the colloquium "the response of state law to the expression of cultural diversity". Bruylant, Bruxelles, pp 663–671

Grote R (2008) The struggle for minority rights and human rights: current trends and challenges. In: König D, Stoll PT, Röben V, Matz-Lück N (eds) International law today: new challenges and the need for reform?: new challenges and the need for reform? Springer Verlag, pp 221–246

Hilliard C, Duranti M (2024) Human rights at the edges of late Imperial Britain: the Tyrer case and judicial corporal punishment from the Isle of Man to Montserrat, 1972–1990. Law History Rev 42:343–366

Iakovidis I, McDonough P (2019) The Molla Sali case: how the European court of human rights escaped a legal labyrinth while holding the thread of human rights. Oxford J Law Religion 8:427–446

Kymlicka W (1995) Multicultural citizenship: a Liberal theory of minority rights. Oxford University Press, Oxford

Lajeunesse S (2025) Cultural rights in motion: legal invisibility, forced migration, and the limits of universality. Soc Leg Stud 34:1–20

Mahajan G (2005) Can intra-group equality co-exist with cultural diversity? Re-examining multicultural frameworks of accommodation. In: Eisenberg A, Spinner-Halev J (eds) Minorities within minorities: equality, rights and diversity. Cambridge University Press, Cambridge, pp 90–112

[25] Hilliard and Duranti (2024), pp. 346–360.

Okin SM (1999) Is multiculturalism bad for women? Princeton University Press, Princeton
Papadopoulou L (2010) Trapped in history: Greek Muslim women under the sacred Islamic law, Annuaire international des Droits de l'homme (AIDH), Vol. V, 2010, religions et droits de l' home. Ant. N. Sakkoulas / Bruylant, Athens, Bruxelles, pp 397–418
Stamatopoulou E (2007) Cultural rights in international law, article 27 of the universal declaration of human rights and beyond. Martinus Nijhoff Publishers, Leiden, Boston
Tsitselikis K (2012) Old and new Islam in Greece from historical minorities to immigrant newcomers. Martinus Nijhoff Publishers, Leiden

Chapter 15
Protecting the Rights of Others and the State's Margin of Appreciation

Contents

It is strongly debated if a person's public manifestation of religious or cultural identity can infringe the rights of third parties or is incompatible with the interests of a state or a state's constitutional values. For example, the controversial issue of wearing religious clothing and symbols in public places has been extensively discussed in political and legal debates. The wearing of religious symbols in public falls under the scope of the right of the manifestation of a person's religious beliefs, though the European Court of Human Rights has repeatedly acknowledged that state interventions in the form prohibitions or restrictions can be justified in order to defend the status of a secular state, gender equality, the rights of others etc.[1] For example, according to the Court the criminal conviction of the members a religious group for wearing a turban, black tunic and rod, in public places out of a mosque amounts to infringement of the Article 9 of the European Convention of Human Rights. The Court also emphasized that the specific case concerned the punishment for the use of certain clothing in open public places and not, like others cases, in public institutions, where the religious neutrality may prevail the right to manifestation of religion.[2]

In the case of *Dahlab v. Switzerland* the Court, considering the prohibition of the wearing of a headscarf by a primary school teacher, held that this prohibition was legitimate in a democratic society as it sought to ensure the school's denominational

[1] ECHR, Leyla Şahin v. Turkey, Application no. 44774/98, 10 November 2005 and ECHR. See also Dogru v. France, Application no. 27058/05, 4 December 2008. In the Dogru v. France case the European Court of Human Rights raised three principal arguments: (a) the lack of a common approach among the Member States, (b) the necessity to place restrictions in order to reconcile the interests of the various groups, (c) the secular nature of the French State. Garlicki (2015), p. 338.

[2] ECHR, Ahmet Arslan and Others v. Turkey, Application no. 41135/98, 23 February 2010.

N. Gaitenidis, *The Rights of Cultural Identity in the Case Law of the European Court of Human Rights*, European Union and its Neighbours in a Globalized World 36, https://doi.org/10.1007/978-3-032-23045-4_15

neutrality and also prevented interference with the religious beliefs of her pupils (who were young children).[3] As Garlicki notes the European Court of Human Rights raised three principal arguments: (a) the particular nature of the applicant's profession: a state school teacher represents the State educational authority and, in consequence enjoys a particular status involving both privileges and obligations, (b) the particular vulnerability of students/pupils affected: the applicant taught very young children who are more easily influenced and (c) the particular nature of the Islamic scarf. In this respect, Garlicki observes that the Court's reasoning conveyed a dual message. On the one hand, the Court grounded its assessment in the specific circumstances of the case, namely the public character of the school and the particularly young age of the pupils, factors which justified a broader scope for state interference with the freedom to manifest religious beliefs. By emphasizing these contextual elements, the Court appeared to leave open the question of how it might have assessed a similar restriction at a higher level of education. On the other hand, the Court referred back to the Swiss Federal Court's reasoning, which entailed a more general and substantive critique of the Islamic headscarf as such. This reference arguably signals that the Strasbourg Court might be inclined to adopt a more restrictive stance in other contexts involving the public display of the Islamic headscarf, beyond the specific educational setting at issue.[4] The children in the *Dahlab case* appear to be a lot more vulnerable due to their young age and susceptibility to influence, which seems to be a crucial element for the Court's decision.[5]

In the *Leyla Şahin v. Turkey* case, no breach of Article 9 was found on account of the exclusion of a university student for wearing a headscarf. The most relevant element in the Court's reasoning was the wide margin of appreciation it accords to the national authorities in this field: "*Where questions concerning the relationship between State and religions are at stake, on which opinion in a democratic society may reasonably differ widely, the role of the national decision-making body must be given special importance […]. It is not possible to discern throughout Europe a uniform conception of the significance of religion in society* […]".[6] The "margin of appreciation" or "margin of discretion" is a doctrine developed by the European Court of Human Rights in the *Handyside v. The United Kingdom* case.[7] According to the doctrine, there is no uniform European conception of morals, therefore, state authorities are in principle in a better position than the international judge to give an opinion on the exact content of these requirements as well as on the necessity of a restriction. The European Court of Human Rights shall only intervene if it clearly

---

[3] ECHR, Dahlab v. Switzerland, Application no. 42393/98, 15 January 2001.

[4] Garlicki (2015), pp. 334–335. Several other cases of the European Court of Human Rights concerned the wearing of religious symbols in public spaces, for example ECHR, Ebrahimian v. France, Application No. 64846/11, 26 November 2015 and ECHR, Hamidovic v. Bosnia and Herzegovina, Application No. 57792/15, 5 December 2017. See more, Gutan (2021), p. 184.

[5] Tamimi (2018), p. 291.

[6] ECHR, *Leyla Şahin v. Turkey*, Application no. 44774/98, 10 November 2005.

[7] ECHR, Handyside v. The United Kingdom, Application no. 5493/72, 4 November 1976.

finds that the state party has failed in that task.[8] One of the reasons for the margin of appreciation doctrine is the recognition that national authorities are generally better equipped to assess the necessity and appropriateness of restrictions and limitations. They have better access to factual information regarding the need for such restrictions and are better placed to evaluate how a particular national measure or decision relates to national constitutional values and legal traditions. Therefore, the Court is typically willing to grant a certain amount of discretion to the States in determining the reasonableness of interferences with Convention rights.[9] Moreover, The European Court has reiterated that the margin of appreciation is quite broader in cases where there is no consensus within the member States of the Council of Europe, either as to the relative importance of the interest at stake or as to the best means of protecting it. "There will also usually be a wide margin if the State is required to strike a balance between competing private and public interests or different Convention rights".[10]

Over the years, the margin of appreciation doctrine has become an integral element of the Court's reasoning and, as pointed out by McGoldrick, it has became an example for other human rights institutions and other international decision-making bodies. However, as a doctrine of the Court's reasoning it has received criticism in the academic, political and judicial sphere. For example, several critics point out that the margin of appreciation leaves room for relativistic interpretation of the European Convention of Human Rights which may endanger the universality of human rights. Also, there is a certain level of unclearness is the doctrine which may violate the principle of legal certainty. Sajó and Uitz comment that the broad margin of appreciation has often resulted in inconsistencies in the case law of the European Court of Human Rights. "*This disregard partly reflects the "official" perception of the proper exercise of individual religious freedom in some member states. It is also related to the self-understanding of many judges—namely, that in the spirit of protecting common European minimum standards the ECtHR should not give direction to member states regarding religious organizations and communities, and on how these entities shall relate to individual religious belief and resulting conduct. Of course, such a self-understanding may have detrimental consequences to individual religious liberty*".[11] On the other hand, the margin of appreciation doctrine, affords to the European Court of Human Rights a necessary level of flexibility, while retaining strong elements of European supervision.[12]

---

[8] Donders (2016), p. 28.

[9] Gerards (2018), p. 498.

[10] ECHR, Evans v. the United Kingdom, Application no. 6339/05, 10 April 2007.

[11] Sajó and Uitz (2020) p. 288.

[12] McGoldrick (2016), pp. 37–39. As Trispiotis notes "*This structural use of the margin of appreciation is all-too-common in cases touching on morals, for instance, cases involving blasphemous art (Otto-Preminger vs. Austria 1994; Wingrove vs. United Kingdom 1996; I.A. vs. Turkey 2005) and has been criticised for its association with moral relativism and for compromising the universality of human rights*". Trispiotis (2019), p. 29. See also, ECHR, Otto-Preminger v. Austria, Application No. 13470/87, 14 January 1993 and ECHR, Wingrove v. The United Kingdom,

The margin of appreciation doctrine is welcomed as a valuable tool for finding a common ground when different legal traditions and cultures intersect or clash. The doctrine is based on the idea that a distinction can be made between defining fundamental rights and the potential limitations of those rights. The European Court of Human Rights believes that the definition of fundamental rights should be the same for all individuals living in the Council of Europe, indicating a shared and uniform minimum standard of fundamental rights protection that aligns with the concept of universal human rights.[13]

The Court was confronted with several similar cases, for example the cases *Ranjit Singh v. France* and *Jasvir Singh v. France,* involving Sikh students wearing Keski (small turban) in schools, as well as in the cases *Aktas v. France*, *Bayrak v. France*, *Gamaleddyn v. France* and *Ghazal v. France* involving Muslim schoolgirls wearing headscarfs. In all these cases, the Court held the claims of manifestly ill--founded, basing its reasoning mainly on the "wide margin of appreciation" of each state and pointed out that it is the duty of national authorities to ensure that, under the principle of pluralism, respect and freedom of others, the manifestation of religious beliefs of students in school premises is not an ostentatious act that would constitute a source of pressure and exclusion. The Court pointed out that the legal provisions do not affect the children's religious beliefs but pursued the legitimate aim of protecting public order and the rights and freedoms of others. Their purpose was to preserve the neutrality and secularity of teaching establishments and they applied to all conspicuous religious symbols. The Court also referred to the role of the principle of secularism (*laïcité*) as a constitutional and fundamental principle of France, which identifies the entire population and its protection seems to be of primary importance, especially in schools. The fact that the applicants in these cases intend to wear a more discreet head covering does not, in the Court's view, diminish the state's discretion. Finally, the Court did not consider the expulsion of the students disproportionate, since the applicants were offered alternative ways of education, such as private schools or home education.[14]

Based on the aforementioned cases Langlaude notes that "*The European Court's position on the prevention of indoctrination and pressure is problematic for the individual believer. The absence of religion in educational institutions, or more specifically religious symbols or religious education may convey the idea that the school system is a bearer of majority values, even Judeo-Christian, under the appearance of impartiality*".[15] The Court's stance regarding "indoctrination" of children through education is also reflected in the *Çiftçi v. Turkey* case. The Court

Application No. 17419/90, 25 November 1996 and ECHR, İ.A. v. Turkey, Application No. 42571/98, 13 September 2005. See also, Gozdecka (2011), pp. 233–248.

[13] Gerards (2018), p. 498.

[14] ECHR, Aktas v. France, Application No. 43563/08, ECHR, Bayrak v. France, Application no. 14308/08, ECHR, Gamaleddyn v. France, Application no. 18527/08, ECHR, Ghazal v. France, Application no.29134/08, ECHR, J. Singh v. France, Application no. 25463/08 and ECHR, R. Singh v. France, Application no. 27561/08, 30 June 2009.

[15] Langlaude (2006), p. 933.

concluded that when a restriction to religious education is intended to ensure that the children have the maturity to attend the classes, it does not constitute an attempt at indoctrination aimed at preventing religious instruction. Therefore, the requirement to have obtained the primary-school leaving certificate in order to enroll in Koranic study classes does not affect the right of parents to advise their children, to exercise with regard to their children natural parental functions as educators, or to guide their children on a path in line with the parents' own religious or philosophical convictions.[16] As Langlaude notes, the Court has consistently reaffirmed its commitment to maintaining neutrality in the education of children, employing particularly strong language when characterizing measures aimed at preventing the indoctrination of pupils. Emphasizing the vulnerability of children, especially their young age and susceptibility to influence, the Court accepted that restrictions on religious education could be justified on the grounds that children are at a developmental stage marked by curiosity and openness to persuasion. This reasoning implicitly suggests that certain forms of religious schooling may be incompatible with a child's right to education. Moreover, Langlaude observes that the legislative framework under scrutiny appears to have been adopted in a broader context of concerns about religious fundamentalism, a consideration that the Court may have implicitly endorsed in its assessment.[17]

More recent jurisprudence confirms this approach. In cases such as *Belcacemi and Oussar v. Belgium* (2021) and *Mikyas and Others v. Belgium* (2024), the Court reiterated that, in the absence of a European consensus, States enjoy a wide margin of appreciation when regulating the public manifestation of religion, particularly in educational settings and where the protection of the rights of others and social cohesion is invoked.[18]

A significant qualification to the wide margin of appreciation afforded to States in matters concerning religious symbols is found in *Lachiri v. Belgium*, a judgment which, as Paul observes, represents an important development in the Court's Article 9 jurisprudence. The case concerned the exclusion of the applicant from a courtroom after she refused to remove her Islamic headscarf while attending proceedings as a member of the public. The European Court of Human Rights found a violation of Article 9, holding that the expulsion constituted an unjustified interference with her freedom to manifest her religion.[19] As emphasized in the judgment and underlined by Paul, the applicant was an ordinary citizen and not a State representative exercising a public function; consequently, she could not be subjected to the same neutrality obligations that bind judges, court officials, or other public servants.[20] The Court explicitly rejected the assumption that the mere wearing of a headscarf in

[16] ECHR, Çiftçi v. Turkey, Application No. 71860/01, 17 June 2004.

[17] Langlaude (2006), p. 935.

[18] ECHR, Belcacemi and Oussar v. Belgium, Application no. 37798/13, 11 July 2017. ECHR, Mikyas and Others v. Belgium, Application no. 50681/20, 9 April 2024.

[19] ECHR, Lachiri v. Belgium, Application no. 3413/09, 18 September 2018.

[20] Paul (2019), pp. 49–52.

a courtroom could be equated with disrespect for the judiciary or a threat to the proper conduct of proceedings, thereby reaffirming that religious neutrality is primarily a duty of the State and its agents, not of private individuals accessing public institutions.

The significance of *Lachiri v. Belgium* extends beyond the mere outcome of the case, as commentators have highlighted its role in clarifying the limits of the margin of appreciation doctrine in the context of religious dress. This was the first time the Court found a violation of Article 9 in a case specifically involving a Muslim woman wearing a headscarf, marking a departure from the trend of mostly unsuccessful challenges to religious dress restrictions at Strasbourg. *Lachiri* underscores that there are genuine limits to the discretion States enjoy in regulating religious attire, particularly where prohibitions are applied to private individuals with no official function and where no risk to public order is established. Yet it also suggests that the judgment contains ambiguous statements that complicate its value as a general precedent on religious symbols regulation.[21]

From a doctrinal perspective, *Lachiri* is particularly noteworthy because, as Paul argues, the Court departed from its previous reliance on a broad margin of appreciation and instead conducted a stricter proportionality review. Unlike earlier cases concerning Islamic dress the Court did not defer to domestic authorities' assessments of necessity, despite the absence of a clear European consensus on courtroom dress codes. Paul highlights that this is the first Islamic dress-related case in which the Court refrained from invoking the margin of appreciation doctrine, a move that signals a recalibration of the balance between State discretion and individual religious freedom. By focusing on the applicant's conduct, status, and the lack of any concrete disruption to public order, the Court narrowed State discretion and affirmed that restrictions on religious manifestation must be supported by compelling reasons. In this sense, *Lachiri* complements earlier case law by delineating a clear boundary: while States may enjoy a wide margin in regulating religious symbols in sensitive institutional contexts such as public education, that margin contracts significantly where restrictions target private individuals who do not exercise public authority. This judgment thus serves as an important corrective within the Court's jurisprudence, reinforcing the protection of individual autonomy and pluralism against excessive reliance on abstract notions of neutrality or public order.[22]

It is therefore safe to assume that when it comes to the question on how public authorities should deal with religious diversity, the European Court of Human Rights acknowledges, by granting a wide margin of appreciation to States, the choice of the extent and form of such regulations must inevitably be left up to a point to the State and the domestic context concerned. The Court's task is to determine whether the measures taken at national level were justified, appropriate and proportionate. As Gerards explains, one of the principal justifications for the margin of appreciation doctrine lies in the assumption that national authorities are, in

[21] Ringelheim (2018).

[22] Paul (2019), pp. 51–52.

general, better placed than an international court to assess both the necessity and the proportionality of restrictions on Convention rights. Domestic authorities typically have more direct access to relevant factual information concerning the social context and practical need for such measures, and they are also better equipped to evaluate how a particular restriction aligns with national constitutional values, historical experiences, and legal traditions. On this basis, the European Court of Human Rights is usually prepared to accord States a certain degree of discretion when determining whether interferences with Convention rights are reasonable and justified.[23] The European Court of Human Rights has confirmed this rationale in several cases.[24]

As Garlicki observes, the doctrine of the margin of appreciation rests on three core premises. First, while the European Convention on Human Rights establishes common and universal standards of protection, it simultaneously allows Member States a degree of choice in the manner in which those standards are implemented. Second, the European Court of Human Rights is required to respect decisions taken by domestic authorities insofar as they remain compatible with these universal standards. Third, the breadth of the margin afforded to States is not fixed, but varies according to the circumstances of each case: in certain contexts national authorities may enjoy a wide margin of appreciation, in others only a limited one, and in some situations no margin at all. Since it is ultimately for the Court to determine the appropriate scope of discretion in each category of cases, the doctrine provides a flexible mechanism for applying general Convention principles to diverse factual and social contexts. Among the factors influencing the width of the margin is the existence of a shared cultural context within a society, understood as a particular constellation of moral, religious, ideological, political, and constitutional values. At the same time, it must be recalled that the Convention itself is grounded in a specific political philosophy and presupposes the universal acceptance of certain fundamental values, most notably tolerance, pluralism, and democracy, which form the core of the Convention system and must be respected by all Member States. The doctrine of the margin of appreciation therefore seeks to accommodate genuine societal diversity while ensuring adherence to these common foundational values.[25]

15.1 Conscientious Objection in Services

Conscientious objection in the provision of services constitutes one of the most sensitive areas in which the manifestation of religious or moral beliefs intersects with the rights and freedoms of others. While freedom of thought, conscience, and religion protects the right to hold and, within certain limits, to manifest personal

[23] Gerards (2018), p. 498.

[24] For example, ECHR, ES v. Austria, Application No. 38450/12, 25 October 2018.

[25] Garlicki (2015), p. 323.

beliefs, the exercise of conscientious objection in professional contexts raises complex questions regarding equality, access to services, and the neutrality of both public authorities and private service providers. The jurisprudence of the European Court of Human Rights demonstrates that conscientious objection is not recognized as an absolute right under Article 9 of the Convention, but rather as a qualified interest that must be balanced against competing rights, particularly the prohibition of discrimination and the effective enjoyment of legally guaranteed services. In this context, the Court has consistently emphasized the importance of proportionality and has afforded States a margin of appreciation when determining how to reconcile individual religious convictions with the protection of the rights of others.

The case *Eweida and Others v. the United Kingdom,* originated in four applications which were brought against the UK by Christians who believed that they had suffered unlawful discrimination at the hands of their respective employers on the grounds of their religious beliefs. Each applicant argued that the state had violated their right to freedom of religion under Article 9. Two of the applicants are Christians who believe that their faith requires them to wear a small cross on a chain visibly around their neck. In both cases, the women's respective employers had refused to allow them to continue in their role unless they removed their cross. The other two applicants refused to provide services to same-sex couples. The Court ruled that in the first case of wearing the cross together with the flight attendant's uniform, there was a violation of Article 9 of the European Convention on Human Rights, while in the case of wearing the cross with a nurse's uniform, the need to protect health prevailed which required the non wearing of jewelry by nursing staff; In the next two cases it was held that the differences in treatment because of sexual orientation demands serious justification and that the same sex couples was in a relatively similar situation with heterosexual couples concerning their need for legal recognition and protection of their relationship. More specifically, the first case concerned a registrar for a local authority who objected to registering same sex partnerships due to her religious beliefs and faced disciplinary action. The second case concerned an employ to a private organization that refused to provide counseling to same sex couples. The European Court of Human Rights noted that a person's manifestation of their belief may impact on others and that this is the reason why this right is qualified in the second paragraph of Article 9 of the European Convention. In this respect it may be limited if such limitation is necessary in a democratic society including for the protection of the rights and freedoms of others. The Court held that an act can be considered as a "manifestation" if it is "intimately linked to the religion or belief". In this respect, according to the Court, there must be a "sufficiently close and direct nexus between the act and the underlying belief". It will not suffice if the act does not directly express the belief or is only "remotely connected to a precept of faith". Whether or not the act is mandated by a recognized religion is irrelevant. Hence, the authorities had wide margin of appreciation, when trying to achieve a balance between the states' obligation to secure the rights of others and the right of applicants to manifest their religion. The Court decided that a proper balance had been achieved and hence, there was not a violation of Article 14 combined with Article 9.[26]

Similarly, in the case *Pichon and Sajous v. France,* the two applicants were joint owners of a pharmacy in rural France. In 1995, they refused to sell contraceptives to three women, who subsequently filed a complaint. The applicants argued before domestic courts that their refusal was justified as no statutory provision required pharmacists to supply contraceptives. The applicants complained to the European Court of Human Rights, asserting that their right to freedom of religion under Article 9 of the Convention had been disregarded by the domestic courts. The European Court of Human Rights held that the applicants' conviction does not violate their rights which are guaranteed by Article 9. The Court has determined that Article 9 of the Convention does not always provide absolute protection for individuals to publicly conduct themselves in accordance with their beliefs, nor does it safeguard every single action or behavior that is motivated or influenced by religion or belief. As the pills were legal, the applicants could "manifest those beliefs in many ways outside the professional sphere".[27] Lamačková observes that the case of *Pichon and Sajous v. France* is of particular importance as it attempts to delimit the exercise of conscientious objection when it conflicts with other human rights and fundamental freedoms. She argues that "*Particularly in the reproductive health care context, states that allow health professionals to exercise conscientious objection must accommodate this in such a way that its exercise does not compromise women's access to health services*".[28]

The decisions in *Grimmark v. Sweden* and *Steen v. Sweden* mark a decisive moment in the European Court of Human Rights' approach to conscientious objection in the context of abortion services. Declaring both applications manifestly ill-founded, the Court accepted that the applicants' refusal to assist in abortion procedures constituted a manifestation of conscience protected under Article 9, but nevertheless held that the resulting interference was justified and proportionate. Central to the Court's reasoning was the State's positive obligation to organise its healthcare system in such a way as to guarantee effective access to lawful abortion throughout its territory, an obligation that was found to outweigh individual claims to conscientious objection.[29] As Domenici observes, the Court relied heavily on the wide margin of appreciation accorded to States in this sensitive area, while at the same time avoiding a full proportionality analysis that would have examined whether less restrictive accommodations were feasible.[30]

In this respect, the judgments represent a retrenchment from the more nuanced approach developed in *Eweida and Others v. the United Kingdom*, where the Court

---

[26] ECHR, Eweida and Others v. the United Kingdom, Applications nos. 48420/10, 59842/10, 51671/10 and 36516/10 15 January 2013. See also McCrea (2014), p. 290.

[27] ECHR, Pichon and Sajous v. France, Application no. 49853/99, 2 October 2001.

[28] Lamačková (2008), p. 7. See also Kastanas (2013), p. 435. See also Ktistakis (2021), p. 533.

[29] ECHR, *Grimmark v. Sweden,* Application no. 43726/17, 11 February 2020. ECHR, Steen v. Sweden, Application no. 62309/17, 11 February 2020.

[30] Domenici (2021), pp. 26–47.

acknowledged that freedom to resign could no longer be treated as an automatic answer to conflicts between professional duties and religious conscience. Instead, *Grimmark* and *Steen* reaffirm a restrictive line according to which Article 9 does not entail a right to conscientious objection where such objection would undermine access to essential public services, particularly in the field of reproductive healthcare.

From a broader normative perspective, the scholarly literature has been critical of the Court's unwillingness to engage with the structural implications of accommodating conscience-based refusals in equality-sensitive contexts. Complementary critiques emerge from equality-law scholarship, which highlights the risks inherent in granting religiously motivated exemptions in the provision of goods and services. As Coyle demonstrates, conscience-based refusal, particularly where they intersect with sexual and reproductive rights, may operate as forms of structural harm that disproportionately affect already vulnerable groups, thereby reinforcing hierarchies of rights under the guise of religious freedom.[31] Domenici argues that by dismissing the applications at the admissibility stage, the Court failed to confront the existence of a European consensus favouring limited forms of accommodation, as well as the possibility of reconciling individual conscience with women's rights through organisational measures that do not compromise access to care.[32] Read together, these analyses underscore that the Court's jurisprudence in *Grimmark* and *Steen* reflects a prioritisation of access, equality, and the protection of third parties over individual claims to conscientious objection, while leaving unresolved deeper questions concerning reasonable accommodation and the internal coherence of Article 9 protection in pluralist democracies.

The Court's jurisprudence on conscientious objection in the provision of services reveals a deliberate and principled prioritisation of equality, access, and the protection of third parties over individual claims to religious exemption in professional contexts. While freedom of conscience remains a foundational element of democratic pluralism, its exercise cannot extend to practices that effectively deny others the enjoyment of legally guaranteed rights, particularly in areas such as reproductive healthcare where access is time-sensitive and structurally uneven. The restrictive approach underscores an understanding of Article 9 that is attentive to the real-world consequences of accommodation and resistant to transforming conscientious objection into a mechanism of exclusion or indirect discrimination. In my view, this line of case law appropriately situates conscientious objection as an exceptional and carefully circumscribed accommodation, rather than as a right capable of reshaping public service provision. At the same time, the Court's reluctance to engage fully with questions of reasonable accommodation leaves unresolved tensions within its Article 9 jurisprudence, suggesting that future cases may yet be required to clarify how individual conscience can be respected without undermining the substantive equality and dignity of service users in pluralist societies.

---

[31] Coyle (2021), p. 83.

[32] Domenici (2021), pp. 40–47.

15.2 The Value of "Living Together"

The case of *S.A.S. v. France*, which challenged the French "burqa ban" on wearing face coverings in public spaces sparkled a new round of debates on the controversial issue of wearing religious symbols in public spaces. The case concerned the rights of individuals to manifest their freedom of religion and private life, a matter which employs a large amount of case law and academic analysis. However, *SAS v France* contains some interesting developments because it considered a blanket ban on covering the face and departures from the Court's previous jurisprudence. In particular, the conclusion that the right to manifest religion may be restricted on the ground of "living together".[33] In *S.A.S. v France*, the applicant challenged the French Law, which prohibits the covering of the face in public. As Berry observes "*the case differs from previous cases concerning the right of Muslim women to manifest religion by wearing religious attire, as the law imposed a blanket ban which extended to the social sphere*". France invoked three grounds for limiting the right to wear burqa: "respect for equality between men and women", "respect for human dignity" and "respect for the minimum requirements of life in society" (also named "*le vivre ensemble*").[34]

The Court provided a detailed reasoning regarding the alleged violations of Articles 8 and 9 of the Convention. It found that the ban of the full-face veil represented an "interference" or a "limitation" of the exercise of both these two rights, but put the emphasis on Article 9 as it found the right of religious freedom to represent the essence of the case. The Court went on to discuss whether the interference could be legitimate per the second paragraph of Article 9 (and an almost similar paragraph in Article 8) which states that the freedom can be subject to "*such limitations as are prescribed by law and are necessary in a democratic society in the interests of public safety, for the protection of public order, health or morals, or for the protection of the rights and freedoms of others*". The Court recognized that the interference with Articles 8 and 9 could be justified under the need to protect the rights and freedoms of others due to the fact that social interaction could be viewed as important in a democratic society where people were "*living together*" and covering the face could interfere with this. The ban was not disproportionate because the criminal sanctions attached to disregarding the ban were minimal.[35]

The Court's decision departs from previous case law examples. Although the outcome of the case may be considered as reducing the rights of Muslim women in France to express their religion, there are aspects of the decision which seem to be setting new standards to the international protection of human rights. For example, the Court's reasoning departs from the earlier decision of *Dahlab v. Switzerland*, in which it was held that the hijab 'appears to be imposed on women. In the *S.A.S. v. France* the Court observed that the covering of the body is a matter which is

---

[33] Rorive (2006), p. 2670.

[34] Berry (2014), para 2.

[35] ECHR, S.A.S. v. France, Application no. 43835/11, 1 July 2014.

inherently a subjective issue, and that this pluralism is essential in a democratic society. Furthermore, the Court's dismissal of the French argument that the "burqa ban" is necessary to protect human dignity also highlights a change in its approach. The Court pointed to the lack of evidence to support the State's assertion that women who wear the full-face veil seek to express a form of contempt against those they encounter or otherwise to offend against the dignity of others. On the contrary, it recognized that the expression of a cultural identity which contributes to the pluralism that is inherent in democracy. It also notes "*the variability of the notions of virtuousness and decency that are applied to the uncovering of the human body*".[36]

On the other hand, The European Court of Human Rights noted that wearing a burqa was deemed incompatible, in French society, with the ground rules of social communication and more broadly the requirements of "living together". As Steinbach observes, the Court did not provide a substantive explanation of how the notion of the "rights and freedoms of others" is conceptually connected to the idea of "living together." Rather than articulating a concrete link between these abstract concepts and identifiable individual rights, the Court limited its reasoning to a single illustrative concern, namely the discomfort allegedly experienced by citizens when interacting with individuals whose faces are covered. In this regard, the Court stated that it could accept the view that persons present in public spaces might be reluctant to see practices or attitudes develop that could fundamentally undermine the possibility of open interpersonal interaction, which, according to what it described as an established consensus, constitutes an essential element of communal life within the society concerned.[37]

In other words the Court considered that wearing of the burqa is retractable religious manifestation that potentially endangers the freedom of others in France. As it mentioned in commentary the notion of living together involves the need for a minority to succumb to the preferences of a majority, thus imposing assimilation to the majority will.[38] It should be noted that a minority disagreed with the conclusion and argued that the decision sacrifices concrete individual rights guaranteed by the Convention to abstract principles. The minority found that the criminalization of the wearing of a full-face veil is a measure which is disproportionate to the aim of protecting the idea of "living together"—an aim which cannot readily be reconciled with the Convention's restrictive catalogue of grounds for interference with basic human rights and they concluded that the ban violated Articles 8 and 9 of the Convention.[39]

As Trispiotis notes "*The emergence of "living together" as a legitimate dimension of the "rights of others" under Articles 8(2), 9(2) and 10(2) ECHR that is capable of justifying state limitations has already attracted vehement criticism in human rights scholarship. More specifically, the ECtHR has been criticized for*

[36] Millet (2015), p. 422.

[37] ECHR, S.A.S. v. France, Application no. 43835/11, 1 July 2014.

[38] Yusuf (2014), pp. 300–302.

[39] Trispiotis (2019), pp. 125–128.

prioritising illicit majoritarian preferences over the individual right to religious manifestation, for yielding to cultural bias and for effectively "bulldozing" a right to personal identity "unless that identity is acceptable and permissible in the eyes of the majority". However, according to Trispiotis the notion of "living together" does not constitute a novelty on the case law of the European Court of Human Rights, but is rather "*closely linked to the republican ideal of fraternity, which reflects a particular kind of social bond between cultural association and democratic citizenship*". In this respect, the notion of "*living together*" represents another manifestation of the core social and democratic values that have already been confirmed be the European Court of Human Rights emphasizing the compelling societal interests of conformity and responsibility.[40]

It is worth noting that the Parliamentary Assembly of the Council of Europe attempted to explicate the normative underpinnings of "*living together*" in Resolution 2076 (2015) and the Recommendation 2076 (2015) on "Freedom of religion and living together in a democratic society".[41] According to the Parliamentary Assembly for many individuals across Europe, religious affiliation constitutes a central component of personal identity and is commonly manifested through worship and adherence to religious practices. The freedom to live in accordance with such practices forms an integral part of the right to freedom of thought, conscience, and religion as guaranteed by Article 9 of the European Convention on Human Rights. This freedom, however, does not exist in isolation. It must be exercised in conjunction with the fundamental rights of others and within a shared social space that enables coexistence and interaction in a democratic society. Consequently, certain limitations on religious practices may be justified, provided that they meet the requirements set out in Article 9(2) of the Convention. Any restriction must be prescribed by law and constitute a necessary measure in a democratic society, pursued in the interests of public safety, the protection of public order, health or morals, or the safeguarding of the rights and freedoms of others. In this context, States Parties are required to strike a fair and proportionate balance between the exercise of freedom of religion and other protected rights, including respect for private and family life, freedom of expression, and the principle of non-discrimination. The Parliamentary Assembly also noted that certain religious practices continue to generate controversy within national communities. Although in different ways, practices such as the wearing of full-face veils, the circumcision of young boys, and ritual slaughter remain highly divisive, and there is no consensus among Council of Europe member States regarding their regulation. Other forms of religious expression may likewise give rise to tensions, particularly in contexts such as the workplace. Against this background, while recognising that States Parties to the European Convention on Human Rights enjoy a wide margin of appreciation in this area, the Parliamentary Assembly has encouraged States to pursue *reasonable*

[40] Trispiotis (2016), p. 581.

[41] Parliamentary Assembly, Recommendation 2080 (2015), Freedom of religion and living together in a democratic society and Parliamentary Assembly, Resolution 2076 (2015), Freedom of religion and living together in a democratic society.

accommodations aimed at ensuring equality in the enjoyment of freedom of religion that is substantive rather than merely formal. In doing so, States are called upon to maintain a conception of neutrality that is inclusive and respectful of diversity, rather than one that privileges uniformity or exclusion.[42]

The notion of "living together" was reconfirmed by the Court in the *Dakir v. Belgium* case. The case concerned a by-law adopted in June 2008 by three Belgian municipalities (Pepinster, Dison and Verviers) concerning a ban on the wearing in public places of clothing that conceals the face. In August 2008, Ms. Dakir, presenting herself as a Muslim who had decided on her own initiative to wear the niqab applied to the Conseil d'État (Council of State) for the annulment of the ban. She claimed, among other things, that the provision expressly concerned the Islamic clothing worn by her and that the resulting ban constituted an interference with her rights. She also contended that the interference had no legitimate aim as secularism was not a constitutional principle and the wearing of the veil could not be subject to a blanket ban. The Court found in particular that the ban imposed by the joint by-law of the municipalities in the Vesdre police area could be regarded as proportionate to the aim pursued, namely the preservation of the conditions of "living together" as an element of the "protection of the rights and freedoms of others. It therefore held that the contested restriction could be regarded as "necessary" "in a democratic society", and that the question whether or not it should be permitted to wear the full-face veil in public places in Belgium constituted a choice of society.[43]

Subsequent case law has confirmed, but not expanded, the approach adopted in *S.A.S. v. France*. In *Belcacemi and Oussar v. Belgium* (2021), the European Court of Human Rights reaffirmed that the preservation of the conditions of "living together" may fall within the protection of the "rights and freedoms of others" and upheld a general ban on face coverings in public spaces as proportionate. At the same time, the Court has refrained from extending this rationale beyond the specific context of full-face concealment and has not relied on "living together" to justify restrictions on other forms of religious dress or symbols. This confirms that the concept functions as a narrowly tailored societal interest rather than a general limitation clause capable of undermining the core of Article 9 protection.[44]

The jurisprudence inaugurated by *S.A.S. v. France* and subsequently reaffirmed in *Belcacemi and Oussar v. Belgium* and *Dakir v. Belgium* has attracted sustained scholarly criticism, particularly regarding the normative indeterminacy of the concept of "living together". Pagotto argues that the Court failed to articulate a robust legal framework capable of grounding this notion within the established structure of Article 9(2) ECHR, relying instead on abstract societal values insufficiently anchored in concrete harm to the rights of others. According to her analysis, the Court's reasoning departs from its traditional insistence on strict proportionality by

[42] Parliamentary Assembly, Resolution 2076 (2015), Freedom of religion and living together in a democratic society, par. 5 and 8.

[43] ECHR, Dakir v. Belgium, Application No. 4619/12, 11 July 2017. See also, Gutan (2021), p. 180.

[44] ECHR, Belcacemi and Oussar v. Belgium, Application No. 37798/13, 11 July 2017.

accepting a generalized conception of social cohesion without requiring evidence that face-covering practices materially impair interpersonal relations in public space[45] (Pagotto 2017, pp. 11–13; 18–19).

A similar critique is advanced by Doomen in his analysis of Belcacemi and Oussar, where he contends that the Court's endorsement of *vivre ensemble* reflects an externally imposed model of citizenship that prioritizes majority conceptions of social interaction over individual self-understanding. He emphasizes that the Belgian and French legislative frameworks endorsed by the Court presuppose that visible facial interaction is a precondition for democratic participation, thereby transforming a contested cultural preference into a legal obligation. This approach, Doomen argues, risks undermining freedom of conscience by conditioning full civic inclusion on conformity with dominant norms of appearance and communication, effectively narrowing the space for pluralism that Article 9 is intended to protect.[46]

More broadly, the academic literature situates the *"living together"* doctrine within a shift toward symbolic constitutional reasoning in the Court's religious freedom jurisprudence. Pagotto observes that these cases exemplify a growing tendency to justify rights restrictions through reference to abstract societal ideals, such as fraternity, trust, and national cohesion, rather than through demonstrable risks to public order or the concrete rights of others. This development, she argues, expands the margin of appreciation to an unprecedented degree while simultaneously weakening judicial scrutiny, thereby allowing states to regulate religious manifestation on the basis of contested identity narratives. As such, the *"living together"* rationale marks a significant recalibration of the balance between individual autonomy and collective values within the Convention system, one that continues to provoke concern regarding the protection of minority identities in pluralist democracies.[47]

The emergence of "living together" as a legitimate ground for restricting fundamental rights marks a significant and potentially troubling shift in the Court's religious freedom jurisprudence. While the objective of fostering social cohesion in pluralist societies is undoubtedly legitimate, grounding limitations on concrete individual rights in abstract and culturally contingent notions of social interaction risks transforming majoritarian sensibilities into legal norms. The Strasbourg Court's acceptance of "living together" in *S.A.S.*, *Dakir*, and *Belcacemi* reflects a willingness to defer to national conceptions of social life that are insufficiently tethered to demonstrable harm to the rights of others. In my view, this approach weakens the protective function of Article 9 by allowing symbolic and identity-based considerations to override individual autonomy, particularly for minority groups whose modes of religious expression deviate from dominant social expectations. Although subsequent case law has confined the application of "living together" to the narrow context of full-face concealment, the doctrinal ambiguity it introduces remains

[45] Pagotto (2017), pp. 11–19.

[46] Doomen (2018), pp. 190–194.

[47] Pagotto (2017), pp. 15–23.

problematic. Unless carefully contained and subjected to rigorous proportionality analysis, the notion risks legitimising assimilationist pressures under the guise of democratic coexistence, thereby undermining the very pluralism that the Convention is meant to safeguard.

References

Berry S (2014) SAS v France: Does Anything Remain of the Right to Manifest Religion?, EJIL:Talk! Blog of the European Journal of International Law

Coyle S (2021) The queer, the cross and the closet: religious exceptions in equality Law as state-sponsored homophobia. Laws 10:83

Domenici I (2021) Antigone betrayed? The European court of human rights' decisions on conscientious objection to abortion in the cases of Grimmark v. Sweden and Steen v. Sweden. Eur J Health Law 28:26–47

Donders Y (2016) Cultural diversity and cultural identity in human rights. In: Wiesand AJ, Chainoglou K, Śledzińska-Simon A, Donders Y (eds) Culture and human rights: the Wroclaw commentaries. De Gruyter Handbook, pp 23–32

Doomen J (2018) The Belgian Burqa ban and the European court of human rights. Religion Human Rights 13:183–201

Garlicki L (2015) The Strasbourg court on issues of religion in the public schools system. In: Hermann-Josef Blanke HJ, Villalón PC, Klein T, Ziller J (eds) Common European legal thinking, essays in honour of Albrecht weber. Springer, pp 321–341

Gerards J (2018) Margin of appreciation and Incrementalism in the case Law of the European court of human rights. Hum Rights Law Rev 18:495–515

Gozdecka DA (2011) Europe's changing approach towards blasphemy: the 'right' not to be offended, sensitive identities and relativism. In: Murphy CC, Green P (eds) Law and outsiders: norms, processes and 'Othering' in the 21st century. Hart publishing, pp 233–248

Gutan B (2021) Cultural rights of migrants - living together in dignity? In: Başak Ç, Bianku L, Motoc J (eds) Migration and the European convention on human rights. Oxford Academic, Oxford, pp 175–195. https://www.ejiltalk.org/sas-v-france-does-anything-remain-of-the-right-to-manifest-religion/

Kastanas H (2013) Article 9. In: Sisilianos LA (ed) European convention on human rights, interpretation by article. Nomiki Vivliothiki, Athens, pp 363–393. (in Greek)

Ktistakis G (2021) Article 9. In: Sarmas I, Kontiadis X, Anthopoulos C (eds) ECHR, interpretation by article. Sakkoulas, Athes—Thessaloniki, pp 533–561. (in Greek)

Lamačková A (2008) Conscientious objection in reproductive health care: analysis of Pichon and Sajous v. France. Eur J Health Law 15(1):7–43

Langlaude S (2006) Indoctrination, secularism, religious liberty, and the ECHR. Int Comp Law Q 55(4):929–944

McCrea R (2014) Religion in the workplace: Eweida and others v United Kingdom. Modern Law Rev 77:277–291

McGoldrick D (2016) A defence of the margin of appreciation and an argument for its application by the human rights committee. Int Comp Law Q 65(1):21–60

Millet FX (2015) Case comment: when the European court of human rights encounters the face: a case note on the Burqa ban in France. ECL Rev 11(2):408–424

Pagotto T (2017) The ban on face covering and the "living together" principle: the Strasbourg court's new social justification for restricting religious freedom. Studia z Prawa Wyznaniowego 20:7–28. p. 11–19

Paul K (2019) Lachiri v Belgium and bans on wearing Islamic dress in the courtroom: an emerging trend. Ecclesiastical Law J 21(48–53):49–52

Ringelheim J (2018) Lachiri v Belgium: Headscarf Ban Imposed on a Civil Party in a Courtroom in Violation of Religious Freedom. Strasbourg Observers, 23 November 2018. https://strasbourgobservers.com/2018/11/23/lachiri-v-belgium-headscarf-ban-imposed-on-a-civil-party-in-a-courtroom-in-violation-of-religious-freedom/
Rorive I (2006) Religious symbols in the public space: in search of a European answer. Cardozo Law Rev 30:2669–2698
Sajó A, Uitz R (2020) Individual religious freedom under the European convention of human rights. In: Mancini S (ed) Constitutions and religion. Edward Elgar Publishing, pp 286–306
Tamimi Y (2018) Human rights and the excess of identity: legal and theoretical inquiry into the notion of identity in Strasbourgh case Law. Soc Leg Stud 27(3):283–298
Trispiotis I (2016) Two interpretations of "living together" in European human rights law. Camb Law J 75(3):580–607
Trispiotis I (2019) Islamophobia as a key contextual factor in human rights adjudication. In: Law I, Easat-Daas A, Merali A, Sayyid S (eds) Countering, Islamophobia in Europe. Palgrave Macmillan, pp 9–31
Yusuf HO (2014) S.A.S. V France: supporting “living together” or forced assimilation. Int Hum Rights Law Rev 3(2):277–302

Chapter 16
Concluding Remarks

Contents

This study demonstrates that the European human rights framework reconciles the protection of cultural identity with the challenges of multiculturalism not by recognising cultural identity as an autonomous right, but by embedding it within the broader system of individual human rights guaranteed by the European Convention on Human Rights. Cultural identity is protected insofar as it contributes to human dignity, personal autonomy, and the free development of the individual, while remaining subject to limits where cultural or religious practices conflict with the rights of others or undermine fundamental democratic values. The jurisprudence of the European Court of Human Rights reveals a model of reconciliation grounded in proportionality, pluralism, and contextual assessment, supported by the margin of appreciation but constrained by minimum Convention standards. Through this approach, the Court seeks to preserve cultural diversity without endorsing cultural relativism, ensuring that multicultural coexistence remains compatible with the universality of human rights and the primacy of human dignity.

The analysis concludes that fundamental rights, and the rights of persons belonging to minorities as an inherent part of the wider framework of human rights, can be used either as arguments in favor of the protection of cultural diversity and identity, or the opposite. Undoubtedly, fundamental rights offer a convenient framework for the negotiation and protection of cultural diversity,[1] as they can ensure a fair balance between the protection of cultural practices and the legitimate limitations on the expression of cultural identity. As Donders concludes "*International human rights law provides many possibilities for individuals and communities to enjoy, maintain and develop their culture, either via the equality principle as well as via cultural rights and the cultural dimension of rights. It is an international legal framework for promoting and preserving not only the diversity between cultures, but also the diversity within cultures. It provides rights to promote and protect culture, but it can also protect against*

[1] Brems (2010), p. 664.

N. Gaitenidis, *The Rights of Cultural Identity in the Case Law of the European Court of Human Rights*, European Union and its Neighbours in a Globalized World 36, https://doi.org/10.1007/978-3-032-23045-4_16

harmful practices or stereotypes".[2] In particular, in the context of the European Convention on Human Rights, in the absence of a special regulation or guarantee, the exercise of the cultural or religious practices is protected through the wider guarantees provided by the Articles of the European Convention of Human Rights.

In a time when identity plays a prominent role in public debates, the Court's approach to identity is crucial. Human rights serve as central moral and political reference points in these debates, often used by opposing political groups and social factions to justify their claims. Under such circumstances, it is essential for the Court to be aware of how it utilizes the notion of identity in its case law. Further research on the Court's approach to identity under different articles of the Convention, as well as insights from other fields of knowledge, can contribute to a more justified and coherent standard in the Court's use of identity.[3] Through the corpus of human rights, the importance of culture for human dignity is confirmed, and cultural identity is protected from negative side effects. However, it is assured that there can be no invocation of fundamental and cultural rights without limits, in a way that justifies and legitimizes the denial or blatant violation of other fundamental rights or freedoms. Despite the fact that a degree of "cultural interpretation" of fundamental rights is reasonable and expected, any attempt to justify violations in the name of culture has no validity.

The European Court of Human Rights has recognized the importance of minority views and beliefs in relation to the application of the Convention. Although it does not require "absolute uniformity", but adopts a fairly "strict" stance on the minimum requirements of the Convention, the Court often attempts to distinguish between "essential "and "non-essential" elements of a culture. While imposing restrictions on the exercise of cultural practices, the Court decides mainly on the proportionality of these measures and their necessity in a democratic, pluralistic society. The "margin of appreciation" granted to national authorities appears to be wider in matters concerning simple moral imperatives, such as special dietary requirements, compared to matters concerning the physical integrity of the individual, such as corporal punishment. However, the judges have not hesitated to impose their own view of European standards, even in cases where different cultural communities exist. The case law of the Court reveals that human rights provide a moral and legal framework for promoting and preserving not only the diversity between cultures, but also the diversity within cultures. In its judgments, the Court seeks to implement the requirement of pluralism and individual rights to diversity in a multicultural society without relinquishing the spirit and common heritage of Europe.[4]

In the *Alekseyev v. Russia* case, which concerned LGBT rights, the Court stated that "*it would be incompatible with the underlying values of the Convention if the exercise of Convention rights by a minority group were made conditional on its*

[2] Donders (2013), p. 138.

[3] Tamimi (2018), p. 296.

[4] Karakaş (2009), pp. 48–53.

being accepted by the majority. Were this so, a minority group's rights to freedom of religion, expression and assembly would become merely theoretical rather than practical and effective as required by the Convention".[5] However, in many cases the European Court of Human Rights is reluctant to prescribe to States how they should deal with cultural diversity, based on their large margin of appreciation.[6]

Apart from reaffirming the importance of culture for human dignity, human rights also provide a frame for shielding cultural diversity from negative side effects. As shown above, cultural rights cannot be enjoyed without limit. They cannot be invoked or interpreted in such a way as to justify the denial or violation of other human rights and fundamental freedoms.[7] As mentioned in the Court's judgement in the case *Young, James & Webster v. United Kingdom "even if sometimes the interest of the individuals need to be subordinated in the group interests, democracy can not lead to the uninterrupted supremacy of the opinion of the majority, but requires a balance that ensures equal treatment for minorities and avoids any abuse of a dominant position*".[8] According to previous observations, the argument of the Court protects individual minority option at two levels: (a) the level of relations between the majority and the minority in the state, (b) the level of relations between people who share a common belonging therefore at the level of the correlations within a group.[9] As Yvonne Donders concludes "*Human rights and cultural diversity may have a mutually beneficial relationship, but this does not mean that, as in all relationships, there will be no complexities or (unexpected) issues that will continue to demand respect, flexibility and adaptability of one and/or the other. While states play a crucial role in this regard and should, indeed, secure conditions, or help to maintain infrastructures, that enable the participation of everyone in a multifaceted cultural life, there cannot be merely top-down approaches. Cultures are determined and developed by individuals and communities, who should always be involved and consulted in cultural laws and policy processes, thereby making these laws and policies more human rights proof*".[10]

In practice, the balancing of respect for religious and cultural expressions and fundamental rights, and everyday multicultural conflicts, is a rather difficult process in modern multicultural states and in the context of "identity politics". However, international and European human rights law is not a set of static texts but a "living instrument"[11] which must respond to the evolving conditions and contemporary social norms. In this respect, the continuous development and interpretation of the

---

[5] ECHR, Aleksevev v. Russia, *Application No.* 4916/07, 21 October 2010. See also, Brems (2021), pp. 196–216.

[6] Gerards (2018), p. 496.

[7] Donders (2010), pp. 15–35.

[8] ECHR, *Young, James & Webster v. United Kingdom, Application No. 7601/76,* 13 August 1981.

[9] Christopoulos (2002), pp. 185–188.

[10] Donders (2016a, b), p. 30.

[11] The European Court of Human Rights has recognized that the ECHR is a living tool: ECHR, Goodwin v United Kingdom Application No. 17488/90, 27 March 1996. Letsas (2016), pp. 106–141.

law of fundamental rights should not constitute a "regression" in the process of consolidating the universal human values which constitute the fundamental basis of the modern European constitutional culture. As Tamimi concludes "*In a time when identity dominates in public debates, the way the Court approaches identity is of utmost importance. Human rights act as central moral and political reference points in these public debates. Indeed, human rights are often used by opposing political camps and social groups to justify and enhance their assertions. Under such conditions, it is imperative that the Court is especially well aware of how it uses the notion of identity in its case law*".[12]

These findings do not prevent the European Court of Human Rights from treating minority rights in a case-by-case basis through the substantive human rights section of the European Convention on Human Rights, even though not in a totally coherent manner. The European Court of Human Rights interprets the special rights of people belonging to minorities, not as minority, but as human rights.[13] After all, the protection of cultural identity is well reflected in cultural dimension of human rights.[14]

The Strasbourg Court's approach to identity claims and cultural diversity varies between strict restrictions and more tolerant accommodation; for this reason the European Court of Human Rights has been criticized by scholars and academic for being unpredictable and inconsistent. Despite its uneven and timid approach, the Court's recognition and support of diversity is valuable in contemporary societies. Diversity governance is seen as a powerful tool to reduce tensions, prevent conflicts, and accommodating diversity so as to maintain social cohesion and prosperity. The Strasbourg's Court, along with the state and other actors, should strengthen their role as promoters of dialogue and cooperation to find solutions beyond reasonable accommodations.[15]

Due to differences in legal traditions, constitutional values, and historical developments, fundamental rights standards in Europe vary, creating a challenge for the European Court of Human Rights to balance the need for uniform and effective rights protection while respecting diversity. The Court is believed to use its famous margin of appreciation doctrine as its primary tool in striking this balance.[16]

Those assumptions lead to the conclusion that certain religious and cultural practices, harmful to human dignity, should be reconceptualized, interpreted and adapted

[12] Tamimi (2018), p. 296.

[13] Christopoulos (2002), p. 189.

[14] **Committee on Economic, Social and Cultural Rights, General Comment 4, The right to adequate housing (Sixth session, 1991), UN Doc. E/1992/23, annex III at 114 (1991), par. 8. Committee on Economic, Social and Cultural Rights, General Comment 14, The right to the highest attainable standard of health (Twenty-second session, 2000), UN Doc. E/C.12/2000/4 (2000), par. 12. Committee on Economic, Social and Cultural Rights, General Comment 12, Right to adequate food (Twentieth session, 1999), UN Doc. E/C.12/1999/5 (1999), par. 7, 8 and 11.**

[15] Medda-Windischer (2021), p. 45.

[16] Gerards (2018), p. 495.

taking into account the imperatives of the contemporary socio-political reality, the value social norms but also the modern trends of human rights law. That is, religious and other cultural minorities cannot remain “locked” in rigid practices and doctrines of the past, when such practices do not respect human dignity; they should adapt to the evolving convergence of international standards of fundamental rights. In this context, the process of “self-adjustment” is proposed in combination with long-term policies of intercultural dialogue, in order to achieve the revision of religious scriptures and customs, with the review of primary sources and the drafting of new interpretations without them being derogatory from their essential value meaning.

At the core of rights related to the protection of cultural identity lies the right of the individual to choose or refuse participation in a culture. This right is recognized in the Council of Europe Framework Convention for the Protection of National Minorities, in Article 3. This concept is based on the perception of the individual as a member of a group, which, however, retains the autonomy to determine their own life. The right of exit can provide the opportunity for an individual to leave oppressive conditions and integrate into a way of life with more personal freedom. The establishment of social and legal institutions and mechanisms for its implementation is necessary for its realization.[17]

It can be concluded that international instruments of fundamental rights protection do not provide protection for any cultural custom or practice, but distinguish between “essential” and “non-essential” elements of a culture. The difficulty therefore lies in defining the dividing line the essential from the non-essential element of a culture, especially in multicultural societies but also between different geographical areas.[18] It is accepted that the main factor for this determination is the concept of human dignity and human value. Since human dignity is, in addition to being legal, an inherent and moral right, it is placed above the cultural peculiarities.[19]

The case law of the European Court of Human Rights reveals a deliberate choice to approach cultural identity not as an autonomous or self-standing right, but as a relational interest protected through the broader architecture of individual human rights. This approach, while often criticised as fragmented or cautious, reflects a principled commitment to placing human dignity, personal autonomy, and equality at the core of cultural protection. The Court’s jurisprudence demonstrates that cultural identity is worthy of protection insofar as it enhances the free development of the individual, but it cannot operate as a shield against scrutiny where cultural or religious practices undermine the fundamental rights of others or the dignity of those within the group itself. In this sense, the Court’s insistence on proportionality and necessity operates as a safeguard against both cultural absolutism and moral relativism.

---

[17] Ben-Porath (2010), p. 1023.

[18] Stamatopoulou (2007), pp. 113–116.

[19] It should be noted that several authors examine the concept of human dignity as inherent in every historical moment, therefore is is dependent and formed by the ethical values adopted by every society. See Tsevrenis (2012), pp. 50–58. Also, Capps (2009), p. 25–35. Also, Luban (2007), pp. 17–18.

At the same time, the Court's extensive reliance on the margin of appreciation, while institutionally understandable, risks diluting the protective force of the Convention in cases where identity claims intersect with entrenched power asymmetries. The jurisprudence examined in this study shows that deference to national authorities has, at times, allowed majoritarian values or dominant cultural narratives to shape the limits of minority protection. This is particularly evident in cases involving religious symbols, "living together," and internal group practices, where abstract societal interests have occasionally prevailed over concrete individual rights. In my view, a more robust engagement with the individual dimension of cultural identity, especially the right to dissent, to opt out, or to refuse participation, would strengthen the Court's capacity to protect pluralism without legitimising assimilationist pressures.

Donders remarks that "*The handling of human rights and cultural diversity therefore requires a multidimensional approach, in terms of instruments and in terms of actors. Apart from legislation, human rights policies and measures in the field of education and social development should be taken. The preparation and implementation of such laws and policies should not only involve state authorities, but as much as possible, the cultural communities concerned as well. Cultural communities have an important responsibility Human rights and cultural diversity require mutual respect: the reception of cultural diversity can only take place in a context in which the cultural community involved shows respect for human rights*".[20] The main challenge of this process is to maintain the stable moral imperatives of a religion without, however, the abusive "mantle" of cultural conservatism and determinism when it constitutes a violation of fundamental rights as well as of the human condition itself.

It is undoubtedly a long-term process which largely depends on the will of a minority group to actively participate in the implementation of changes and in intercultural dialogue between the different cultures found in a state and in consultation with national and supranational authorities. Therefore, legal and political interventions are necessary, in order to limit or prohibit practices that are incompatible with fundamental rights. These interventions, however, should be in line with the fundamental European constitutional principles and with a view to protecting and promoting human dignity and personal autonomy.

A central conclusion of this book is that the protection of cultural identity under the Convention must be understood as inseparable from the protection of individuals *within* cultures. The jurisprudence analysed confirms that the Court is increasingly attentive to the phenomenon of "minorities within minorities" and to the risks posed by collective norms imposed without genuine consent. While cultural belonging is often essential to personal identity, it cannot justify the erosion of individual autonomy or the imposition of legal regimes based solely on group affiliation. The negative dimension of cultural rights, the right not to be treated as a member of a

[20] Donders (2016a, b), p. 381.

group, or not to adhere to its practices, emerges as a cornerstone of contemporary human rights protection and as a necessary corrective to communitarian excesses.

Finally, this study maintains that the future development of the Court's approach to cultural identity depends on its ability to reconcile diversity with a stable core of European constitutional values. Cultural practices must remain open to reinterpretation and adaptation in light of evolving human rights standards, without being fossilised under claims of tradition or authenticity. Intercultural dialogue, reasonable accommodation and participatory governance are essential tools in this process, but they cannot replace clear legal boundaries where human dignity is at stake. In my view, the enduring contribution of the European Convention system lies precisely in its refusal to privilege culture over humanity: cultural diversity is protected not as an end in itself, but as a living expression of human freedom, capable of change, critique, and renewal within a democratic society governed by the rule of law.

References

Ben-Porath S (2010) Exit rights and entrance paths: accommodating cultural diversity in a Liberal democracy. Perspect Polit 8(4):1021–1103

Brems E (2010) Human rights as a framework for negotiating/protecting cultural differences: an exploration in the case-law of the European court of human rights. In: Foblets MC, Gaudreault--DesBiens JF, Renteln AD (eds) Cultural diversity and the law: state responses from around the world? Proceedings of the colloquium "the response of state law to the expression of cultural diversity", Brussels, September 2006 (with the support of the Francqui foundation). Bruylant, Bruxelles, pp 663–716

Brems E (2021) Islamophobia and the ECtHR, a test case for positive subsidiarity for the protection of Europe's long-term migrants? In: Başak Ç, Bianku L, Motoc J (eds) Migration and the European convention on human rights. Oxford Academic, Oxford, pp 196–216

Capps P (2009) Human dignity and the foundations of international law. Hart Publishing, Oxford

Christopoulos D (2002) Otherness as a power relationship, aspects of Greek, Balkan and European experience. Kritiki, Athens (in Greek)

Donders Y (2010) Do cultural diversity and human rights make a good match? Int Soc Sci J 61(199):15–35

Donders Y (2013) International human rights and cultural diversity: balancing act. Romanian J Comp Law 4(2):123–138

Donders Y (2016a) Cultural diversity and cultural identity in human rights. In: Wiesand AJ et al (eds) Culture and human rights: the Wroclaw commentaries. De Gruyter Handbook, pp 23–32

Donders Y (2016b) Human rights and cultural diversity: too hot to handle. Netherlands Q Human Rights 30(4):377–381

Gerards J (2018) Margin of appreciation and Incrementalism in the case law of the European court of human rights. Hum Rights Law Rev 18:495–515

Karakaş I (2009) The European convention on human rights and respect for diversity. In: Directorate General of Human Rights and Legal Affairs (ed) Human rights in culturally diverse societies: challenges and perspectives, conference proceedings, the Hague 12–13 November 2008. Council of Europe, Strasbourg, pp 48–53

Letsas G (2016) The ECHR as a living instrument: its meaning and its legitimacy. In: Føllesdal A, Wilhelms W, Ulfstein G (eds) *Constituting Europe* the *European court of human rights in a national*, European and global context. Cambridge University Press, Cambridge, pp 106–141

Luban D (2007) Legal ethics and human dignity. Cambridge University Press, Cambridge

Medda-Windischer R (2021) Religious and linguistic minorities and the European court of human rights: between restrictive measures and concerted solutions. Europa Ethnica 78(1–2):36–47
Stamatopoulou E (2007) Cultural rights in international law, article 27 of the universal declaration of human rights and beyond. Martinus Nijhoff Publishers, Leiden-Boston
Tamimi Y (2018) Human rights and the excess of identity: legal and theoretical inquiry into the notion of identity in Strasbourg case law. Soc Leg Stud 27(3):283–298
Tsevrenis VK (2012) Human dignity. Sakkoula Publications, Athens-Thessaloniki (in Greek)

References

Allen QCR (2007) Article13 EC, Evolution and Current Contexts. In: Meenan H (ed) Equality Law in an Enlarged European Union. Cambridge University Press, Cambridge, pp 38–72
Anagnostopoulou D (2019) The prohibition of hate speech in the international framework of the United Nations. In: Kouroupis K, Karagouni V (eds) Consolidating the European Area of Justice, The Protection of Fundamental Rights – Justice Training Program for a European Area of Justice. Nomiki Vivliothiki, pp 169–181. (in Greek)
Arnardóttir OM (2017) Vulnerability under Article 14 of the European Convention on Human Rights: Innovation or business as usual? *Oslo Law Review 4*(3):150–171
Askitis A (2020) Molla Sali (ECHR): Greece's "velvet condemnation" for the application of sharia to the inheritance disputes of Greek Muslims, (in Greek)
Ayton-Shenker D (1995) The Challenge of Human Rights and Cultural Diversity, United Nations Background Note http://www.un.org/rights/dpi1627e.htm
Barry B (2001) Culture and Equality: An Egalitarian Critique of Multiculturalism. Polity Press, Cambridge
Barth WK (2008) On Cultural Rights, The Equality of Nations and the Minority Legal Tradition. Martinus Nijhoff Publishers, Leiden
Bauer N (2020) Neutralité de l'État et dissensions ecclésiales : réflexions à partir d'un arrêt récent de la Cour européenne, Revue du droit des religions. http://journals.openedition.org/rdr/1127
Bekker JC (1989) Seymour's Customary Law in Southern Africa, 5th edn. Juta & Co. Ltd, Cape Town
Belavusau U (2012) Fighting Hate Speech through EU Law. Amsterdam Law Forum 4(1):20–25
Benedi Lahuera S (2009) Race Equality and TCNs, or How to Fight Discrimination with a Discriminatory Law. European Law Journal 15(6):738–756
Ben-Porath S (2010) Exit Rights and Entrance Paths: Accommodating Cultural Diversity in a Liberal Democracy. Perspectives on Politics 8(4):1021–1103
Berry S (2014) SAS v France: Does Anything Remain of the Right to Manifest Religion?, EJIL:Talk! Blog of the European Journal of International Law
Bougiakiotis E (2018) *E.S. v Austria*: Blasphemy Laws and the Double Standards of the European Court of Human Rights, U.K. Const. L. Blog, https://ukconstitutionallaw.org/
Bradley N (2018) Essentialism in the Concept of Culture: Gauging Belief. Journal of Intercultural Communication 21:1–21
Bratza N (2022) The 'Precious Asset': Freedom of Religion Under the European Convention on Human Rights. Ecclesiastical Law Journal 14:256–271

N. Gaitenidis, *The Rights of Cultural Identity in the Case Law of the European Court of Human Rights*, European Union and its Neighbours in a Globalized World 36, https://doi.org/10.1007/978-3-032-23045-4

Brems E (2010) Human rights as a framework for negotiating/protecting cultural differences: an exploration in the case-law of the European Court of Human Rights. In: Foblets MC, Gaudreault-DesBiens JF, Renteln AD (eds) Cultural diversity and the law: state responses from around the world; proceedings of the Colloquium "The Response of State Law to the Expression of Cultural Diversity". Bruylant, Bruxelles, pp 663–671

Brems E (2021) Islamophobia and the ECtHR, A Test Case for Positive Subsidiarity for the Protection of Europe's Long-term Migrants? In: Başak Ç, Bianku L, Motoc J (eds) Migration and the European Convention on Human Rights. Oxford Academic, Oxford, pp 196–216

Bribosia E, Rorive I, Waddington L (2013) Reasonable Accommodation beyond Disability in Europe?. European Network of Legal Experts in the Non-discrimination field. European Commission, Directorate-General for Justice, Belgium. https://tandis.odihr.pl/bitstream/20.500.12389/21768/1/07881.pdf

Bromell D (2022) Regulating Free Speech in a Digital Age - Hate, Harm and the Limits of Censorship. Springer, London

Brzozowski W (2020) Papageorgiou and Others v Greece: Exemption from a Mandatory Course in Religion and the Art of Reading between the Lines. Ecclesiastical Law Journal 22(3):355–360

Capps P (2009) Human Dignity and the Foundations of International Law. Hart Publishing, Oxford

Chaib SO (2016) Religious Accommodation in the Workplace: Improving the Legal Reasoning of the European Court of Human Rights. In: Foblets MC, Katayoun Alidadi K (eds) A Test of Faith? Religious Diversity and Accommodation in the European Workplace. Routledge, New York, pp 33–58

Chainoglou K (2017) The Right to Historical Truth and Historical Memory versus Historical Revisionism and Denialism: A Human Rights Analysis. In: Chainoglou K, Strawson J, Collins B, Phillips M (eds) Injustice, Memory and Faith in Human Rights. Routledge, Abingdon, pp 136–150

Chen VHH (2014) Cultural identity *Key Concepts in Intercultural Dialogue, 22*. https://centerforinterculturaldialogue.files.wordpress.com/2014/07/key-concept-cultural-identity.pdf

Christopoulos D (2002a) Otherness as a power relationship, Aspects of Greek, Balkan and European experience. Kritiki, Athens. (in Greek)

Christopoulos DK (2002b) Otherness as a power relation, Aspects of the Greek, Balkan and European experience, Series: Minority Group Research Center: Series of Studies Series Leader: Tsitselikis K, Christopoulos D. Kritiki, Athens (in Greek)

Christopoulos DK (2006) The right to self-determination. In: Naskou-Perraki P, Kistakis G (eds) The Greek Cases in Strasbourg, Volume I, 1991-2001. Ant. N. Sakkoulas, Thessaloniki Athens, pp 369–379. (in Greek)

Cismas I (2014) Religious Actors and International Law. Oxford University Press, Oxford

Cittadino F (2019) Incorporating Indigenous Rights in the International Regime on Biodiversity Protection: Access, Benefit-sharing and Conservation in Indigenous Lands. Brill, Leiden

Coyle S (2021) The Queer, the Cross and the Closet: Religious Exceptions in Equality Law as State-Sponsored Homophobia. Laws 10:83

Cuche D (2001) The concept of culture in the social sciences. Typothito - G. Dardanos, Athens (in Greek)

Daes EIA (2008) Indigenous Peoples, Keepers of our past – Custodians of our future. IWGIA, Copenhagen

Dagtoglou P (1991) Constitutional Law, Individual rights, vol. A'. Antonis N. Sakkoulas, Athens-Komotini (in Greek)

de Varennes F, Kuzborska E (2015) Human Rights and a Person's Name: Legal Trends and Challenges. Human Rights Quarterly 37(4):977–1023

Di Federico G (2011) Fundamental Rights in the EU: Legal Pluralism and Multi-Level Protection After the Lisbon Treaty. In: Di Federico G (ed) The EU Charter of Fundamental Rights, From Declaration to Binding Instrument. Springer, London, pp 15–54

Dieter BK (2006) The Protection of the Right to Education by International Law Including a Systematic Analysis of Article 13 of the International Covenant on Economic, Social and Cultural Rights. Martinus Nijhoff Publishers, Leiden

Dinstein Y (1992) Freedom of Religion and Religious Minorities. In: Dinstein Y (ed) The Protection of Minorities and Human Rights. Martinus Nijhoff Publishers, Leiden, pp 145–169

Domenici I (2021) Antigone Betrayed? The European Court of Human Rights' Decisions on Conscientious Objection to Abortion in the Cases of Grimmark v. Sweden and Steen v. Sweden. European Journal of Health Law 28:26–47

Donders Y (2002) *Towards a Right to Cultural Identity*? Antwerp, Intersentia, Bruxelles

Donders Y (2003) Protection of cultural rights in Europe: none of the EU's business. Maastricht Journal of European and Comparative Law 10(2):117–148

Donders Y (2010) Do cultural diversity and human rights make a good match? International Social Science Journal 61(199):15–35

Donders Y (2013a) Cultural Pluralism in International Human Rights Law: The Role of Reservations. In: Vrdoljak AF (ed) The Cultural Dimension of Human Rights. Oxford University Press, Oxford, pp 205–239

Donders Y (2013b) International human rights and cultural diversity: balancing act. Romanian Journal of Comparative Law 4(2):123–138

Donders Y (2016a) Cultural Diversity and Cultural Identity in Human Rights. In: Wiesand AJ, Chainoglou K, Śledzińska-Simon A, Donders Y (eds) Culture and Human Rights: The Wroclaw Commentaries. De Gruyter Handbook, pp 23–32

Donders Y (2016b) Human rights and cultural diversity: too hot to handle. Netherlands Quarterly of Human Rights 30(4):377–381

Donders Y (2016c) Protecting the home and adequate housing: living in caravan or trailer as human right. International Human Rights Law Review 5(1):1–25

Donders Y (2018) Towards a Right to Cultural Identity? Yes, Indeed! Diritti Umani e Diritto Internazionale 12(3):523–548

Doomen J (2018) The Belgian Burqa Ban and the European Court of Human Rights. Religion and Human Rights 13:183–201

Dube N (2024) Wa Baile v. Switzerland: An implicit acknowledgment of racial profiling as structural discrimination. Strasbourg Observers, https://strasbourgobservers.com/2024/03/26/wa-baile-v-switzerland-an-implicit-acknowledgment-of-racial-profiling-as-structural-discrimination/

Eisenberg A (2009) Reasons of Identity, A Normative Guide to the Political and Legal Assessment of Identity Claims. Oxford University Press, Oxford

Encyclopedia Britannica (2023) The Editors of Encyclopaedia. "Silesia summary". https://www.britannica.com/summary/Silesia. Accessed 25 June 2023

EU Network of Independent Experts on Fundamental Rights (2006) *Commentary of the Charter of Fundamental Rights.* http://ec.Europe.eu/justice/fundamental-rights/files/networkcommentaryfinal_en.pdf

European Court of Human Rights (2022) Fact sheet: Hate speech, June 2022: https://www.echr.coe.int/documents/fs_hate_speech_eng.pdf

Evans M (2017) The Freedom of Religion or Belief in the ECHR since Kokkinakis: Or Quoting Kokkinakis. Religion & Human Rights 12:83–98

Farget D (2012) Defining Roma identity in the European court of human rights. International Journal on Minority and Group Rights 19(3):291–316

Farrior S (2024) Basu v. Ger. and Muhammad v. Spain (Eur. Ct. H.R.). International Legal Materials 63(1):94–141

Fenwick H (2005) Civil Liberties and Human Rights. Cavendish Publishing Limited, London

FRA (2018a) Handbook on European non-discrimination law – 2018 edition. Publications Office of the European Union, Luxembourg. https://fra.europa.eu/sites/default/files/fra_uploads/fra-2018-handbook-non-discrimination-law-2018_en.pdf

FRA (2018b) Unmasking bias motives in crimes: selected cases of the European Court of Human Rights https://fra.europa.eu/sites/default/files/fra_uploads/fra-2018-unmasking-bias-motives-paper_en.pdf

FRA, Ensuring justice for hate crime victims: professional perspectives, Publications Office of the European Union, Luxembourg https://fra.europa.eu/sites/default/files/fra_uploads/fra-2016-justice-hate_crime-victims_en.pdf

Francioni F (2011) The Human Dimension of International Cultural Heritage Law: An Introduction. The European Journal of International Law 22(1):9–16

Fredman S (2001) Combating Racism with Human Rights: The Right to Equality. In: Fredman S (ed) Discrimination and Human Rights, The Case of Racism. Oxford University Press, Oxford, pp 9–44

Garay A (2008) Association les Témoins de Jéhovah versus France The Jurisprudence of the European Court of Human Rights on Religious Activities and Taxation Issues. Religion & Human Rights 3(2):185–190

Garlicki L (2015) The Strasbourg Court on Issues of Religion in the Public Schools System. In: Hermann-Josef Blanke HJ, Villalón PC, Klein T, Ziller J (eds) Common European Legal Thinking, Essays in Honour of Albrecht Weber. Springer, New York, pp 321–341

Gatti M (2019) Autonomy of Religious Organisations in the European Convention of Human Rights and European Union Law. In: Rossi LS, Di Federico G (eds) Fundamental Rights in Europe and China. Regional Identities and Universalism. Editoriale Scientifica, Napoli, pp 132–153

Geller J, Gergely D (2013) Vona v.Hungary: Freedom of association and assembly can be restricted to protect Minority Rights. Strasbourg Observers academic blog. https://strasbourgobservers.com/2013/08/07/vona-v-hungary-freedom-of-association-and-assembly-can-be-restricted-to-protect-minority-rights/

Gerards J (2018) Margin of Appreciation and Incrementalism in the Case Law of the European Court of Human Rights. Human Rights Law Review 18:495–515

Giannakoula A (2018) The Criminal Law dealing with Racism: Current Challenges and Targets. In: Deligianni C, Gaitenidis N, Koniaris V (eds) Protection of Fundamental Rights: Contemporary Issues in the European Space. Papazisis Publications, Athens, pp 89–110. (in Greek)

Gordon JS (2015) Human Rights and Cultural Identity. Baltic Journal of Law & Politics 8(2):112–135

Gozdecka DA (2011) Europe's changing approach towards blasphemy: The 'Right' not to be offended, sensitive identities and relativism. In: Murphy CC, Green P (eds) Law and Outsiders: Norms, Processes and 'Othering' in the 21st Century. Hart publishing, pp 233–248

Grammatikas V (2019) International Protection of Minorities. In: Naskou Perraki P (ed) Human Rights, International and Regional Protection. Sakkoulas, Athens, pp 109–120. (in Greek)

Grote R (2008) The Struggle for Minority Rights and Human Rights: Current Trends and Challenges. In: König D, Stoll PT, Röben V, Matz-Lück N (eds) International Law Today: New Challenges and the Need for Reform?: New Challenges and the Need for Reform? Springer Verlag, pp 221–246

Gutan B (2021) Cultural Rights of Migrants - Living Together in Dignity? In: Başak Ç, Bianku L, Motoc J (eds) Migration and the European Convention on Human Rights. Oxford Academic, Oxford, pp 175–195

Hall S (1997) Cultural Identity and Diaspora. In: Woodward K (ed) *Identity and Difference*. SAGE Publications, pp 51–59

Henrard K (2007) Equal rights versus special rights? Minority protection and the prohibition of discrimination. European Commission Directorate-General for Employment and Social Affairs. Office for Official Publications of the European Communities, Luxembourg

Henrard K (2016) The European Court of Human Rights, Ethnic and Religious Minorities and the Two Dimensions of the Right to Equal Treatment: Jurisprudence at Different Speeds? Nordic Journal of Human Rights 34(3):157–177

Herbach M, Siampakou N (2024) Faith and fury: Rising anti-blasphemy extremism in Europe and its legal implications. International Centre for Counter-Terrorism. https://www.icct.nl/publication/faith-and-fury-rising-anti-blasphemy-extremism-europe-and-its-legal-implications
Hilliard C, Duranti M (2024) Human Rights at the Edges of Late Imperial Britain: The Tyrer Case and Judicial Corporal Punishment from the Isle of Man to Montserrat, 1972–1990. Law and History Review 42:343–366
Iakovidis I, McDonough P (2019) The Molla Sali Case: How the European Court of Human Rights Escaped a Legal Labyrinth While Holding the Thread of Human Rights. Oxford Journal of Law and Religion 8:427–446
Kanellopoulos PI (2010) The law of the European Union, Treaty of Lisbon, 5th edn. Sakkoula, Athens - Thessaloniki (in Greek)
Karakaş I (2009) The European Convention on Human Rights and respect for diversity. In: Directorate General of Human Rights and Legal Affairs (ed) Human Rights in Culturally Diverse Societies: Challenges and Perspectives, Conference proceedings, The Hague 12-13 November 2008. Council of Europe, Strasbourg, pp 48–53
Kastanas H (2013) Article 9. In: Sisilianos LA (ed) European Convention on Human Rights, Interpretation by Article. Nomiki Vivliothiki, Athens, pp 363–393. (in Greek)
Kekes J (1996) The Morality of Pluralism. Princeton University Press, New Jersey
Kerikmäe T (ed) (2014) Protecting human rights in the EU: controversies and challenges of the Charter of Fundamental Rights. Springer, Heidelberg
Kim SY (2021) Les vulnérables: evaluating the vulnerability criterion in Article 14 cases by the European Court of Human Rights. Legal Studies 41(4):617–632
Kostakopoulou D (2010) Introduction. In: van Oers R, Ersbøll E, Kostakopoulou D (eds) A Re-definition of Belonging?, Language and Integration Tests in Europe. Martinus Nijhoff Publishers, Leiden, Boston, pp 1–23
Kovács P (2016) Indigenous Issues under the European Convention of Human Rights, reflected in an Inter-American Mirror. The George Washington International Law Review 48(4):781–806
Ktistakis G *(2021) Article 9*. In: Sarmas I, Kontiadis X, Anthopoulos C (eds) ECHR, Interpretation by Article. Sakkoulas, Athes – Thessaloniki, pp 533–561. (in Greek)
Kuhn PY (2019) Reforming the Approach to Racial and Religious Hate Speech Under Article 10 of the European Convention on Human Rights. Human Rights Law Review 19:119–147
Kukathas C (1992) Are there any Cultural Rights? Political Theory 20(1):105–139
Kukathas C (2003) The Liberal Archipelago: A Theory of Diversity and Freedom. Oxford University Press, New York
Kymlicka W (1989) *Liberalism, Community, and Culture*. Oxford University Press, Oxford
Kymlicka W (1995) *Multicultural Citizenship: A Liberal Theory of Minority Rights*. Oxford University Press, Oxford
Kymlicka W (2001) *Politics in the Vernacular: Nationalism, Multiculturalism, and Citizenship*. Oxford University Press, Oxford
Lajeunesse S (2025) Cultural Rights in Motion: Legal Invisibility, Forced Migration, and the Limits of Universality. Social and Legal Studies 34:1–20
Lamačková A (2008) Conscientious Objection in Reproductive Health Care: Analysis of Pichon and Sajous v. France. European Journal of Health Law 15(1):7–43
Langlaude S (2006) Indoctrination, Secularism, Religious Liberty, and the ECHR. International and Comparative Law Quarterly 55(4):929–944
Lenzerini F (2014) The Culturalization of Human Rights Law. Oxford University Press, Oxford, New York
Lenzerini F (2016) Cultural Identity, Human Rights, and Repatriation of Cultural Heritage of Indigenous Peoples. The Brown Journal of World Affairs 23(1):127–141
Letsas G (2016) The ECHR as a Living Instrument: Its Meaning and its Legitimacy. In: Føllesdal A, Wilhelms W, Ulfstein G (eds) *Constituting Europe* The *European Court of Human Rights in a National*, European and Global Context. Cambridge University Press, Cambridge, pp 106–141
Levy TJ (2000) The Multiculturalism of Fear. Oxford University Press, Oxford

Luban D (2007) Legal Ethics and Human Dignity. Cambridge University Press, Cambridge
Lund CC (2011) In Defense of the Ministerial Exception. North Carolina Law Review 90:1–72
Mahajan G (2005) Can intra-group equality co-exist with cultural diversity? Re-examining multicultural frameworks of accommodation. In: Eisenberg A, Spinner-Halev J (eds) Minorities within Minorities: Equality, Rights and Diversity. Cambridge University Press, Cambridge, pp 90–112
Mancini S, de Witte B (2008) Language Rights as Cultural Rights: A European Perspective. In: Francioni F, Scheinin M (eds) Cultural Human Rights. Martinus Nijhoff Publishers, Leiden, Boston, pp 247–284
Marks SP (2003) Defining Cultural Rights. In: Iin Bergsmo M (ed) Human Rights and Criminal Justice for the Downtrodden – Essays in honour of Asbjorn Eide. Martinus Nijhoff Publishers, The Hague, pp 293–324
McCrea R (2014) Religion in the Workplace: Eweida and Others v United Kingdom. The Modern Law Review 77:277–291
McCrudden C (2003) The New Concept of Equality, Academy of European Law, Trier pp. 2–24, http://www.era-comm.eu/oldoku/Adiskri/02_Key_concepts/2003_McCrudden_EN.pdf
McGoldrick D (2016) A defence of the margin of appreciation and an argument for its application by the human rights committee. International and Comparative Law Quarterly 65(1):21–60
McKean W (1983) Equality and discrimination under international law. Clarenden Press, Oxford
Medda-Windischer R (2021) Religious and Linguistic Minorities and the European Court of Human Rights: Between Restrictive Measures and Concerted Solutions. Europa Ethnica 78(1–2):36–47
Meyer-Bisch P (1993a) Les droits culturels forment-ils une catégorie spécifique de droits de l'homme? In: Meyer-Bisch P (ed) Les droits culturels, une catégorie sous développée de droits de l'homme. Editions universitaires, Fribourg, pp 17–43
Meyer-Bisch P (ed) (1993b) Les droits culturels, une catégorie sous développée de droits de l'homme. Editions universitaires, Fribourg
Millet FX (2015) Case Comment: When the European Court of Human Rights Encounters the Face: A Case Note on the Burqa Ban in France. ECL Review 11(2):408–424
Naskou Perraki P (1999) The case law of the European Court of Human Rights on the protection of religious freedom in Greece. EEEurD:785–814. (in Greek)
Naskou Perraki P (2006) Religious Freedom. In: Naskou-Perraki P, Kistakis G (eds) Greek Cases in Strasbourg, Volume I, 1991-2001. Ant. N. Sakkoulas, Thessaloniki, pp 321–353. (in Greek)
Naskou Perraki P, Tzivaras I (2021) The Right to Education. Sakkoulas, Athens-Thessaloniki (in Greek)
Nieuwenhuis A (2000) Freedom of speech: USA vs Germany and Europe. Netherlands Quarterly of Human Rights 18(2):195–214
Nugraha IY, Regules JM, Vrancken M (2022) Vavřička and Others v. The Czech Republic. American Journal of International Law 116(3):579–585. https://doi.org/10.1017/ajil.2022.36
Nyman-Metcalfin K (2014) The Future of Universality of Rights. In: Kerikmäe T (ed) Protecting human rights in the EU: controversies and challenges of the Charter of Fundamental Rights. Springer, Heidelberg, pp 21–35
Riagáin Ó (2001) Many Tongues but One Voice: a Personal Overview of the Role of the European Bureau for Lesser Used Languages in Promoting Europe's Regional and Minority Languages. In: O'Reilly C (ed) Language, Ethnicity and the State. Palgrave, New York, pp 20–39
Okin SM (1999) Is Multiculturalism Bad for Women? Princeton University Press, New Jersey
OSCE (2022) Hate Crime Laws: A Practical Guide, 2nd edn. OSCE. Office for Democratic Institutions and Human Rights (ODIHR), Warsaw. https://www.osce.org/files/f/documents/1/4/523940.pdf
Ostrovsky AA (2005) How the Margin of Appreciation Doctrine Preserves Core Human Rights within Cultural Diversity and Legitimises International Human Rights Tribunals. Hanse Law Review 1(1):47–64

Otis G, Laurent A (2013) Indigenous land claims in Europe: The European Court of Human Rights and the decolonization of property. Arctic Review on Law and Politics 4(2):156–180

Ouald Chaib S (2012) Religious accomodation in the workplace: improving the legal reasoning of the European court of human rights. In: Alidadi K, Foblets MC, Vrielink J (eds) A test of faith? Ashgate, Religious diversity and accommodation in the European workplace, pp 33–58

Pagotto T (2017) The Ban on Face Covering and the "Living Together" Principle: The Strasbourg Court's New Social Justification for Restricting Religious Freedom. Studia z Prawa Wyznaniowego 20:7–28. p. 11–19.

Panagiotidis NM (2005) Rights and Minorities. Grafis, Alexandroupoli (in Greek)

Panagopoulou Koutnatzi F (2021) Article 8. In: Sarmas I, Kontiadis X, Anthopoulos C (eds) ECHR, Interpretation by Article. Sakkoulas, Athes – Thessaloniki, pp 423–463. (in Greek)

Papadopoulou L (2010) Trapped in history: Greek Muslim Women under the Sacred Islamic Law, Annuaire International des Droits de l'homme (AIDH), Vol. V, 2010, Religions et droits de l' home. Ant. N. Sakkoulas / Bruylant, Athens, Bruxelles, pp 397–418

Papaioannou M (2013) The protection of cultural property in Public International Law, in search of the human dimension, Doctoral Dissertation, Panteion University, Department of International and European Studies, Athens (in Greek)

Papapolychroniou S (2008) Interpretative pluralism as a condition for inclusion of minority values in law: the example of religious minorities in Greece and the "dominant" religion. In: Christopoulos D (ed) The unrecognized issue of minorities in the Greek legal order. Minority Groups Research Center, Kritiki Publications, Athens, pp 89–126. (in Greek)

Pararas PI (2011) *Constitutional culture* and human *rights*. Ant. Sakkoulas, Athens - Komotini (in Greek)

Patten A, Kymlicka W (2003) Language Rights and Political Theory. Oxford University Press, Oxford

Paul K (2019) Lachiri v Belgium and Bans on Wearing Islamic Dress in the Courtroom: An Emerging Trend. Ecclesiastical Law Journal 21(48–53):49–52

Pech L (2009) The Law of Holocaust Denial in Europe: Towards a (qualified) EU-wide Criminal Prohibition, Jean Monnet Working Paper 10/09, NYU School of Law, pp. 1–53. http://www.jeanmonnetprogram.org/papers/09/091001.pdf

Pegorier C (2018) Speech and Harm: Genocide Denial, Hate Speech and Freedom of Expression, International. Criminal Law Review 18(1):97–126

Pentassuglia G (2011) Towards a Jurisprudential Articulation of Indigenous Land Rights. European Journal of International Law 22(1):165–202

Peroni L (2012) Erasing Q, W and X, erasing cultural differences. In: Brems E (ed) Diversity and European Human Rights: Rewriting Judgments of the ECHR. Cambridge University Press, Cambridge, pp 445–469

Peroni L (2014) The European Court of Human Rights and Intragroup Religious Diversity: A Critical Review. Chi.-Kent. L. Rev:663–687

Peršak N (2022) Criminalising Hate Crime and Hate Speech at EU Level: Extending the List of Eurocrimes Under Article 83(1) TFEU. Criminal Law Forum 33(2):85–119

Petty AR (2016) Religion, Conscience, and Belief in the European Court of Human Rights, 48, vol 802. George Washington International Law Review, pp 807–893

Pierce AJ (2012) Collective Identity, Oppression, and the Right to Self-Ascription. Lexington Books, United Kingdom

Pietrobon A (2020) State Negationism and the Rule of Law. In: Gattini A, Garciandia R, Webb P (eds) Human Dignity and International Law. Brill, Leiden, pp 164–174

Pikramenos MN (2019) What does it mean that I can freely develop my personality? (in Greek). https://www.syntagmawatch.gr/my-constitution/ti-simainei-oti-boro-na- anaptyxo-elefthera-tin-prosopikotita-mou/

Pitt G (2007) Religion or belief: aiming at the right target. In: Meenan H (ed) Equality Law in an Enlarged European Union. Cambridge University Press, Cambridge New York, pp 202–230

Pollis A (1999) Greece: A Problematic Secular State. In: Tsitselikis K, Christopoulos D (eds) Legal Issues of Religious Otherness in Greece, Center for Research on Minority Groups. Ed. Kritiki & KEMO, Athens, pp 165–197. (in Greek)

Prevedourou E (2021) Article 14. In: Sarmas I, Kontiadis X, Anthopoulos C (eds) ECHR, Interpretation by Article. Sakkoulas, Athes – Thessaloniki, pp 720–764. (in Greek)

Prott L (2002) Individual or Collective Rights for Cultural Heritage in the Information Society? Museum International, Heritage issues in the information society 2 LIV(4):7–12

Ringelheim J (2010) Minority Rights in a Time of Multiculturalism—The Evolving Scope of the Framework Convention on the Protection of National Minorities. Human Rights Law Review 10(1):99–128. https://doi.org/10.1093/hrlr/ngp038

Ringelheim J (2012) Chapman redux: The European Court of Human Rights and Roma traditional lifestyle. In: Brems E (ed) Diversity and European Human Rights: Rewriting Judgments of the ECHR. Cambridge University Press, Cambridge, pp 426–444

Ringelheim J (2018) Lachiri v Belgium: Headscarf Ban Imposed on a Civil Party in a Courtroom in Violation of Religious Freedom. Strasbourg Observers, 23 November 2018. https://strasbourgobservers.com/2018/11/23/lachiri-v-belgium-headscarf-ban-imposed-on-a-civil-party-in-a-courtroom-in-violation-of-religious-freedom/

Roberts CK (2020) The Negative Aspect of the Freedom to Manifest Religion or Belief in the Educational Context in Greece. Oxford Journal of Law and Religion 9(1):208–211

Rokša Zubčevič A, Bender S, Vojvodid J (2017) Media regulatory authorities and hate speech. Council of Europe. https://edoc.coe.int/en/media/7431-media-rgulatory-authorities-and-hate-speech.html

Romainville C (2014) Cultural diversity as a multilevel and multifaceted legal notion operating in the law on cultural policies. International Journal of Cultural Policy 22(2):273–290

Rorive I (2006) Religious Symbols in the Public Space: In Search of a European Answer. Cardozo Law Review 30:2669–2698

Roy O, Annicchino P (2013) Human Rights between Religions, Cultures, and Universality. In: Vrdoljak AF (ed) The Cultural Dimension of Human Rights. Oxford University Press, Oxford, pp 7–25

Ruiz Vieytez E (2012) Minority marriage and discrimination: Redrafting Muñoz Díaz v. Spain. In: Brems E (ed) Diversity and European Human Rights: Rewriting Judgments of the ECHR. Cambridge University Press, Cambridge, pp 401–425

Ruiz Vieytez E (2024) Religious diversity, minorities and human rights: gaps and overlaps in legal protection. Religions 15(1). https://doi.org/10.3390/REL15010087

Sajó A, Uitz R (2020) Individual religious freedom under the European Convention of Human Rights. In: Mancini S (ed) Constitutions and Religion. Edward Elgar Publishing, pp 286–306

Seglow J (2011) Theories of Religious Exemptions. In: Calder G, Ceva E (eds) Diversity of Europe, Dilemmas of differential treatment in theory and practice. Routledge, London, pp 52–64

Shelton D (2016) On Identity. George Washington International Law Review 49(1):1–18

Silverman H, Ruggles F (2007) Cultural Heritage and Human Rights. In: Silverman H, Ruggles F (eds) Cultural Heritage and Human Rights. Springer, USA, pp 5–22

Stamatopoulou E (2006) Cultural rights and contemporary realities: the right to participate in cultural life. Armenopoulos 9:1391–1041. (in Greek)

Stamatopoulou E (2007) Cultural Rights in International Law, Article 27 of the Universal Declaration of Human Rights and Beyond. Martinus Nijhoff Publishers, Leiden

Stavrinaki T (2013) First Protocol, Article 2. In: Sicilianos LA (ed) European Convention on Human Rights, Interpretation by Article. Nomiki Vivliothiki, Athens, pp 693–706. (in Greek)

Stavrinaki T (2017) Article 10. In: Sisilianos LA (ed) European Convention on Human Rights, Interpretation by Article. Nomiki Vivliothiki, pp 475–518. (in Greek)

Steinbach A (2015) Burqas and Bans: The Wearing of Religious Symbols under the European Convention of Human Rights. Cambridge Journal of International and Comparative Law 4(1):29–52

Strasbourg Observers academic blog (2013) Mann Singh wins turban case in Geneva after losing in Strasbourg https://strasbourgobservers.com/2013/11/19/mann-singh-wins-in-geneva-after-losing-in-strasbourg/
Stratilatis C (2014) On the distinction between statements of fact and value judgments: A comment on Petrenco v. Moldova. Annuaire International des Droits de l'Homme VIII:725–749
Swiebel J (2009) The European Union's Policies to Safeguard and Promote Diversity. In: Prügl E, Thiel M (eds) Diversity in the European Union. Palgrave Macmillan, London, pp 21–36
Tamimi Y (2018) Human Rights and the Excess of Identity: Legal and Theoretical Inquiry into the Notion of Identity in Strasbourgh Case Law. Social & Legal Studies 27(3):283–298
Tavernier P (1994) Minorités et facteur de tensions en Europe. In: Grigoriou P (ed) Questions de minorités en Europe. Presses Interuniversitaires Européennes, Bruxelles, pp 17–33
Telalian M (2002) European Framework Convention for the Protection of National Minorities and its personal scope of application. In: Affredsson G, Stavropoulou M (eds) Justice Pending: Indigenous Peoples and Other Good Causes, Essays in Honour of Erica-Irene A. Daes. Martinus Nijhoff Publishers, The Hague, pp 117–136
Téson F (1985) International Human Rights and Cultural Relativism. Virginia Journal of International Law 25:869–898
Thornberry P (2002) Treatment of minority and indigenous issues in the European Convention on Human Rights. In: Affredsson G, Stavropoulou M (eds) Justice Pending: Indigenous Peoples and Other Good Causes, Essays in Honour of Erica-Irene A. Daes. Martinous Nijhoff Publishers, The Hague, pp 137–168
Topidi K (2021) Religious Minority Identity in the Work of the Advisory Committee of the Framework Convention for the Protection of National Minorities: A Multifaceted Challenge in Evolution. Religions 12:1–18
Torbisco-Casals N (2016) Multiculturalism, Identity Claims, and Human Rights: From Politics to Courts. The Law & Ethics of Human Rights. 10(2):367–404
Tridimas T (2006) The General Principles of EU Law, 2nd edn. Oxford University Press, Oxford
Tridimas T (2022) The General Principles of EU Law, 3rd edn. Oxford University Press, Oxford
Trispiotis I (2016) Two interpretations of "living together" in European human rights law. The Cambridge Law Journal 75(3):580–607
Trispiotis I (2019) Islamophobia as a Key Contextual Factor in Human Rights Adjudication. In: Law I, Easat-Daas A, Merali A, Sayyid S (eds) Countering, Islamophobia in Europe. Palgrave Macmillan, pp 9–31
Tsevrenis VK (2012) Human dignity. Sakkoula Publications, Athens-Thessaloniki (in Greek)
Tsitselikis K (1996a) Minority Languages and "Minoritization", the law as a regulatory factor. In: Glossas KE (ed) "Strong" – "Weak" languages in the European Union - Aspects of Linguistic Hegemony - Proceedings of the Conference, pp 213–224. (in Greek)
Tsitselikis K (1996b) The international and European regime for the protection of the linguistic rights of minorities and the Greek legal order. Sakkoulas, Athens. (in Greek)
Tsitselikis K (2012) Old and New Islam in Greece From Historical Minorities to Immigrant Newcomers. Martinus Nijhoff Publishers, Leiden
Tsolakou Th (2010) Commentary on the ECtHR decision of 11.10.2007, Bekir Ousta and others v. Greece, Aristovoulos Manesis Group, pp. 1–12, (in Greek). http://constitutionalism.gr/site/wp-content/mgdata/pdf/9tsolakoubekir2752010.pdf
Vagias M (2019) Freedom of thought, conscience and religion. In: Naskou Perraki P, Human Rights, International and Regional Protection. Sakkoulas, Athens, pp 493–501. (in Greek)
Venice Commission (2010) Blasphemy, insult and hatred: finding answers in a democratic society, Science and technique of democracy, No. 47. Council of Europe Publishing, Strasbourg
Vertovec S, Wessendorf S (2006) Cultural, religious and linguistic diversity in Europe: An overview of issues and trends. In: Penninx R, Berger M, Kraal K (eds) *The Dynamics of International Migration and Settlement in Europe*. University of Amsterdam Press, Amsterdam

von Bogdandy A (2008) The European Union as Situation, Executive, and Promoter of the International Law of Cultural Diversity – Elements of a Beautiful Friendship. The European Journal of International Law 19(2):241–275
Vrdoljak AF (2011) Cultural Heritage in Human Rights and Humanitarian Law. In: Ben-Naftali O (ed) International Human Rights and Humanitarian Law. Oxford University Press, Oxford, pp 250–302
Weiler JHH (2009) Fundamental Rights and Fundamental Boundaries: Common Standards and Conflicting Values in the Protection of Human Rights in the European Legal Space. In: Kastoryano R (ed) An Identity for Europe, The Sciences Po Series in International Relations and Political Economy. Palgrave Macmillan, New York, pp 73–101
Wolff T (2021) True Believers? – Sincerity and Article 9 of the European Convention on Human Rights. European Constitutional Law Review 17(2):259–286
Xanthaki A (2010) Multiculturalism and International Law: Discussing Universal Standards. Human Rights Quartely 32(1):21–48
Yea-Wen C, Hengjun L (2016) Cultural Identities. Oxford Research Encyclopedias:1–25. https://doi.org/10.1093/acrefore/9780190228613.013.20
Yusuf HO (2014) S.A.S. v France: Supporting "living Together" or Forced Assimilation. International. Human Rights Law Review 3(2):277–302
Yves Kuhn P (2019) Reforming the Approach to Racial and Religious Hate Speech Under Article 10 of the European Convention on Human Rights. Human Rights Law Review 19:119–147
Zaręba S (2025) The Getty Trust Case: Human Rights, Property Issues, and Cultural Heritage Protection. Santander Art and Culture Law Review:207–222
Zechenter EM (1997) In the Name of Culture: Cultural Relativism and the Abuse of the Individual. Journal of Anthropological Research 53(3):319–347

Case Law

Case law of the European Court of Human Rights

Belgian Linguistic Case (Case relating to certain aspects of the laws on the use of languages in education in Belgium), Application Nos. 1474/62, 1677/62, 1691/62, 1769/63, 1994/63, 2126/64, 23 July 1968
ECHR, A.M. and Others v. Russia, Application no. 47220/19, 6 July 2021
ECHR, Abdu v Bulgaria, Application no. 26827/08, 11 March 2014
ECHR, Ádám and Others v. Romania, Application No. 81114/17, 13 October 2020
ECHR, Ahmad v. The United Kingdom (1982) 4 EHRR 126
ECHR, Ahmet Arslan and Others v. Turkey, Application no. 41135/98, 23 February 2010
ECHR, Aksu v. Turkey, Applications Nos. 4149/04 and 41029/04, 15 March 2012
ECHR, Aktas v. France, Application No. 43563/08, 30 June 2009
ECHR, Alekseyev v. Russia, *Application No.* 4916/07, 21 October 2010
ECHR, Alujer Fernández and Caballero García v. Spain, Application no. 53072/99, 14 June 2001
ECHR, Angelini v. Sweden, Application No. 10491/83, December 3, 1986
ECHR, *Angelova and Iliev v. Bulgaria,* Application No. 44862/04, 26 July 2007
ECHR, Antayev and others v Russia, Application no. 37966/07, 3 July 2014
ECHR, Appel-Irrgang v. Germany, Application No. 45216/07, 6 October 2009
ECHR, Arrowsmith v. United Kingdom, Application No. 7050/75, Comm. Rep. 1978

ECHR, Assenov and Others v. Bulgaria, Application no. 90/1997/874/1086, 28 October 1998
ECHR, Association Les Témoins de Jéhovah v. France, Application no. 8916/05, 30 June 2011
ECHR, avezcrkava "Riječživota" and Others v. Croatia, Application no. 7798/08, 9 December 2010
ECHR, B.S. v. Spain, Application no. 47159/08, 24 July 2012
ECHR, Basu v. Germany, Application no. 215/19, 18 October 2022
ECHR, Baylac-Ferrer and Suarez v. France, Application No. 27977/04, 25 September 2008
ECHR, Bayrak v. France, Application no. 14308/08, 30 June 2009
ECHR, Beard v. the United Kingdom, Application No. 24882/94, 18 January 2001
ECHR, Begheluri and others v Georgia, Application no. 28490/02, 7 October 2014
ECHR, Bekir-Ousta and others v. Greece, Application No. 35151/05, 11 October 2007
ECHR, Belcacemi and Oussar v. Belgium, Application no. 37798/13, 11 July 2017
ECHR, Beyeler v. Italy, Application no. 33202/96, 5 January 2000
ECHR, Bouton v. France, Application no. 22636/19, 13 October 2022
ECHR, *Bruno v. Sweden,* Application no. 32196/96, 28 August 2001
ECHR, Buckley v. the United Kingdom, Application No. 20348/92, 7 February 1992
ECHR, Bulgakov v. Ukraine, Application No. 59894/00, 11 September 2007
ECHR, Burghartz v. Switzerland, Application No. 16213/90, 22 February 1994
ECHR, Buscarini and Others v. San Marino, Application No. 24645/94, 18 February 1999
ECHR, C.O.G.G. and Others v. Lithuania, Application No. 17764/22 (pending)
ECHR, Campbell and Cosans v. the *United Kingdom*, Application No. 7511/73, 23 March 1983
ECHR, Campell and Cosans v. the United Kingdom, Application No. 7511/76, 7743/76, 25 February 1982
ECHR, Catan and Others v. Moldova and Russia, Application Nos. 43370/04, 8252/05, 18454/06, 19 October 2012
ECHR, Chaa´re Shalom ve Tsedek v. France, Application no. 27417/95, 27 June 2000
ECHR, Chagos Islanders v. United Kingdom, Application No. 35622/04. 11 December 2012
ECHR, Chapman v. the United Kingdom, Application No, 27238/95, 18 January 2001
ECHR, Chassagnou ao v. France, Application No. 25088/94, 29 April 1999
ECHR, Christians Against Racism and Fascism v. the United Kingdom, Application No. 8440/78, 16 July 1980
ECHR, Çiftçi v. Turkey, Application No. 71860/01, 17 June 2004
ECHR, Cisse v. France, Application No. 51346/99, 9 April 2002
ECHR, Ciubotaru v. Moldova, Application no. 27138/04, 27 April 2010
ECHR, Collins and Akaziebie v. Sweden, Application No. 23944/05, 8 March 2007
ECHR, Costello-Roberts v. the *United Kingdom*, Application No. 13134/87, 25 March 1993
ECHR, Coster v. the United Kingdom, Application No. 24876/94, 18 January 2001
ECHR, CW v. the United Kingdom, Application No.18187/91, 10 February 1993
ECHR, Cyprus v. Turkey, Application No. 25781/94, 10 May 2001
ECHR, D. v. France, Application no. 10180/82, 6 December 1983
ECHR, *D.H. and Others v. Czech Republic,* Application No. 57325/00, 13 November 2007
ECHR, Dahlab v. Switzerland, Application no. 42393/98, 15 January 2001
ECHR, Dakir v. Belgium, Application No. 4619/12, 11 July 2017
ECHR, Djavit An v. Turkey, Application No. 20652/92, 20 February 2003
ECHR, Dogru v. France, Application no. 27058/05, 4 December 2008
ECHR, Doğu Perinçek v. Switzerland, Application no. 27510/08, 15 October 2015
ECHR, Ebrahimian v. France, Application No. 64846/11, 26 November 2015
ECHR, Emin and others v. Greece, Application No. 34144/05, 27 March 2008
ECHR, Erbakan v. Turkey, Application no. 59405/00, 6 July 2006
ECHR, Erdagoz v. Turkey, Application No. 21890/93, 22 October 1997
ECHR, ES v. Austria, Application No. 38450/12, 25 October 2018
ECHR, Evans v. the United Kingdom, Application no. 6339/05, 10 April 2007
ECHR, Eweida and Others v. the United Kingdom, Applications nos. 48420/10, 59842/10, 51671/10 and 36516/10 15 January 2013

ECHR, Ezelin v. France, Application No. 11800/85, 26 April 1991
ECHR, Fanrfan Temel and Others v. Turkey, Application No. 36458/02, 3 March 2009
ECHR, Fédération chrétienne des témoins de Jéhova de France v. France, Application no. 53430/99, 6 November 2001.
ECHR, Fener Rum Patrikligi (Ecumenical Patriarchate) v. Turkey, Application no. 75909/01, 15 June 2010
ECHR, Fernández Martínez v. Spain, Requête no 56030/07, 15 mai 2012
ECHR, Folgerø and Others v. Norway, Application No. 15472/02, 29 June 2007
ECHR, G and E v. Norway, *Application no. 9278/81 and 9415/81,* 3 October *1983*
ECHR, Gamaleddyn v. France, Application no. 18527/08, 30 June 2009
ECHR, Garaudy v. France, Application no. 64496/17, 7 July 2003
ECHR, Gatis Kovalkovs v. Latvia, Application no. 35021/05, 31 January 2012
ECHR, Ghazal v. France, Application no. 29134/08, 30 June 2009
ECHR, Giniewski v. France, Application no. 64016/00, 31 January 2006
ECHR, Gjikondi and others v. Greece, Application no. 17249/10, 21 March 2018
ECHR, Goodwin v United Kingdom Application No. 17488/90, 27 March 1996
ECHR, Gorzelik and others v. Poland, Application no. 44158/98, 17 February 2004
ECHR, Gough v. The United Kingdom, Application no. 49327/11, 28 October 2014
ECHR, Griechische Kirchengemeinde München und Bayern eV v. Germany, Application no. 52336/99, 18 September 2007
ECHR, Grimmark v. Sweden, Application no. 43726/17, 11 February 2020.
ECHR, Groppera Radio AG and Others v. Switzerland, *Application No.* 10890/84, 28 March 1990
ECHR, Guillot v. France, Application No. 22500/93, 24 October 1996
ECHR, Gündüz v. Turkey, Application no. 35071/97, 4th December 2003
ECHR, H.W.P. and K. v. Austria, Application no. 12774/87, 12 October 1989
ECHR, Halvar FROM v. Sweden, 4 March 1998 Application No. 34776/97
ECHR, Hamidovic v. Bosnia and Herzegovina, Application No. 57792/15, 5 December 2017
ECHR, Handolsdalen Sami Village and Others v. Sweden, Application No. 39013/04, 30 March 2010
ECHR, Handyside v. The United Kingdom, Application *No.* 5493/72, 7 December 1976
ECHR, Hasan and Chaush v Bulgaria, Application no. 30985/96, 26 October 2000
ECHR, Hasan and Eylem Zengin v. Turkey, Application No. 1448/04, 9 October 2007
ECHR, Hingitaq 53 and Others v. Denmark, *Application no. 18584/04, 12 January 2006*
ECHR, Hizb Ut-Tahrir v. Germany, Application No. 31098/08, 19 July 2012
ECHR, Hoffman v. Austria, Application No. 12875/87, 23 June 1993
ECHR, Holy Synod of the Bulgarian Orthodox Church (Metropolitan Inokentiy) and Others v. *Bulgaria,* Application nos. 412/03 and 35677/04, 22 January 2009
ECHR, I.A. v. Turkey, Application no. 42571/98, 13 September 2005
ECHR, Incal v. Turkey, Application No. 22678/93, 9 June 1998
ECHR, Inhabitants of Alsemberg and Beersel v. Belgium, Application No. 1474/62, 26 July 1963
ECHR, Izzettin Dogan and Others v. Turkey, Application no. 62649/10, 26 April 2016
ECHR, J. Singh v. France, Application no. 25463/08, 30 June 2009
ECHR, Jabari v. Turkey, Application No. 40035/98, 11 July 2000
ECHR, Jacobski v. Poland, Application no. 18429/06, 7 March 2011
ECHR, Jane Smith v. the United Kingdom, Application No. 25154/94, 18 January 2001
ECHR, Jersild v.Denmark, Application No. 15890/89, 23 September 1994
ECHR, Johtti Sapmelaccat R Y and Others v. Finland, Application no. 42969/98, 18 January 2005
ECHR, Jones v. the United Kingdom, Application no. 42639/04, 13 September 2005
ECHR, *Juma Mosque Congregation and others v.* Azerbaijan, Application no. 15405/04, 8 January 2013
ECHR, Kamasinski v. Austria, Application No. 9783/82, 19 December 1989
ECHR, Karlsson v. Sweden, Application no. 12356/86, 8 September 1988

ECHR, Karlsson v. Sweden, Application no. 12356/86, decision of the Commission, 8 September 1988
ECHR, Kemal Taşkın and Others v. Turkey, Application Nos. 30206/04, 37038/04, 43681/04, 45376/04, 12881/05, 28697/05, 32797/05, 45609/05, 2 February 2010
ECHR, Kjeldsen, Busk Madsen and Pedersen v. Denmark, Application nos. 5095/71; 5920/72; 5926/72, 7 December 1976
ECHR, *Kokkinakis v. Greece,* Application no. 14307/88, 25 May 1993
ECHR, Könkämä and 38 Other Sami Villages v. Sweden, Application no. 27033/95, 25 November 1996
ECHR, Kosteski v. Former Yugoslav Republic of Macedonia, Application No. 55170/00, 13 July 2006
ECHR, Kovačević v. Bosnia and Herzegovina, Application No. 17764/22 (pending)
ECHR, Lachiri v. Belgium, Application no. 3413/09, 18 September 2018
ECHR, *Larrisis and Others v. Greece,* Application No s. 23372/94; 26377/94; 26378/94, 24 February 1998
ECHR, Lautsi and Others v. Italy, Application No. 30814/06, 18 March 2011
ECHR, Lavida and Others v. Greece, Application no. 7973/10, 30 May 2013
ECHR, Le Mailloux v. France, Application no. 18108/20, 5 November 2020
ECHR, Lee v. the United Kingdom, Application No. 25289/94, 18 January 2001
ECHR, Leela Förderkreis e.V. and Others v. Germany, Application No. 58911/00, 6 November 2008
ECHR, Lehideux and Isorni v. France, Application No. 24662/94, 23 September 1998
ECHR, Leyla Şahin v. Turkey, Application no. 44774/98, 10 November 2005
ECHR, Lidija Kuharec alias Kuhareca v. Latvia, Application No. 71557/01, 7 December 2004
ECHR, Ligue des Musulmans de Suisse and Others v. Switzerland, Application no. 66274/09, 8 July 2011
ECHR, Lombardi Vallauri v. Italy Application no. 39128/05, 20 October 2010
ECHR, Mann Singh v. France Application no. 24479/07, 13 November 2008
ECHR, Manoussakis and others v. Greece, Application no. 18748/91, 26 September 1996
ECHR, Mehmet Nuri Ozen and Others v. Turkey, Application Nos. 15672/08, 24462/08, 27559/08, 28302/08, 28312/08, 34823/08, 40738/08, 41124/08, 43197/08, 51938/08 and 58170/08, 11 January 2011
ECHR, Members of the Gldani Congregation of the Jehovah's Witnesses and Others v. Georgia, Application No. 71156/01, 3 May 2007
ECHR, Mentzen v. Latvia Application No. 71074/01, 7 December 2004
ECHR, *Metropolitan Church Of Bessarabia And Others* v. *Moldova,* Application no. 45701/99, 27 February 2002
ECHR, Mikulic' v. Croatia, Application No. 53176/99, 7 February 2002
ECHR, Mikyas and Others v. Belgium, Application no. 50681/20, 9 April 2024
ECHR, Milanović v. Serbia, Application no. 44614/07, 14 December 2010
ECHR, Molla Sali v. Greece, Application no. 20452/14, 19 December 2018
ECHR, Muhammad v. Spain, Application no. 34085/17, 18 October 2022
ECHR, Muñoz Díaz v. Spain, Application no. 49151/07, 8 December 2009
ECHR, Nachova and others v, Bulgaria, Application nos. 43577/98 and 43579/98, 6 July 2005
ECHR, Nationaldemokratische Partei Deutschlands v. Germany, Application No. 25992/94, 29 November 1989
ECHR, Norwood v. the United Kingdom, Application no. 23131/03, 16 November 2004
ECHR, Obst v. Germany, Application no. 425/03, 23 September 2010
ECHR, Omeredo v. Austria, Application No. 8969/10, 20 September 2011
ECHR, Oršuš and Others v. Croatia, Application no. 15766/03, 16 March 2010
ECHR, Osmanoğlu and Kocabaş v. Switzerland, Application No. 29086/12, 10 January 2017
ECHR, Otto-Preminger-Institut v. Austria, Application no. 13470/87, 20 September 1994
ECHR, Ouardiri v. Switzerland, Application no. 65840/09 28 June 2011
ECHR, Ouranio Toxo and others v. Greece, Application No. 74989/01, 20 October 2005

ECHR, Papageorgiou and Others v. Greece, Applications nos. 4762/18 and 6140/18, 31 October 2019

ECHR, Pavel Ivanov v. Russia, Application no. 35222/04, 20 February 2007

ECHR, Peringek v. Switzerland, Application No. 27510/08, 15 October 2015

ECHR, Philip Williamson and Others v. the United Kingdom, Application No. 55211/00, September 2000

ECHR, Pichon and Sajous v. France, Application no. 49853/99, 2 October 2001

ECHR, Podkolzina v. Latvia, Application N o. 46726/99, 9 April 2002

ECHR, *Pretty v. the United Kingdom,* Application *No.* 2346/02, 29 July 2002

ECHR, Putistin v. Ukraine, Application No. 16882/03, 21 November 2013

ECHR, R. Singh v. France, Application no. 27561/08, 30 June 2009

ECHR, Raëlien Suisse v. Switzerland, Application no. 16354/06, 13 July 2012

ECHR, Refah Partisi (Prosperity Party) and Others v.Turkey, Applications nos. 41340/98, 41342/98, 41343/98 and 41344/98, 13 February 2003

ECHR, Religionsgemeinschaft der Zeugen Jehovahs and Others v. Austria, Application no. 40825/98, 31 July 2008

ECHR, *Rommelfanger v* the Federal Republic of Germany, Application No. 12242/86, 6 September 1989

ECHR, S.A.S. v. France, Application no. 43835/11, 1 July 2014

ECHR, Sagir and Others v. Greece, Application no. 34724/18, 24 June 2025

ECHR, Sakir v. Greece, Application no. 48475/09, 24 May 2016

ECHR, Sampanis and Others v. Greece, Application No. 32526/05, 5 June 2008

ECHR, Sampanis and others v. Greece, Application no. 59608/09, 11 December 2012

ECHR, Schüth v. Germany, Application no.1620/03, 23 September 2010

ECHR, Sejdić and Finci v.Bosnia and Herzegovina, Application nos. 27996/06 and 34836/06, 22 December 2009

ECHR, Sekmadienis Ltd. v. Lithuania Application no. 69317/14, 31 January 2018

ECHR, Serif v. Greece, Application no. 38178/97, 14 December 1999

ECHR, Seven Individuals v. Sweden, Application No. 8811/79, 13 May 1982

ECHR, Sidiropoulos and others v. Greece, Application No. 26695/95, 10 July 1998

ECHR, Šimunić v. Croatia, Application No. 20373/17, 22 January 2019

ECHR, Soulas and Others v. France, Application no. 15948/03, 10 July 2008

ECHR, Spetz and Others v. Sweden, Application no. 20402/92, 12 October 1994

ECHR, Spetz and Others v. Sweden, Application no. 20402/92, decision of the Commission of 12 October 1994

ECHR, Stankov and the United Macedonian Organization Ilinden v. Bulgaria, Application nos. 29221/95 and 29225/95

ECHR, Stec and Others v. the United Kingdom, Applications nos. 65731/01 and 65900/01, *12 April 2006*

ECHR, Steen v. Sweden, Application no. 62309/17, 11 February 2020

ECHR, Stjerna v. Finland, Application No. 18131/91, 25 November 1994

ECHR, *Stoica v. Romania*, Application No. 42722/02, 4 March 2008

ECHR, Sud Fondi Srl v. Italy, Application no. 75909/01, 20 January 2009

ECHR, Supreme Holy Council of the Muslim Community v. Bulgaria, Application no. 39023/97, 16 March 2005

ECHR, Svyato - Mykhaylivska Parafiya v. Ukraine, Application No. 77703/01, 14 June 2007

ECHR, Tagiyev and Huseynov v. Azerbaijan, Application no. 13274/08, 5 December 2019

ECHR, Tagiyeva v. Azerbaijan, Application no. 31613/12, 7 July 2022

ECHR, Taştan v. Turkey, Application no. 63748/00, 4 March 2008

ECHR, The J. Paul Getty Trust and Others v. Italy, Application no. 35271/19, 2 May 2024

ECHR, The Muonio Saami Village v. Sweden, Application no. 28222/95, 15 February 2000

ECHR, The United Communist Party of Turkey and Others v. Turkey, Application No. 19392/92, 30 January 1998

ECHR, The *United Macedonian Organization Ilinden – PIRIN and Others v. Bulgaria,* Application no. 59489/00, 20 October 2005
ECHR, The United Macedonian Organization Ilinden and Others v. Bulgaria, Application no. 59491/00, 9 September 2004
ECHR, Thlimmenos v. Greece, Application No. 34369/97, 6 April 2000
ECHR, Timishev v. Russia, Applications nos. 55762/00 and 55974/00, 13 December 2005
ECHR, Tothpal and Szabo v. Romania, Application nos. 28617/13 and 50919/13, 19 February 2019
ECHR, Tourkiki Enosi Xanthis and others v. Greece, Application No. 26698/05, 27 March 2008
ECHR, Tyrer v. the *United Kingdom*, Application No. 5856/72, 25 April 1978
ECHR, Ülke v. Turkey, Application no. 39437/98, 24 January 2006
ECHR, Ulusoy and Others v.Turkey Application No. 34797/03, 3 May 2007
ECHR, Valsamis v. Greece, Application no. 21787/93, 18 December 1996
ECHR, Vartic v. Romania, Application no. 14150/08, 7 January 2014
ECHR, Vavřička and Others v. the Czech Republic, Applications nos. 47621/13 and 5 others, 8 April 2021
ECHR, Vereinigung Bildender Künstler v. Austria, Application no. 68354/01, 25 January 2007
ECHR, Vona v. Hungary, Application no. 35943/10, 9 July 2013
ECHR, W v. The United Kingdom, Application No. 11095/84, 7 March 1989
ECHR, Wa Baile c. Suisse, Requêtes nos 43868/18 et 25883/21, 20 février 2024
ECHR, Williamson v. the United Kingdom, Application no. 27008/95, decision of the Commission of 17 May 1995
ECHR, Wingrove v. the United Kingdom, Application no. 17419/90, 25 November 1996
ECHR, X v. Austria, Application No. 8142/1978, 10 October 1979
ECHR, X. v the United Kingdom, Application no. 8160/78, 12 March 1981
ECHR, X. v. the United Kingdom, Application no. 5270/72, 20 December 1974
ECHR, X. v. the United Kingdom, Application no. 7215/75, November 5, 1981
ECHR, Yordanova and Others v. Bulgaria, Application No. 25446/06, 24 April 2012
ECHR, *Young, James & Webster v. United Kingdom, Application No. 7601/76,* 13 August 1981

Case Law of the Court of the European Union

Judgment of the Court of 17 December 1970, Internationale Handelsgesellschaft mbH v Einfuhr- und Vorratsstelle für Getreide und Futtermittel, Case 11-70, ECLI:EU:C:1970:114
Judgment of the Court of 28 October 1975, Roland Rutili v Ministre de l'intérieur, Case 36-75, ECLI:EU:C:1975:137
Judgment of the Court (First Chamber) of 14 October 2004, Omega Spielhallen- und Automatenaufstellungs - GmbH v Oberbürgermeisterin der Bundesstadt Bonn, C-36/02, ECLI:EU:C:2004:614
Judgment of the Court (First Chamber) of 27 January 2005, Europe Chemi-Con (Deutschland) GmbH v Council of the European Union, C-422/02 P, ECLI:EU:C:2005:56
Judgment of the Court (Second Chamber) of 10 July 2008, Centrum voor gelijkheid van kansen en voor racismebestrijding v Firma Feryn NV, C-54/07, ECLI:EU:C:2008:397
Judgment of the Court (Grand Chamber) of 16 July 2015, "CHEZ Razpredelenie Bulgaria" AD v Komisia za zashtita ot diskriminatsia, C-83/14, ECLI:EU:C:2015:480
Judgment of the Court (Grand Chamber) of 14 March 2017, Samira Achbita and Centrum voor gelijkheid van kansen en voor racismebestrijding v G4S Secure Solutions NV, C-157/15, ECLI:EU:C:2017:203
Judgment of the Court (Grand Chamber) of 15 July 2021, IX v WABE eV and MH Müller Handels GmbH v MJ, Joined Cases C-804/18 and C-341/19, ECLI:EU:C:2021:594

Judgment of the Court (Second Chamber) of 13 October 2022, S.C.R.L. (Vêtement à connotation religieuse), C-344/20, ECLI:EU:C:2022:774
Judgment of the Court (Grand Chamber) of 11 September 2018, IR v JQ, C-68/17, ECLI:EU:C:2018:696

Decisions of the UN Human Rights Committee

(Mann) Singh v. France, HRC, 26/09/2013, CCPR/C/108/D / 1928 /2010
Ahmad v. Inner London Education Authority [1978] QB 38
Bikramjit Singh v France, Communication No. 1852/2008, UN Doc. CCPR/C/106/D/1852/2008
Coeriel et al v. the Netherlands, Communication No. 453/1991, UN Doc. CCPR / C / 52 / D / 453/1991
Ivan Kitok v. Sweden, Communication No. 197/1985, CCPR/C/33/D/197/1985 (1988)
Sandra Lovelace v. Canada, Communication No. 24/1977: Canada 30/07/81, UN Doc. CCPR/C/13/D/24/1977

Case law of the European Commission of Social Rights

ECSR, *Quaker Council for European Affairs v. Greece* (coll. compl. No. 8/2000), 25 April 2001

Reference Texts

Documents of the European Union

Council Directive 2000/43/EC of 29 June 2000 implementing the principle of equal treatment between persons irrespective of racial or ethnic origin, OJ L 180, 19.7.2000, pp. 22–26
Council Directive 2000/78/EC of 27 November 2000 establishing a general framework for equal treatment in employment and occupation, OJ L 303, 2.12.2000, pp. 16–22
Council Directive 2004/113/EC of 13 December 2004 implementing the principle of equal treatment between men and women in the access to and supply of goods and services, OJ L 373, 21.12.2004, pp. 37–43
Council Directive 93/104/EC of 23 November 1993 concerning certain aspects of the organization of working time, OJ L 307, 13.12.1993 p. 18–24
Council Directive 93/119/EC of 22 December 1993 on the protection of animals during their slaughter and/or killing, OJ L 340 of 31.12.1993, pp. 21–34
Council Framework Decision 2008/913/JHA of 28 November 2008 on combating certain forms and expressions of racism and xenophobia by means of criminal law, OJ L 328, 6.12.2008, p. 55–58
Council Regulation (EC) No 1099/2009 of 24 September 2009 on the protection of animals at the time of killing (Text with EEA relevance), OJ L 303, 18.11.2009, p. 1–30
Directive 2004/38/EC of the European Parliament and of the Council of 29 April 2004 on the right of citizens of the Union and their family members to move and reside freely within the territory of the Member States amending Regulation (EEC) No 1612/68 and repealing Directives

64/221/EEC, 68/360/EEC, 72/194/EEC, 73/148/EEC, 75/34/EEC, 75/35/EEC, 90/364/EEC, 90/365/EEC and 93/96/EEC (Text with EEA relevance), OJ L 158, 30.4.2004, p. 77–123
Directive 2006/54/EC of the European Parliament and of the Council of 5 July 2006 on the implementation of the principle of equal opportunities and equal treatment of men and women in matters of employment and occupation (recast), OJ L 204, 26.7.2006, p. 23–36.
European Parliament resolution of 15 January 2013 on development aspects of intellectual property rights in genetic resources: implications for poverty reduction in developing countries (2012/2135(INI))
European Parliament resolution on female genital mutilation (2001/2035(INI))
European Parliament, 29 February 1996, *Resolution on cults in Europe*; and Council of Europe, Parliamentary Assembly, Recommendation 1412, *Illegal activities of sects,* 22 June 1999.
Report from the Commission to the European Parliament and the Council on the implementation of Council Framework Decision 2008/913/JHA on combating certain forms and expressions of racism and xenophobia by means of criminal law, COM(2014)27 final

Documents of the Council of Europe

Advisory Committee on the Framework Convention for the Protection of National Minorities, Commentary on Education under the Framework Convention for the Protection of National Minorities, ACFC/25DOC(2006)002, Strasbourg, 2 March 2006. http://www.coe.int/t/dghl/monitoring/minorities/3_FCNMdocs/PDF_CommentaryEducation_en.pdf
Advisory Committee on the Framework Convention for the Protection of National Minorities, Commentary on the Language Rights of Persons belonging to National Minorities under the Framework Convention for the Protection of National Minorities, ACFC/44DOC (2012) 001 rev, Strasbourg, 24 May 2012, http://www.coe.int/t/dghl/monitoring/minorities/3_fcnmdocs/PDF_CommentaryLanguage_en.pdf
Council of Europe, Protocol No. 12 to the Convention for the Protection of Human Rights and Fundamental Freedoms, Explanatory Report, (ETS No. 177) Rome, 4.XI.2000
European Charter for Regional or Minority Languages, Explanatory Memorandum, ETS No. 148, Strasbourg 1992, par. 10-11, http://www.coe.int/t/dg4/education/minlang/textcharter/Charter/Explreport_gr.pdf
Parliamentary Assembly, Recommendation 2080 (2015), Freedom of religion and living together in a democratic society
Parliamentary Assembly, Recommendation No. R (97) 20 of the Committee of Ministers on "hate speech"
Parliamentary Assembly, Resolution 2036 (2015), Tackling intolerance and discrimination in Europe with a special focus on Christians
Parliamentary Assembly, Resolution 2076 (2015), Freedom of religion and living together in a democratic society
Council of Europe, Parliamentary Assembly Resolution Resolution 1510 (2006), Freedom of expression and respect for religious beliefs
Council of Europe, Parliamentary Assembly Recommendation 1805 (2007), Blasphemy, religious insults and hate speech against persons on grounds of their religion

Documents of the United Nations

Committee on Economic, Social and Cultural Rights, General Comment 4, The right to adequate housing (Sixth session, 1991), UN Doc. E / 1992/23, annex III at 114 (1991)

Committee on Economic, Social and Cultural Rights, General Comment 14, The right to the highest attainable standard of health (Twenty-second session, 2000), UN Doc. E / C.12 / 2000/4 (2000)

Committee on Economic, Social and Cultural Rights, General Comment 12, Right to adequate food (Twentieth session, 1999), UN Doc. E / C.12 / 1999/5 (1999)

Economic and Social Council, UN Sub-Commission on the Promotion and Protection of Human Rights, Commentary Of The Working Group On Minorities To The United Nations Declaration On The Rights Of Persons Belonging To National Or Ethnic, Religious And Linguistic Minorities, E/CN.4/Sub.2/AC.5/2005/2, 4 April 2005

General Assembly, A/60/399, Report of the Special Rapporteur of the Commission on Human Rights on freedom of religion or belief, Asma Jahangir, 30 September 2005

General UN Office of the High Commissioner for Human Rights (OHCHR), Fact Sheet No. 18 (Rev.1), Minority Rights, February 1998, No. 18 (Rev.1)

Human Rights Committee, General Comment 22, Article 18 (1993), CCPR/C/21/Rev.1/Add.4

Human Rights Committee, General Comment 22, Article 18 (Forty-eighth session, 1993). Compilation of General Comments and General Recommendations Adopted by Human Rights Treaty Bodies, UN Doc. HRI/GEN/1/Rev.1 at 35 (1994)

Human Rights Council, Promotion and protection of the rights of indigenous peoples with respect to their cultural heritage, A/HRC/30/53

Human Rights Council, Report of the independent expert in the field of cultural rights, Farida Shaheed, A/HRC/17/38, 21/03/2011

Human Rights Council, Report of the Special Rapporteur on freedom of religion or belief, Asma Jahangir - Missionto Sri Lanka, E/CN.4/2006/5/Add.3

UN Human Rights Council, Combating defamation of religions: resolution / adopted by the Human Rights Council, 15 April 2010, A/HRC/RES/13/16

UN Committee on Economic, Social and Cultural Rights, General Comment on the Right to Education (Art. 13), 8 December 1999, 21st sess., UN Doc. E / C.12 / 1999/10 (1999)

UN General Assembly GA res 60/167, Human rights and cultural diversity, 7 March 2006

UN Human Rights Committee (HRC), CCPR General Comment No. 22: Article 18 (Freedom of Thought, Conscience or Religion), 30 July 1993, CCPR/C/21/Rev.1/Add.4

UN Human Rights Committee (HRC), CCPR General Comment No. 23: Article 27 (Rights of Minorities), 8 April 1994, CCPR/C/21/Rev.1/Add.5

UN Office of the High Commissioner for Human Rights, Fact Sheet No. 23, Harmful Traditional Practices Affecting the Health of Women and Children, August 1995, No. 23

FSC
www.fsc.org
MIX
Papier aus verantwortungsvollen Quellen
Paper from responsible sources
FSC® C105338

If you have any concerns about our products,
you can contact us on
ProductSafety@springernature.com

In case Publisher is established outside the EU,
the EU authorized representative is:
Springer Nature Customer Service Center GmbH
Europaplatz 3, 69115 Heidelberg, Germany

Printed by Libri Plureos GmbH
in Hamburg, Germany